H.H. Dhruva

Baroda State Delegate

At The VIII International Congress of Orientalists, Stockholm and Christian

H.H. Dhruva

Baroda State Delegate
At The VIII International Congress of Orientalists, Stockholm and Christian

ISBN/EAN: 9783337903244

Printed in Europe, USA, Canada, Australia, Japan

Cover: Foto ©Suzi / pixelio.de

More available books at **www.hansebooks.com**

BARODA STATE DELEGATE

AT

the VIII. International Congress of Orientalists
Stockholm (Sweden) and Christiania (Norway)

(1889.)

BY

H. H. DHRUVA

B. A. LL. B. (Bom.), D. L. A. (Sweden), M. R. A. S.
(London and Bom.), M. P. T. S., &c., &c.
City Joint Judge and Sessions Judge, Baroda.

PREFACE.

Native States seldom seem to have taken any interest in the International Congresses of Orientalists except perhaps in the last two or three. At the time of the VII. Congress that assembled at Vienna, in Austria, in 1887, when the arrangements for sending an Indian to it by the Supreme Government fell through, the Princes of Kattyawar were said to have contributed their mite to the deputation of Professor Ramkrishna Gopal Bhandarkar. But that was not an independent nor a voluntary action of theirs. Nor is it at the same time a fact that these Congresses have ever taken any notice of our Chiefs, nor have they applied to them for support or sympathy. It was the Maharaja of Vijayanagara that contributed liberally towards the publication of the Second Edition of the Rig Veda with the great commentary of Sàyana, once a minister of one of the ancestors of His Highness. Similarly it is the Maharaja Siyaji Rao Gaikvad of Baroda who has patronized the preparation and publication of the archœological volumes of Dabhoi, Patan, Modera, and Siddhapur Antiquities, the first of which has been long since out. The extensively liberal and just policy of His Highness the Maharaja is too well pronounced to demand any detailed account here. The Sanskrit Library every day being enlarged by the collection and addition of rare Sanskrit Mss. and printed works, the Baroda Museum getting to be formed and completed on a good scale, the Prâchîna Kâvya Mâlâ publications in 30 volumes at a cost of Rs. 12000 and the translations into Gujcrati and Marathi of Selections from Sanskrit Literature, and the S'râvanî Dakshnas and Examinations are some of the eloquent evidences of the living interest taken by our enlightened Prince.

It is on account of this intelligent interest in our Sanskrit Language and Literature and such Orientalism, that His Highness the Gaikvad of Baroda was the first Prince that was directly invited to join the Congress and to be present at it or to send a Pandit Representative Delegate of his there, by the August Patron of the Assemblage, H. M. King Oscar II. of Sweden and Norway and the invitation was right royally responded to by the Premier Prince of Western India by his deputing one of his district Judicial officers to represent His Highness at the gathering. The interesting correspondence is given as an appendix further on.

His Highness's deputation met with a hearty reception at the court of Norway and Sweden as well as at the hands of the Congress at Stockholm and Christiania. King Oscar II. honoured the delegate with the distinguished decoration of the Gold Medal (and diploma) of *Literis (at) Artibus*. A place of honour was given to his paper on *Rekha Ganita* which was the first that was read in the Aryan Section at Stockholm and a vote of thanks was passed for His Highness's act of deputation by that body at Christiania at the close of its work. The whole body of the Congress also cheerily drank the health of Maharaja Siyaji Rao with that of other Kings of Europe and the East at the closing Public Dinner at Gotten-

berg. The interest thus nobly begun to be taken by
the Ruler of this State has been followed up by His
Highness's enrolling himself among the Members of
the Royal Asiatic Society of Great Brittain and Ireland and by the still more generous support accorded
to the Congress that met in London last year in
September and which was honoured by the presence of
His Highness's brother Srimant Sampat Rao Gaikvad.
And we are indebted to His Highness's Government
also for this reprint of the Papers and Poems read
at the VIII. Congress meetings and the allied writings. Although the VIII. Congress met 4 years ago,
the Proceedings of the Session have not yet been
ready and it will yet be time, one cannot say how
long, when they will at all see the light. The matter of this publication was broached to the late la-
mented Huzoor Assistant Rao Bahadur G. K. Bhatva-
dekar B. A. LL. B., who took it up in right earnest,
and on the motion of my friend Rao Bahadur Hargo-
vinddas Dwarkadas, Director of Vernacular Instruction, obtained the necessary sanction for it. I am also
obliged to his successor, the present Naib Divan Rao
Bahadur Yeshvantrao Vasudev Athalye M. A. LL.
B. for his continuing the same support and interest
in the work.

The present publication labours under one defect.
We had not the original Papers read at the Congress
and the copies on hand were rather indifferent. Consequently several errors seem to have crept in for which
we ask our learned reader's kind indulgence. I cor-

rect some of them and add important notes in a handy introduction that I attach hereto. The delay in the publication is more to be laid at my door than to that of any other, as the laborious duties of a Judge left me little time to devote an undivided attention to the seeing through print of this work. I must here thank the authorities of the Press who have done much of the proof correction to my great relief and satisfaction.

H. H. DHRUVA.

INTRODUCTION.

It would not be uninteresting to give by way of introduction short notes on the Appendices published hereafter, as annextures illustrative of some portions of the Papers reprinted in this volume as also corrective of some errors or misapprehensions that might have crept in them at first, under new light obtained through further discussion of the themes or closer and fuller studies of and researches in their fields.

(1) THE CONGRESS AND THE DELEGATE.

Appendix (A) gives the history of the author's deputation as also the opinions of those best able to judge on the spot, of his work. They speak for themselves and require no comment. Nor does Appendix (B.) containing the Delegate's message to the August Patron of the Congress, King Oscar II. from his Chief, His Highness the Gaikvad of Baroda.

(2) SANSCRIT ELEMENTS OF EUCLID: GEOMETRY.

Appendix (c. and D.) are of a far more instructive and interesting character. It sets forth at the outset a summary of the discussion on the first Paper read at the Congress, that is, on the Elements of Euclid's Geometry, in 15 books, of Pandit Jagannâtha Samrât of Jeypur. And what follows clearly shows who of the disputants are correct and how far. The notes could have been enlarged and made more extensive and instructive. But as there is shortly to be a publication of the *Rekha Ganita* in the Bombay Sanskrit Series, as sanctioned by the Bombay Government educational authorities, they have been reserved for that edition.

In order to ascertain the true facts about the survival of the books of Euclid and their early editions I made a rather prolonged stay at Stockholm in examining some of the older editions at the Royal Library as well as at the Library of the Astronomical Observatory there on the 19th of September 1889. I also addressed letters of enquiry in regard to the point to several eminent scholars in Europe, who have kindly vouchsafed to me the information at their command which will all be engrossed in the edition in the Bombay Sanscrit Series. Dr. Rost of the India Office, London, Prof. Macdonell of Oxford, Prof. Wallis of Cambridge, Dr. Burgess of Edinburgh, Dr. Kern of Leyden, Prof. Weber of Berlin and Prof. Carllides of Athens are some of these friends whose names I needs must give here in all justice and thankfulness.

. The earliest Latin edition at the Astronomical Observatory, Stockholm, is in two parts, one of the first nine books, and the other, of the last nine from Books VII. to XVI. and this last was published at Frankfurt in 1654 A. C. While there is an earlier Greek and Latin Edition of A. C. 1560 of only the first six books with commentaries, there is such an Oxford edition in 15 books of the year 1703 A. C. The earliest Swedish edition of Georg Brandt is of the year 1718 A. C.

The collections of editions at the Royal Library

at Stockholm are still earlier, dating so far back as A. C. 1470 and after. And the one in fifteen books is dated A. C. 1482, counting 489 Propositions in all. The *Rekha Ganita* has but 478 Propositions in circa 1720 A. C., and Adelard's 15 books have 493 Propositions in A. C. 1482. And Clavis's 16 books of A. C. 1536 have 500 Propositions according to Basil, 465 according to Heiburg, 486 according to Peyrard, and 498 according to August. The work of Adelard abovementioned was but a translation from Arabic, made in 1130 A. C., first published by Campain at Venice in 1482 A. C. which passed through several editions later at different places in Europe. Thus even in Europe the earliest printed work on Euclid was indebted to Arabic. And the information collected in the Appendix also goes to give an Arabic original as the basis of Jagannâtha Samrât's *Rekha Ganita*. The Researches of the late Pandit Durgâprasâda Sarmâ of Jaypur, with whom I had an interesting correspondence in Sanskrit, between 2nd June 1890 and 22nd February 1891, also, tend to the same conclusion. The Pandit informs me that there still exist the Samrât heirs, by name, Mathurânâtha &c., enjoying grants of villages from the Prince to their ancestor, the Geometrician, but they unfortunately are not blessed with his learning. Neither they nor the State seems to possess a good original Ms. of the work. It is to Pandit Durgâprasâda's find that we owe the discovery of Euclid being the original author whose Elements of Geometry Jagannâtha Samrât translated. One of the Mss. lent to me by the Pandit has at the beginning a note thus "अषोक्लीदृशाख्यं रेखाग-णितं लिख्यते"

The author of *Rekha Ganita* has also written other works such as the *Siddhanta-Samrat,* giving a description of Astronomical instruments, and *Siddhanta-Kaustubha* both incomplete and *Goliya Rekha Ganita* or Spherical Geometry. The first of these evinces a marked acquaintance of the writer with Arabic authors and their works, whom and which he largely quotes. (This work has references also to our *Rekha Ganita.*) It can only mean that the present work too was derived from the Arabic as its European representatives were in the 12th and the 15th centuries.

In the light of these materials we arrive at the following conclusions which may be put by the side of those of the paper read before the Congress in order to correct them where they need correction.

(1) That the author of *Rekha Ganita* was well conversant with Arabic works and writers.

(2) That he translated perhaps his *Rekha Ganita* from an Arabic Original.*

(3) That the work was Euclid's Elements of

---

* What that Arabic Original was and written by whom, cannot be determined. Even the Arabic Original of Adelard's Euclid of 1130 A. C. also cannot be fixed. For it cannot be the work of Nasir Alauddin Altusi (Vide p. 23 post) who wrote it in the 13th century. Again Nasir's Euclid was in 13 books while that of Adelard was in 15 Books.

Geometry and there existed no Indian work of the kind to serve as its basis.†

(4.) That still there was no European work or any work in any European Language of the kind which the Samrât could have translated.

(5.) And that there is no such European work at the Jeypur State Library that Dr. Burgess speaks of.

And still in the face of the ancient S'úlva Sútras in existence, a total absence of a knowledge and cultivation of the Elements of Geometry in India cannot be asserted. Perhaps these Elements had not reached the stage of those of Euclid's as the progress in the field was cut short by the overthrow of the Sacrifices, that originated them, on the rise and spread of the Jaina and Bauddha cults.

I cannot rightly close this part of the Introduction without showing my great satisfaction at the work of *Rekha Ganita* having attracted the notice of such a scholar as Mr. L. Wilkinson before me, to whom then is properly due the honour of the first discovery of the work. Sufficient will be my reward if I have been

---

† Except it be the Sanskrit rendering of Euclid by Alberuni about 1050 A. C. The great Moslum scholar tells us in his *Indica* about it in these terms: "Most of their books are composed in *Sloka* in which I am now exercising myself, being occupied in composing for the Hindus a translation of Euclid and of the Almajest" (Vide. Sachan's Translation, Vol. I. p. 137). How interesting indeed the find of this Alberuni's Sanskrit metrical Euclid would be! The *Sidhanta Samrat* of Jagaunâtha Samrât mentions frequent references to one *Almajest*. Can it be the one rendered into Sanskrit *Sloka* by Alberuni?

instrumental in giving it that European, nay world-wide, publicity to it, that will no doubt be fruitful of good results in the advancement of the knowledge of the Science, which the work lacked before. Now to return to our Appendices once more.

(3.) THE GUJERATI LANGUAGE.

Appendix (E) gives some popular songs and specimens of provincialisms current in Màlavâ, Hârânti, and Kattyawad, which go to prove the contention of the paper that the Language of this province has a far greater extent for its currency, and it can lay a fair claim to a big share in the honour of being considered with Hindi the dominant or chief, if not the parent language, in regard to these provincial dialects. A collection of some popular Cutchi Kafis, now with me, would, if published by these, have shown the same partnership between Gujerati and Sindhi in regard to the Cutchi and Jadeji dialects. These dialects are as it were the connecting links between the main branches of the Aryan Indian Vernaculars. Such a connecting link would be met with in the duplicate dialect spoken about Burhanpur, Nandurbar, and on the confines of Gujerat, Konkan, Màlavâ and Mahârâshtra for the Gujerati and Marathi Languages. Thus the whole round of the circle is closed by Hindi, Sindhi, Gujerati, and Marathi which can be fully and well studied then and then only if we take these links or transitional dialects that close up the breaches between them.

One has to be very careful in the study of these languages as the materials sometimes coming to hand are of a very deceptive character. Jain and Bardic writings are of such a conservative character that one cannot be sure of either their Antiquity or modernity, in the absence of any other evidence, from their mere forms only. And out of literary compositions, the Râsâu of Chand Bardâi is eminently of such a character. This would be more fully understood from my paper on the Gujerati Language of the 14th and 15th centuries and from its Appendices shortly to be published in the Proceedings of the London Congress of Orientalists of 1892. Meanwhile it would be but fair to draw the reader's attention to Dr. Buhler's views on the same in Appendix (A) 9.

(4) BARODA ANTIQUITIES.

As the Kâthi Vansâvali and the Statements of Coins and Inscriptions have been sufficiently discussed in the paper, they have been omitted in this reprint. Had there been more time at our command we would have taken them up there. But as it is we reserve them for the Baroda Manual of Antiquities shortly to be prepared.

The Editors of the *Gujerat Darpan, Buddhi Prakas'a* and *Gujerati,* as also the *Poona Sarvajanika Sabha Quarterly Journal,* deserve our best thanks for their honouring some of the writings here published, or giving their translations or substances, in prominent places in their columns. I cannot better close this introduction than with a cordial invitation to my brother scholars to occupy and cultivate the field of studies and research here opened.

BARODA,
15th June 1893. } H. H. DHRUVA.

THE VIII. INTERNATIONAL CONGRESS OF ORIENTALISTS.*

In the year 1889 the VIII. International Congress of Orientalists that assembled at Stockholm (Sweden) and Christiania (Norway) between the 2nd and the 11th of September last, and the Universal Exhibition of Paris, commemorative of the Centenary of the French Republic, were the great attractions of Europe. People from all parts of the world flocked to these centres of European Civilization and Progress. The sights were unique and unrivalled in their variety, grandeur and educating influences. While the one represented the highest results of mechanical and scientific progress and material advancement, the other was illustrative of the great energy and intellect of the West, perhaps of the World, bestowed on the study of the Light and Learning of the East, and of Antiquity generally. While the one was inaugurated by one of the most prominent Republics of Europe and the World,—that of France, the other was brought together at the invitation of one of the most intelligent and cultivated Princes of the North, King Oscar II. of Nor-

---

* This paper was written for the Poona Lecture Series, 1890, and was originally printed in the Quarterly Journal of the Poona Sarvajanic Sabha.

1

way and Sweden. The Universal Exhibition was a right
imperial work, although it basked under the sunshine
of a Republic, while the Congress was purely demo-
cratic in spirit and constitution, although it smiled under
a royal patronage. But both of them were representative of the intellect, energy and application of the West.

The Congress of Orientalists had for its compeers
and contemporaries other Congresses also, the hundred
and one of Paris, that formed appanages of the Universal Exhibition ; as also the Vegetarian Congress,
that met at Cologne, about the 15th of September.
But the Orientalist Congress of the North far excelled and surpassed those of the South in every respect.
All the four quarters and continents of the World had
sent their representatives to the ancient land of Scandinavia ; there, all the leading religions of the world had
got their followers. Of these, Europe among the former,
and Christianity among the latter figured prominently.
There were 459 European, 16 American, 13 Asiatic and
5 African scholars present. If we re-arrange these
numbers according to race, the Aryans far out-number-
ed the Semitics and the Negraics, there being only
one Abyssinian and 9 Semitics, the rest being Aryans
or Indo-Germans. The Japanese, Fins and Magyars
are not separately classed here. Of the Indo-Germanic
races, the Teutoni-Gothic races of the North and the
West formed more than 75 p. c. in number i. e. 380 out
of a total of 492 members present. The Grœco-Latin
races had only 37 scholars and the Sclavonic only 19, the
mixed having 44. The distribution of the numbers

according to religion consisted of 2 Brahmins, 2 Buddhists, 1 Zoroastrian, and 9 Islamites, the rest being Christians. In Europe again, geographically speaking, the North and the West far exceeded the South and the East, there being 402 of the former and 90 of the latter. These figures show the interest of the subject as distributed ethnically, geographically, and according to race, locality, and religious creeds. They also show us at a glance how the Orientals, for whom the subjects discussed at the Conference ought to have the most attraction, are the most apathetic about them, or are so slow and backward in taking a real and living interest in them. While the Brahmin, the Jain, the Buddhist or the Moulvi does not appreciate the worth of the rare Mss. lying with him, and while he consigns them even to the flowing waters of rivers, or sells them to the grocer for packing pills and powders in them; while the most important of our coins, copperplates or inscriptions, the palm-leaf mss. or papyri, are allowed to rot and perish in obscurity, they fetch and command fancy prices in the distant West. The arts and lores, that are forgotten and lost in their lands of birth, receive a strange resurrection in distant lands, where it could never have been expected or imagined, that they would attract any notice. The East, therefore, is not a little indebted to the West for having thus rekindled the light that was almost entirely extinct in its first home.

The registered number of members of the Congress was close upon 710, while the number actually present was 492. The members present at Berlin, Leyden, and Vienna in 1881, 1883, and 1886 were 290, 454, and 424 respectively. The proportion of local members to the general total, *viz.*, of 141, Sweden, and 62, Norway, *i. e.* 203 in all, to 492, also was an evident improvement, if we look at 117 Germans out of 290, in Berlin, 160 Hollanders to 454, in Leyden and 117 Austrians to the total of 424 in Vienna. The percentage was 45 in 1881, 35 in 1883 and 27 in 1886, and it rose last year to 40. There was also an improvement in the part taken by the Oriental, and especially Indian, members. While Mr. S. P. Pandit M. A. was the only Indian scholar present in the first Congress in England, Pandit Shyamji Krishnavarma and Mr. Ramdas Chhabildas, Barrister-at-Law, were present at Leyden ; while Pandita Ramabai attended at Berlin, Prof. R. G. Bhandarkar M. A. Ph. D., was present at Vienna ; there were 3 pure Indians at the last Congress, and Dr. P. Peterson, M. A. D. Sc. Professor, Elphinstone College, figured prominently with them. Mr. J. J. Modi B. A. read two papers before the General Section, and two before the Aryan Section, and, he was decorated with a Gold Medal of *Literis et Artibus.* There was a paper, read by me before the Aryan Section, Stockholm, on the 3rd of September 1889, and two papers before the same at Christiania, on the 10th of the same month. My first was on the *Sanskrit Elements of Euclid's Geometry* ; The other two were on (1) *the Neo-Vernaculars of Western India with special reference to Ancient and Mediæval Gujerati Grammar (Mugdhavbodha-Mauktika) written in V. S. 1450,* (A. D. 1394,) and (2) *the Anti quities of the Baroda State and the Light they shed on Gujerat History.* There were also two Sanskrit Poems, specially composed for the occasion and recited by me, one at Stockholm, and the other at Christiania. Lastly we had good reason to congratulate ourselves, that this time, India was wholly represented by the Bombay Presidency at the Congress, and the two important discoveries of the Sanskrit Euclid and the Buddhistic work on Logic, the Nyâyabindu of Dharmottaraâchârya brought to light by Dr. Peterson, were also made by scholars from this side of India.

The large number of members, attending the Congress this year, as noticed above, may have been partly due to the Universal Exhibition, that had drawn people from every point of the Earth. There was, further, another novel feature of the Congress, *viz.,* the part taken therein by the fair sex. This was not entirely formal nor idle nor unimportant. There was an interesting paper read by Madame Sofie von Torma in Section I. b.

The following Universities had sent delegates to the Congress; Halle 1. Griefswald 3, Giessend 1, and Jena 1, in Germany ; Vienna 3, Univerité Allemande de Prague 1, in Austro—Hungary ; Munich 2, in Bavaria ; Copenhagen 2, in Denmark ; John Hopkins de Baltimore and Browneof de Providence 1 in the United States ; Helsingfors 1, Finland ; Oxford 2, Cambridge 1 and London 1, in England ; Edinburgh 2, in Scotland ; Bombay 1, in India ; Universite Pontificale de Rome

1, in Italy; St. Petersburg 2, and Kassan 1, in Russia; Upsala 1, and Lund 1, in Sweden. Similarly learned Societies had sent delegates viz., the Deutsche Morgenländische Gesllschaft had sent 1 and Orientalische Gesellschaft 2, in Germany; K. K. Handels Museum 1, L' Instruction Publique de Vienne 1, Ungarische Academie der Wissen Schaften 1, and K. K. Natural historisches HofMuseum 1, in Austro-Hungary; Societe d' Archèologie de Bruxelles 1, Belgium: China Branch of the Royal Asiatic Society 2, China; Smithsonian Institution 1, the United States, America; Societe Finno-ungroise de Helsingfors 1, Finland; Societe Asiatique á Paris 1 and Societe d' Anthropologie á Paris 1 as also Academie d' Hippone á Bone 1, France; Royal Asiatic Society of Great Britain and Ireland 4, Society of Biblical Archœology 3, Palestine Exploration Fund 1, India Office 1, Christian Knowledge Society 1, in Great Britain and Ireland; Asiatic Society of Bengal 1, India; Reale Academia de' Lincie 1, Bibliotheque du Vatican 1, Academia Reale delle Scienze á Torino 1, Italy; Koninkligh Institutut Voor de Taal 1, Landn Volken-Kunde van Nederlandsch Indïe á la Haye 3, Holland; and Society Impèriale Archèologique 1 Russia. Several Foreign Governments too had deputed their representatives. Austro-Hungary had sent 9, Baden 1, Baroda 1, Bavaria 4, Bosnia and Herzegovina 2, Brazil 1, Denmark 2, Egypt 4, France 2, the Government of India 2, Italy 3, Japan 1, the Netherlands 4, Persia 1, Portugal 1., Roumania 1, Russia 1, Royaume de Saxe 1, Duches Saxe Coburg Gotha 1, Siam 1 and Turkey 2. This contributed largely to making the Congress a highly effective and right royal assembly.

The reception accorded to the Congress by its August Patron, the King of the Goths and the Vandals, of Norway and Sweden, King Oscar II, as well as by the people of Norway and Sweden, may safely be said to have had no parallel in the history of the reception of any past Congress. The illuminations and fire-works, pleasure trips, grand dinners and festivals, with music and opera, telephone and swimming bath entertainments, and what not,—everything was made extremely pleasant and agreeable to the learned scholars assembled there. The reception would never fade away from the memory of those to whom it was accorded. The festivities were so continuous and varied that the Congress gathering has been described to have' been more a holiday trip than a real working assembly. The Organization Committee and the local authorities have been blamed for this. But I would rather like to thank them for the kind and good feeling shown by the Prince and the People of the North, who are famous for their hospitality and love and liking of foreigners. The honour that was thus paid to this collected representative humanity was unprecedented in the annals of the world. It was more cordial than that paid to any popular ruler of mankind or to a successful general returning crowned with all the glories and trophies of war. And yet there was no foolish idolatry or tall hero-worship. If there was any worship, it was that of Intellect and Humanity, the triumph of Progress in matters that are more divine than human. So in this direction too there was a clear departure and marked advance. Again that the work of the brain absolutely needed change and rest, relaxation and relief, will be seen from what follows.

The Congress worked in five Sections : I. Semitic ; II. Aryan ; III. African ; IV. Central and Extreme Asia ; and V. Malayasia and Polynnesia. The Semitic Section was again subdivided into two sub-sections (a) the Arabic and Islamite, and (b) other Semtic⁚ Languages, and Cuneiform Writings and Inscriptions &c. The African Section concerned itself mainly with Egyptology, while Sanscrit and Zend engrossed an overwhelmingly greater part of the attention of the Aryan Section, although among the modern Vernaculars, Gujerati, and the Beluchi and Hunza dialects too, had no inconsiderable share of it. The papers and work distributed over these Sections were written by 86 persons out of 492. Of these there was only 1 lady as noticed above, and she came from Austro-Hungary. Of the remaining 85, there was only 1 Brahmin, I myself ; only 1 Parsi, Mr. J. J. Modi ; and 2 Japanese, among the Asiatics ; and 4 Egyptians among the Africans. There were 14 Germans, 14 Frenchmen, 10 Swedes, 7 Austrians, 5 Englishmen, 5 Italians, 2 from the United States, 2 Dutchmen, 2 Norwegians, 2 Danes, 2 Russians 1 Welshman, 1 Greek, 1 Swiss, 1 Belgian ; the nationalities of the rest being unknown. Here too we see that not only do the Teutonic races muster strong, but their work also forms a very large bulk of the total. Sweden and Norway too have been doing not a little.

But France and Germany, followed by Austria and Italy, are to the fore as usual. It is greatly to be regretted that Great Britain and Ireland figure so little in this field in spite of all their resources and facilities.

There we e in all about 106 papers read by these 86 persons; 48 being in French and 37 in German, while there were perhaps about 2 in Italian and 18 in English. It was not only the programme, catalogues and bulletins and speeches that gave the Congress a French or German character but this larger proportion of papers also confirmed this impression. It was indeed no compliment to the world-pervading English language that is striving to be a universal tongue, and to the races speaking English, that they should have been dwarfed down so insignificantly as they were on the present occasion. Although there was a larger proportion of English-speaking and English-knowing members in the Congress, the language was ignored, so to say, not only at the meetings of the Sections, and of the whole Congress, but even at the table and on festive occasions. The convenience of the majority had, no doubt, the first claim to be consulted and attended to At the same time it is clear that tradition, more than actual convenience, vertually governed the choice of the common or predominent language. French is gradually becoming less and less the *lingua franca* of the Continent and the German and Italian languages will never occupy the place thus vacated by this indisputably senior member. The vacancy thus caused should largely be filled by English, and as in the long run, it will drive

2

away, or at least cast into the shade, every other language of the world, English deserves to be the learned
or literary language of the future world, as Greek was of
the Ancient and Latin of the subsequent ages in the
West, and Sanskrit in the East. And the sooner we
do it the better, as the proposed change is likely to
bring the results of learned research in this exten_
sive field easily within the reach of everybody who
cares to study the subject. Besides it would economise
the time and labour spent in the study of more languag_
es than one, not necessarily required for a correct
understanding or study of the results of antiquarian
research.

It will not be uninteresting here to take stock of
what progress the present Congress has made over
the last, in what direction and fields this progress
has been made and what results have been achieved
by European research. While Section I (a) counted 21
papers on the list and the same Section (b) 22, the
Aryan Section had but 18, the African 13, the Central
and Extreme Asian 10, and Malayasia and Polynesia
but 2. Every one will regret that so little work was
brought by the Aryan Section to the Congress in spite
of its innumerable resources and facilities and in spite
of its unbounded field and horizon, clearer and more
open than those of the others. And even, this work
was not of a substantial or critically scientific character.
While Archœology and Mythology occupied a large
share of the above, and Comparative Philology and
Study of Languages had their due share, no strata of

Oriental Philosophies or Sciences were unearthed in the way in which Prof. Oppert in Section 6 (*b*) was seen working for the Chaldean Astronomy and Astrology, and Dr. Inouyẽ in Section IV for Chinese Philosophy. We had only Dr. Deussen's remarks on the depth of Aryan Philosophy on the नासदासीत् Hymn, and a paper on the Sanskrit Euclid. But even these did not go deep enough. They probed the subjects but superficially.

If we look at the papers announced, or read, as can be seen from the bulletins published by the Committee, there is a sad want of further and more critical enquiry into the really difficult fields of Oriental study and research with regard to the Philosophies or the Darshans. In them we have advanced not an inch from where we were with Colebrook nor in the Purans from where we were with H. H. Wilson. Beyond the Sacred Books of the East and a few publications here in the Bombay Sanskrit Series and the Calcutta Bibliotheca Indica Series, we have done almost nothing in the Vedic, Brahmanic and Upanished and Sutra Literature. There are still dark continents to be explored, more unknown than the interior of Africa or Australia, some parts of America or the Arctic and Antaratic regions. We still want our Livingstones, Stanleys and Nodelskjolds. Tantric Literature is a jungle still dense and not even distantly approached. Of course, our dramas and poems, our tales and stories, our fables and fictions are more largely understood than before. Our coins are disciphered in larger numbers, copper plate grants

and stone and other inscriptions have been more thoroughly read and annotated and edited and our epics
and some of our Sutras of domestic or sacrificial rites
and some of the Smritis and Upanishads are more
clearly and correctly interpreted. The progress made
by us in Comparative Mythology, Comparative Theo-
logy and Comparative Philology is not inconsiderable,
although we have much work still left unaccomplished
in all these directions. The languages, both living and
dead, classical and vernacular, still require to be more
largely studied, understood and investigated. But the
thick crust of the earth of Sanscrit and other Oriental
Literature—the accumulated result and formation of
long ages of activity—has not been penetrated even to
a thousandth part, to say the least, of the depth. We
are yet groping about the outskirts. But we have
some unlimited and boundless strata to examine. Although we cannot shut our eyes to the great work done
by the Scholars of the West, and the bright light they
have shed on the dark depths, we cannot help noticing
what a vast deal they have still left for native investi-
gation to accomplish.

All the past Congresses have assembled in Europe,
far from the scenes and sources of the subjects of
research and studies. The fountain-heads of inspiration
lie very far from them. The originals are hidden from
their view. They have got their materials in many
cases second hand, which only very distantly resemble
the originals. The copies no doubt are faithful, but they
are copies after all, and no Oriental Congress for re-

search can be really Oriental until and unless it has repaired to their native sources and homes. The East must and should invite the West to itself, if it wants to be correctly understood, appreciated, and studied. The Governments of China, Japan and Siam, of India, Persia, Turkey and Egypt, have a duty to perform to themselves and to the nations they represent for they are the subjects of the studies and enquiries. And it will be only then that the full extent and magnitude of the work of research will be apprehended. When the stream will thus be made alternately to flow and reflow from the East to the West and from the West to the East, what looks now hazy from a distance will get clearer, what is indistinct will look bright, what is crude and unsightly will appear perfect and proportionate. New vistas will open, fogs and mists will melt away and the real unobscured light from Orient will shine superb.

Many a Philosophy of the East is but imperfectly understood in Europe. The Phonetics are still a difficulty. The French and the German, the Swedish and the Russian languages can never be perfectly mastered from books, grammars and manuals. Much less can Sanskrit, whether Vedic or Classic, Arabic, Persian, Chinese, Japanese, or the modern vernaculars of India be so studied. What applies to Phonetics also holds good in the case of shades of meanings, turns of expression and idioms. The local associations and the associations of ideas and thoughts also must be learned here in their respective homes.

Before closing this general view of the Congress, I must mention the names of the leading scholars of Europe who were present at the Congress, and especially in the Aryan Section. The old veteran Professors Max-Muller and Weber, advancing fast on the other side of sixty, appeared still to retain their full strength and vigour. So also the eminent Zend scholar Prof. Spiegel. The Aryan Section honoured themselves in honouring. these three leading spirits with their Chairmanship. The Orientalists and the general world would no doubt have liked to hear something more about them beyond their presiding over the section meetings or beyond their speeches. There were also several well-known Indian Europeans, if I be allowed the use of such a term. I have already alluded to Dr. Peterson more than once. Dr. Buhler was another and he still commands the high and well-deserved position of a great epigraphist of Ashoca and other inscriptions. Dr. Kielhorn and Dr. Burgess also were still unflagging in their interesting work. There were again Professor Rendall of the British Museum, Dr. Rost of the India Office, and Dr. Leitner of Woking Institute ; and the brother Codringtons were there among others.

The Italian scholar Count Angelo Gubernatis— whose name is still fresh in our memory since his last visit—was there as active as when he recounted in his sonorous voice the result of his thought and study in Indian Mythology. Among the German scholars, the name of Dr. Deussen deserves to be mentioned with reverence for his deep love and patient study of Indian Philosophy. In my conversation with him, I learnt with great pleasure his division of the civilization of the world into Indo-Germanic, Semitic, and Egyptian. All the three commenced with Polytheism, and ended with Monotheism or rather Monism. With the first, Polytheism developed into Monotheism philosophically, with the second, fanatically, and with third, mechanically. The second comprises Judaism and Islamism. Christianity, although born in Judaism, was more really the result of the action of Aryanism on the latter. Zoroastrism, largely influencing Judaism during the captivity of the Jews, softened down its severity and tempered it into Christianity. Buddhism contributed largely to the development of Christian forms and rituals. The fanaticism of the Inquisition and the middle ages was due to the Semitic trace in Christianity. Islamism was a reaction of Judaism against the Aryanized Christianity. Professor Deussen's appreciation of Poetry and Drama, Philosophy and Mythology, as distinguishing marks of the Aryan civilization was also a happy one.

It was not less interesting to hear Dr. Buhler's view ·of the Indian caste system; he, unlike other scholars, would like to see it preserved but largely modified and liberalized. It is a distinctive institution of Aryanism. It had its existence in Europe upto very recent times in the Scottish clans, and the French *dishonorables* at the close of the last century were the Pariahs of Liberal France. The course of events has developed Individualism in Europe, levelling all barriers of classes against masses. Europe has lost a good deal with its one-sided and extreme development of Individualism, while here in India the out-and-out iron hardness of the caste system has done no little harm. What is wanted is an easy and pliable opening for the innate powers and strength of the lower strata of the Indian Society, without dislodging and dismembering the higher ones. In a small paper like this, all that was read, done, and discussed at the Congress can never be compressed to-gether. It is neither my aim here to recount everything that took place from day to day at the various sittings of the Congress. But in the rather diffused *resume* above given, I have tried to present the salient points and features of an institution which is likely to shape not a little the knowledge, not only of India and the East, but also of the whole world.

Apart from this literary and scientific value, the Congress has its social and political usefulness. It creates a love of peace among the leading men of the several nationalities of the world. And it can never fail to exert its influence over a wider circle. Contact and mutual knowledge are invariably the parents of mutual good will and fellowship. The awkwardness and angularities of local pride and prejudice are sure to wear away. And a very desirable levelling of prejudice must result from their contact. Travels to distant countries and the personal acquaintance of those lands and peoples again have their own intrinsic value as great educating influences.

It is only under such circumstances and auspices, that the East and the West can be brought face to face to learn, to love and respect each other. On the one hand, there are vast treasures of which the owners do not know the full value. On the other hand, there are the great explorers from foreign lands who crave to interpret the present with the help of the past. Both have to learn and gain considerably from each other. The principles of self-help and individual action and liberty of thought, act and speech constitute the strength of the West; deep spirituality, keen imagination, great austerity of life and love of study constituted the glory of the East. The untiring energy, the unfailing earnestness, the strong will and determination, the unshaken purpose of Europe are largely required in our country of the Rising Sun. The patience, calmness and coolness of judgment of the East will add no little tone to the other. Steam, electricity, and the other physical powers are no ordinary measures of the strength of Europe. The material wealth and greatness of those distant countries are of no common proportions. The magnificence, the might and the magnanimity of those lands and peoples deserve all the attention that we can bestow on them, and they are right worthy acquisitions. The virtues of the West merit a worthy wedlock with those of the East. Everywhere there are two sides to a picture,—and a close study of the best forms of ancient and modern life can alone teach us to avoid the dark spots wherever they exist, and to admire the

3

bright side wherever it shines. These mutual meetings are conducive to the good of either party.

There is much to study in Europe for our people not only in the moral and material world but in other respects also. The arts and sciences supply a vast field for the enlargement of our knowledge and powers. The anthropological, ethnographical and other museums of Europe are a life's study in themselves, where we can institute comparison of arts, industries, dress, living, habits and customs of different countries and people. The natural scenery and social peculiarities of various lands and nations bring new light to us. The mode of building houses of wooden planks and rafters in Norway and Switzerland reminds us of our own wooden houses. Knitting and needle-work, tapestry and wood carving of Sweden and Norway have frequently called to my mind similar handicrafts of India. The lake, mountain and woodland scenery of Sweden, Norway and Switzerland would call to our mind scenes in Guzerat, the Deccan, Kashmir and the Himalayas. Norway is the Deccan without Konkan. Semmering in Austria reminds us of the Kasara and Khandala Ghauts. Everything that enlightens the mind, that enlarges the heart, that elevates the soul, that strengthens affections, that creates nations, that raises and enlarges empires, kingdoms and republics, is found as a living and active force in Europe, and they are matters of the past in most cases in the East. There we find "sermons in stones, tongues in trees, and good in everything," as the Swan of Avon sings. May our Indians learn to study these things and assimilate the best of them with their system !

The Elements of Euclid's Geometry in Sanscrit in 15 Books by Jagannatha Samrat
(Circa A. D. 1720 to 1728.)

I owe it to my friend Rao Bahadur Justice Janârdan Sakhârâm Gâdgil B. A., LL. B., F. T. S. of the High Court of Judicature, Baroda State, to be able to present this work to the learned assembly here. The work, I trust, will have a universal interest, both for the Orientalist Scholars as well as the *Savants*, inasmuch as it brings to light the so-called lost Books of Euclid's Elements of Geometry. We know from the invaluable works of Potts and Todhunter only the first six books of Euclid with fragments of the eleventh and the twelfth. The latter writer in his notes appended to his edition of Euclid's Elements* gives a bird's-eye view of the history and survival of the work in Europe. The burning of the Alexandrian Library—that contained very precious works of ancient arts, sciences, literature and philosophy of the East, and the West —by Khalif Omar is said to have destroyed this and other mathematical works of general instruction and it is therefore that the work is not found in its complete form in the West. So if India and the Sanskrit language have been instrumental in preserving what is irrecoverably lost elsewhere, it is no small heirloom that they are now going to give to the world in the form of this *Rekha Ganita,* or Mathematics of Lines, Geometry

---

* Vide pp. 250 et seq.

in Fifteen Books. This work proves to us that it was
not only Arithmetic and Algebra, which originated with
them and Astronomy, that the Indian Aryans cultivated
but they did Geometry as well. Without it, the
Science of Mathematics would be incomplete. The circle would be wanting in one of its most important arcs.
The author of this work very beautifully describes that
Brahmadeva or the Supreme God imparted this *Silpa
Shastra*, (Engineering Scienee, as my friend Mr. Justice
Gadgil renders it in the notes he has kindly placed at
my disposal), to Visva Karmâ or the Universal Artificer
and it descended from him, from teacher to disciple, to
recent times. We shall see further on whether the Science
was new to the Indian Aryans and received by them
from abroad or they had the elements thereof in some
form or another already. I can do no better than
give in the words of Mr. Justice Gadgil himself, how the
manuscript of the work under notice, was brought to light.
"The original Ms. was found in the Library of the late
celebrated Bàl Gangâdhar Shâstri Jâmbhekar by Abâ
Shâstri Bakre. I got a copy made of the Ms."—which
original kindly lent to me by the gentleman, I hold in
my hand at present. Mr. Justice Gadgil's Copy was made
in V. S. 1942 (A. C. 1886). The date of the original
Ms. now with me is V. S. 1886 (A. D. 1830) "Kârtek
(*Sans* Kârtika) Sudi (*Sans* Sudi) 5", in the words of the
writer. Although the Ms. was found in possession of a
Maratha Brahmin, and I got it from Baroda in the last
week of June, within three weeks of my leaving India
for this Congress, yet it appears to have belonged

to Upper India, perhaps to Rajputana as the words "Kârtek and Sudi" indicate. Who can tell what hands it has changed, or what vicissitudes it has passed through? Col. Tod tells us in his *Râjasthan* + that Sawae Jey Sing's "profligate descendent the late Jugutt-Sing" distinguished himself by scattering to the wild winds and the four quarters the best collections of his illustrious predecessor. The writer notes, " the noble treasures of learning which Jeysing had collected from every quarter, the accumulated result of his own research and that of his predecessors, were divided into two portions, and one-half was given to a common prostitute, the favorite of the......The most remarkable manuscripts were till lately hawking about Jeypoor". And probably our Ms. was one of them. Thank heaven that it at least has escaped the sorrowful wreck that has overtaken many. But looking to its date V. S. 1886, it was perhaps not the subject of the tyrant's wreckless destructions ; for Juggut Sing, ruled between A. C. 1803 and 1820.$ What had escaped the Conflagration of Khalif Omar, also escaped destruction by King Juggut Singh. My friend Dr. Peterson informs me that he has seen a Ms. of a *Rekha Ganita* at Jeypore * when he visited the place last. Shortly before leaving India I have addressed a letter to the Secretary of the Royal Library for a loan of the copy and if I get it, it will be of no small service to

+ Cf. Vol. II. p. 320,

$ Vol. II. of Tod Raj. p. p. 326-27.

* and also at Ulwar.

us to compare and collate it with our present Ms. and correct some of the copyist's mistakes that have crept in, and to supply the figures for some of the propositions that are wanting. The present Ms. extends over 144 double pages and a portion more. Each single page contains 29 lines on an average and each line contains an average of 25 letters. The copy is written in bold beautiful Devanagari characters, and the text contains some mistakes in writing, as I have already mentioned.

The geometrical figures for most of the propositions are very neatly drawn. I say most of the propositions, because for some of them, they are wanting, as mentioned above.

While our present Euclid in English as in Todhunter's work contains 196 propositions, this Sanskrit Euclid contains (478) four hundred and seventy eight. The first six books in both the recensions, the English and the Sanskrit, contain an equal number of propositions, (viz· 48 in the First Book, 14 in the Second, 16 in the Fourth, 25 in the Fifth and 33 in the Sixth), except in the Third which contains 37 in the English one while it has 36 in the Sanskrit. The Seventh, Eighth, Ninth, Tenth, Eleventh, Twelfth, Thirteenth, Fourteenth and Fifteenth Books in Sanskrit contain 39, 27,* 38, 109, 41, 15, 21, 10 and 6 propositions respectively. The fragments of Books XI and XII in English, I may add, contain but 21 and 2 propositions respectively in

---

* The number of propositions is specified at the opening of each Book. Book VIII specifies 25 Propositions but it actually gives 27.

Prof. Todhunter's work. I have in the above enu-
meration not counted separately the more than one
case (method of proof) of some of the propositions in
either of the two recensions.

Of these 15 Books, Euclid (B. C. 323 to 283)
is said to have written 13 to which two more were
added by Hypsides of Alexandria.* The work of Euclid in 13 Books was translated into Arabic by Nasir
Alà Uddin al Tusi in the Thirteenth Century. The
earliest editions of Euclid in Europe + appear to be those
of 1703 and 1781 of Oxford and of 1788 of London.
The Oxford edition of 1703 was by David Gregory.
"As an edition of the whole of Euclid's works this
stands alone, there being no other in Greek". (De
Morgan). It appears to have been in Greek. It was
followed by the Greek edition of the first Six Books of
Euclid with a Latin translation by Gulielmus Cameron
published at Berlin in 1824 and 1825 in two volumes.
Then came the edition of Ferdinande August again
of Berlin published in two volumes in 1826 and 1829,
containing all the 13 books of Euclid with a collection
of various readings. "A third volume which was to
have contained the remaining works of Euclid, never
appeared." % Prof. Todhunter remarks that the well

---

* Cf. Tod Hunter's Euclid p. 250.

+ In India the earliest Gujerati versions were those of Col.
G. R. Jervis translated from the works of W. Hutton (A. D. 1855)
3rd edition and of Messrs James Graham and Nundshanker Tulja-
shanker, of Book I (Edition A. D. 1858). For still earlier European
editions, vide Postscript, May 1890.

% Cf. Todhunter's Euclid pp. 250-1.

known publishers Messrs. Trubner and Co. have promised an edition of the whole of Euclid but it has not appeared.* The two volumes of 1781 and 1788 above mentioned go under the name of "The Elements of Euclid with disertation" by James Williamson. Other translations of Euclid &c. are not noticed here as they do not contain anything new beyond the above editions. But it would not be fair to pass over these editions and the earlier ones that contain notes on the elements of Euclid as (1) an Examination of the First Six Books of Euclid's Elements by William Austin, Oxford 1781; (2) Euclid's Elements of Plane Geometry with copious notes by John Walker, London 1827; (3) The First Six Books of Euclid with a Commentary by Dionysius Lardner, 4th Ed. London 1834; and (4) Prof. DeMorgan's Short Supplementary Remarks on the First Six Books of Euclid's Elements, in the Companion to the Almanac for 1894§.

The *resume* above given tells us that the elements of Geometry have never appeared in all the fifteen books, either in the West or in the East, in any language, Greek or Arabic, Latin or English, German, Portuguese or French. + Nor has any translation or discussion, annotation or explanation been attempted or given of any books beyond the seventh, except that James Williamson gave a translation into English of the first thirteen books in 1781 and 1788. §§ It is these

* This has lytely appeared.
§ Cf. Todhunter. ibid.
+ Vide Pestscript.
§§ To this may be added Nusir Alá Uddin Al Tusi's Arabic Translation above noticed.

facts therefore that give a special value and interest to the work of Jagannâth Samrât.

The contents of the first Six Books are too well known to demand any detailed notice. But it is interesting to note that the Sanskrit Geometry does not give the three Postulates and gives only two of the Axioms, viz., that all right angles are equal and that two straight lines cannot enclose a space. The First Book gives the definitions of *Bindu* or a point, *Rekha* or a line *Dharatala Bhumi* or *Kshettra* or superfices, which are described as *Sama* or plane and *Vishama* or curved : angles, *Konas* also are divided into *Sama* or plane and *Vishama* or curved. They are *Sama Konas* proper or right angles and *Alpa Konas* or acute angles and *Adhika Konas* or obtuse angles. *Rekhas* are lines which are also *Sama* or straight and *Kutila* or *Vakra* or curved. *Kshettra* or *Dharatala* figures again are *Tribhujas* or triangles or trilaterals (*Bhujas, Asras, Bahus,* meaning sides), *Chaturasras* or *Chaturbhujas* or quadrilaterals and *Vrittas* or circles and *Chapa Karnas* or semi-circles. Triangles are again *Samatribahuka,* equilateral, *Samaduibahuka,* isosceles, and *Vishamabahuka,* scalene ; as also *Sama Kona,* right-angled, *Nyuna Kona,* acute-angled and *Adhika Kona* obtuse-angled. Quadrilaterals are *Sama Kona Sama Chaturbhuja,* squares, *Vishama Chaturbhuja* or *Vayata,* oblong, *Visama Kona Sama Chaturbhuja,* rhombus and *Vishama Kona Vishama Chaturbhuja,* rhomboid. Trapeziums and trapezoids, polygons and multi-laterals are not given nor defined. *Bindu* or *Madhya Bindu* or the center of a circle is *Kendra.*

4

The diamater is *Vyasa*. *Sutra* is a radius and *Pali* the circumference. There are also terms for an arc, a sector, a base, a hypotenuse &c. Parallel lines are also *Samantarala Rekhas*. These are the only definitions and terms of the First Book in our Sanskrit work. Books II, III, IV, VIII, IX, XII, XIII. XIV, XV, have no definitions. Books V, VI, VII have definitions suited to their subject and purpose. In Book VII numbers (*ankas*) are defined and they are *Laghvanka, Brihadhanka, Samanka,* even—and it is twofold, *Sama Sama,* even divisible by even, as 8 and *Sama Vishama* even divisible by odd, Vishamanka, as 6, odd divisible by odd, as 9 and *Prathamanka,* as 11, indivisible either by odd or even. The other *Ankas* are *Yuganka, Militanka, Bhinnanka. Varga* and *Ghana* are square and cube. *Kshettrafala* and *Ghanafala* are square and cube areas. *Ghata* is a root. There are *Gunya Gunanka* or *Bhuja* and *Sajatiya* and *Purnanka* or an integer as 6. Book X similarly gives *Rekhas* or lines as *Bhinna-Varga, Kalpita Kevala-Bhinna, Bhinnabhinna Varga, Milita Varga.* There are also *Kshetrafala Mulada Rasi* and *Karani.*

While Proposition VII., Book I, is proved in one way, V is proved in two ways, as also XI. XII, XVII. XXI, XXVI, XXIX. (proved by 8 propositions and by itself as two sets) XXVIII, XXXV. The corollary of a proposition is separately proved. Propositions XX and XXIV are proved in 3 ways. The penultimate proposition of the Book i. e. XLVII is proved in about 14 ways!!! In Book II, Propositions I to

IX and XI are each proved in two ways and Proposition X in three ways. In Book III, Proposition XXX is proved in more ways than one, and Propositions II, VIII, X to XV, and XXXIII are each of them proved in 2 ways. In Book IV, Proposition XIII is proved in 4 ways, while Proposition II of Book VI is proved in three ways and Propositions VI, IX, X, XV, XVIII, XXIX and XXXI are each of them proved in two ways. In Book VII, Proposition XIV and XVIII are each them proved in 2 ways. In Book X, Propositions I and XII are so proved, and also in Book XI, III, and in Book XIII, XV; while Proposition IX in Book XII is proved in three ways. This, in short, is a summary of the contents of the fifteen books. I do not wish it be understood as complete as I have not yet been able to go fully through the work, nor have I been able to compare these with the Arabic or the European Versions of the work. I hope to make up for these defects in the edition of the work, with an English Translation and notes, that I am shortly to publish in conjunction with my brother Mr. K. H. Dhruva B. A., Ahmedabad, India. But a passing glance will tell us what important treasure has alighted on our view. A critical study and examination of the work will no doubt bring forward important facts and results in the field of our knowledge of the Science of Numbers, Lines, Angles and Areas. Books VII, VIII and IX are said to treat of numbers and so do the books in Sanskrit before us. Book X concerns itself with the consideration of the com-mensurable and the in-commensurable magnitudes and it is the longest in the Elements.

We see the same here also. Book XI, XII, and XIII, mainly treat of Solid Geometry. Jagannatha's work also treats of the same, and to these may be added Books XIV and XV, which deal with Spherical Geometry as well. The contents of the Work as given above and of the Books as also the same number and order of Propositions in the first six Books point to the same original of the present work, viz. the Greek, i. e. what we know as the writing of Euclid. The use of letters in the several propositions and figures also go to prove the same fact. The letters are अ *a,* ब *b,* द *d,* ग *g,* ह *h* as representing the Greek alphabets Alpha, Gema, Delta Epsilon-and झ *z,* व *v,* स *s,* त *t* श *sh,* छ *chh, kha* ख, *f* फ, *l* ळ, न *n,* य *y,* म *m,* &c. Let us see what the author himself has to say on the head, and this launches us into the question of the age and authorship of the work.

The writer of the work is a Brahmin, by name Jagannâth Samrât, more than once alluded to above. As the writer informs us, he lived in the time of King Jayasinhadeva whom he calls, and eulogizes as, Sri Rajarajeswara. He is the same as King Sawai Jaysing, the founder of Jaipur, of whom Col. Tod says that "In spite of his many defects Jay Sing's name is destined to descend to posterity as one of the most remarkable man of his age and nation. " * He was the founder of Jaypur in A. C. 1728.§ He ruled for 40 years and died in V. S. 1799 (A. C. 1743). × He was a patron of

* Col Tod's Rajasthana II. 319.

§ Cf. Ibid p. 319.

× Cf. Ibid pp. 310 and 320.

of learning and Jain Vidhyâthara was the principal Pundit of his Court as also our author whom Col. Tod does not seem to mention. He was himself no mean author. He was at the same time a mathematician, an astronomer, and a historian.

He ordered observatories to be constructed at Delhi, Jaypur, Oojein, Benares, and Mathura "upon a scale of Asiatic grandeur, and their results were so correct as to astonish the world".§ You can still see the Observatory at Benares in all its completeness and mathema_ tical accuracy, overlooking the Ghaut or Bank of the Ganges. He was a scholar and savant as also a states- man and warrior. The part played by him in the wars of succession after the death of Aurengzib was no insignificant one. He was a prominent figure-head in the Triple Alliance of Marwar, Meywar and Amber, that wrested from the Emperor and his partizans the annulment of the notoriously tyrannical capitation tax or the *Jezeya Vera*, called Janârdana by our Pandit. $

Mahamudsha who came to the throne in 1720 A. C. called him from his favourite pursuits and appointed him his Lieutenant for the Provinces of Agra and Malwa. % This accounts for the King's erection of observatories at the several places, especially those at Mathura, Delhi, Benares and Oojein. He was asked to prepare the tables by the Emperor to which he devoted

§ Cf. Tod's Rajasthan II. 311.

$ Col. Tod's Rajasthan I. 310 264 XIV et. seq. Ch. XV. also p. 318. Il 311.

% Cf. Tod's Rajasthana II. 34.

7 years. (A. C. 1721 to 1728). The work is called
Zeh Mahamadshahi by him. In order to secure correct
results and perfect accuracy he had engaged a learned
Portuguese missionary, by name Padre Manual, and
through him he indented upon the services of Xavier
de Silva who was sent to him by King Emannuel of
Portugal. He had also sent several skilful persons
to the Court. Xavier de Silva is said to have com-
municated to the Rajput Prince, says Col. Tod, the
Tables of Dela Hire published in A. C. 1792. In 1729
he determined the obliquity of the ecliptic to 23m. 28s.
within 28s. of what was determined to be in the year
following by Godwire. Its accuracy was further put
to the test in 1793 by Dr. W. Hunter. Col. Tod. further informs us that he "caused Euclid's Elements, the
treatises on Plane and Spherical Trigonometry......XI
to be translated into Sanskrit." § In the exact translation from the work of the king also he mentions the
the name of Euclid thus :—"the demonstrations of Euclid are an imperfect sketch of the forms of His contri-
vance."—(meaning that of the Supreme Artificer.)+
Apart from the lieutetenancy that he held under Mah-
mudshah, and the part he played earlier in the Triple
Alliance, his own dominion was greatly enlarged by
him. From a small principality much encroached upon
by enemies at home and abroad, he raised it to a power
in Rajputana. His prowess and bravery were equally
remarkable. On the elevation of Shahalum Bahadur

---

§ Col. Tod. Rajasthana II. 311 et. seq.
+ Col. Tod. Rajasthana II. 313.

Shah, Amber was sequestrated for his opposition and an imperial governor was sent to take possession thereof. But Jaysing entered his state sword in hand, drove out the Emperor's garrison and formed a league with Ajitsingh of Marwar for their mutual preservation.* All this is solid ground of History. Now let us see what our author says. The work opens with some of introductory verses and every Chapter but Chapters II, III, V closes with a verse which is descriptive of the work being written at the order of the said Kiug Jaya Singh Deva by Jagan Nàth Samràt. I subjoin one below :—

श्रीमद्भामाधिरान प्रभुवर जयसिंहस्य तुष्टयै द्विजेन्द्र
श्रीमत्सम्राट् नगन्नाथ इति समभिद्यारुहितेन प्रणिते
ग्रंथेऽस्मिन्नाम्निरेखागणित इति सुकोणावबोध प्रदात
यर्घ्यायोऽभ्येतृमोहापह इह विरति घत्त संख्या बभुव

It can be translated thus :—

"The fifteenth book came to a close in this Rekha Ganita or Geometry which destroys the *moha* or delusion of a student, and which gives instruction of good Lord Jaya Singha Deva, his August Majesty the King of Kings."

From the above we can gather that the writer was a Brahmin of eminence, that he held a high position at the Court of King Jaya Singh who was a great monarch, and that he wrote this Geometry for the satisfaction of the King.

The opening verses state the same facts with rather fuller details. The first verse is a salutation to

---

* Cf. Tod's Rajasthan pp, 1 318 al c. a. II. 311.

Ganpati, the Indian God of Wisdom, and the second to Lakshmi, Nrisinha—the God Vishnu in his incarnation of man-lion—and his spouse Lakshmi, the Goddess of Beauty and Wealth, also to Vakdevi or the Goddess of Speech, and to his Guru or Preceptor, well-versed in the Science of Mathematics. Verses 3. 4. 5 are historical and descriptive of the King. I subjoin and translate them below :—

श्री गोविंद समाद्ययादि विबुधान् वृन्दाटविं निर्गतान्
यस्तंत्रैव निराकुलं शुचिमना भावः खशक्त्यानयत्
म्लेच्छान् मान समुन्नतान् खतरसा निर्जित्य भूमंडले
जीयाच्छी जयसिंहदेव नृपतिः श्रीराजराजेश्वरः ॥ ३
करं जनार्दनं नाम दूरीकृत्य खतेजसाप्नो
भ्राजते दुःसहोदरीणां यथा ग्रैष्मो दिवाकरः—४.
येनेष्टं वाजपेया धैर्महादानानि षोडश
दत्तानिद्विजवर्य्येभ्या गोग्रामगजवाजिनः—५.

(V. 3.) May he live in this world the Auspicious Rajarajeswara x or king of kings. Jayasinhadeva, who of a pure heart, took back through his prowess just there Sri Govinda and other Brahmins (or gods) that were cast out of Vrindâtavi (or Vrindâvana) after having defeated the Mlechhas that were overbearing through pride by his own power.

(V. 4.) He shines like the Summer Sun, unbearable to enemies having done away with his own splendour (influence) the impost pressing hard on the people, Janardana by name.

x   Cf. Sawai Jeya Singh of Col. Tod.

(V. 5.) Who has performed Vâjapeya and other *yajnas* or sacrifices and who has given the sixteen kinds of gifts viz. cows, villages, elephants and horses to the best of Brahmins.

In all these facts the writer is amply borne out by the historical researches of Col. Tod. If Govinda &ca. were Brahmins, we do not know more about them. If they were gods, meaning idols of Govinda i. e. Vishnu &c. overthrown by Sultan Mahomed, Alauddin &c. at Mathurâ, then the author means a re-installation of them by the King which can be between A. C. 1719 and 1728 or rather 1720 and after, when in the latter case he was in power at the Court of Delhi and when he was the Emperor's lieutenant for the Provinces of Agra and Malva.* The conquest of Jaya Sing, here described, may imply either his successes over the Syeds or over the imperial soldiers at Amber referred to above. All these make no common soldier and warrior of King Jayasinhadeva, very worthily Rajârajeswaia. Here there is no fulsome praise of a bard—but a justly offered encomium by an accurate and grateful mathematician to his patron.

The fact of King Jayasinhadeva's hand in the annulment of the *Jezeyavero* described in Verse 4 is also a matter of history. This may refer to the event when the triple alliance of Marwar, Meywar and Amber having him at its head, secured, perhaps at the point of the sword, the repeal of the odious tax at the hand of Ferokshere in A. C. 1719. But this does not appear to have

---

* Vide Tod's Rajasthana supra.

5

lasted long. For, we know a second repeal in the time
of Mahamudshah when King Jayasing came to power
between A. C. 1720 and 1728. Col. Tod speaking of
this remarks "nor was he blind to the interests of his
nation or the honor of Amber and his important offices
were made subservient to obtaining the repeal of that
disgraceful edict, the *Jezeya*, and the authority to sup-
press the infant power of the Jats, long a thorn in the
side of Amber."* The year of this second repeal is not
mentioned. But perhaps our author means the first,
for he does not allude to the observatories established
by the King at Mathura &c. while he eulogizes the act
of the reinstitution of Govinda &ca. in Vrindâtavi quite
close to it. The author does not speak of the foundation
of Jeypur &c. that took place in V. S. 1784 (A. C. 1728).§
These are important facts for us to determine the age of
the work and the date of its composition. It can safely be
laid somewhere between "the three years of uninter-
rupted quiet" which the King "appears to have enjoyed"
"taking no part in the struggles which terminated in A.
D. 1721." Of course it was after A. C. 1719, the date
of the first repeal of the impost of *Jezeya*. It was perhaps before A. C. 1721 from which year the King was
engaged in writing and working out his Mahomed-Shai
Tables for the following years. The year A. C. 1720
therefore seems to be the year of the composition of
the work before us.

(Verse 6) is:—

---

* Rajasthan II. 314.

§ Ibid II. 319.

तस्य श्री जयसिंहस्य तुष्टयै रचयाति स्फुटम्
द्विज : सम्राट् जगन्नाथो रेखागणितमुत्तमम्

This need not be translated, as its meaning is included in the verse above given and translated. About the year A. C. 1720 the King was engaged in his philosophical pursuits which can be no other than mathematical and astronomical. The preparation of the table was a task imposed upon him by his imperial master who showered upon him honours and emoluments unasked. The performance of the sacrifices and the giving of gifts of horses, elephants, cows and villages, all indicate a quiet state of enjoyment by the King. These sacrifices are also referred to by Col. Tod. "Amongst the vanities of the founder of Amber, it is said that he intended to get up the Ceremony of the Asva Medha Yâga or sacrifice of the horse, a rite which, his re-searches into the traditions of his nation must have informed him, had entailed destruction of all who had attempted it from the days of Janmejaya the Pandu to Jeichund the last Rajput monarch of Kanouj. It was a virtual assumption of universal supremacy."§ This was perhaps an accomplished fact if we interprete the verse rightly. And it was only then that the term Râja Râjeswara was properly applicable to him. This also must be before the year of his vassalage or promotion at the Court of Delhi in A. C. 1721 and after. And that too brings down our work to the year before it i. e. A. C, 1720.

We can now very well go to verses 7-8-9 that I

§ Rajasthana II. 20.

give and translate below :—

अपूर्वं विदितं शास्त्रं यत्र कोणावबोधनात्
क्षेत्रेषु जायते सम्यग् व्युत्पत्ति र्गणिते तथा ७
शिल्पशास्त्रमिदं प्रोक्तं ब्रह्मणा विश्वकर्मणे
पारंवर्यवशादितदागतं धरणीतले ८
तद् विच्छिन्नं महाराज जयसिंहाज्ञया पुनः
प्रकाशितं मया सम्यग् गणकानंतहेतवे ९

(V. 7). This wonderful science is known (where) understanding is got of areas from a knowledge of the angles as well as in mathematics.

(V. 8). Brahmâ or the Supreme God revealed this engineering science to Viswa Karmâ, the Universal Artificer, and it came to the earth in succession (from teacher to pupil)*.

(V. 9.) That was lost or destroyed; I again published it well for innumerable mathematicians or for the Mathematician Ananta, at the command of the Great King Mahârâja Jaya Sinha.

Here is a view quite in contrast with the one, given before, of a Greek origin of the work. As is usual with our writers they trace everything to the first originator and author of things, and so also has been the case here. While the King mentions Euclid by name and his demonstrations, his Pandit wishes to give here an Indian origin for it. Perhaps the light afforded to the former in his contact with Padre Manual was not with-

---

* Cf. The term used by King Jaya Sinha in his tables. Introduction of Mahommedshahi.

in the reach of the latter and he perhaps did not know the writer while he was adopting his writing. Perhaps King Emmanuel of Portugal had not yet sent Xavier De Silva with the tables of De La Hire and other Western lore. And so perhaps the Greek edition of Euclid of A. C. 1703 published at Oxford had not reached India to be the basis of the Indian work. Perhaps no European version of Euclid was the basis of the Indian Work as they are found to be in 13 Books, while the present work is in 15 Books. Possibly Pandit Jagannath had before him the Arabic Version of Nasir that his master might have got from the Court of Delhi. But the same objections apply to that supposition also. It also is in 13 Books. Nasir also has been named in the present work, &c. Then there is every reason to conclude that there was an Indian tradition of the work that was lost in the midst of obscurity. While the West had preserved only 13 Books and that too saw the light in the biginning of the Eighteenth Century, the far East had preserved all the fifteen. With the exception of the letters used, there is nothing Greek about it. The work appears to have been adopted and assimilated in the Indian system. The technical terms already noticed and detailed above are pure Sanskrit, except perhaps Kendra and Pali (the centre and circumference of a circle). According to our authority there were works extant on the Science in India. There was a regular school of Geometricians that taught the Science from generation to generation of students and teachers.

But even then that was well nigh extinct and here there was a renaiscence, that of other Mathematical Sciences.

A nation that could create Arithmetic and Algebra could not have been ignorant of Geometry which too deals with numbers and quantity. (Vide Books VII, VIII, IX, X). A nation that has made great advances in Astronomy could not do without the Science of lines, angles and arcs. The writer himself speaks of a larger use of this Science beyond that of the determination of areas from angles—viz : for wider mathematics (vide V. 7). Pandit Dayânand Saraswati was of opinion that *Yajnas* were instrumental in the keeping up of the study of Geometry. The *Kalpa Sutras* dealing with the *Yajnas*, and especially the *Silpa Sastras* contained germs of the Science and much of the dark unexplored continent of *Tantric* Literature perhaps contains important *debries* of this *vichhinna*, dilapidated, destroyed, lost Science. Then it is also possible that there was an Indian foundation on which the present edifice was built on a foreign plan and with outlandish materials. The alternative proofs of several propositions and technical phraseology give a colour to the author's view. But more light is needed to determine the question—which can with our present knowledge be very well kept open.

But with all that, our position with regard to the work is not a whit changed, and so I take this the pleasant opportunity of presenting to the learned world, the Elements of Geometry, which we may very well term Euclid in the Sanskrit garb written by a Brahmin of Brahmins, Samrāt Jagannath, at the Court of King Jaya Singh-deva Raja Rajeswara, in A. C. 1720-1 within 17 or 18 years of the publication of the first Greek edition of Euclid at Oxford. May it prove to be of value to Science and Scholarship !

The Neo-Vernaculars of Western India.

In continuing the vista of research in the Philology and Literature of the Neo-Vernaculars of India, opened by my friend M. Grieson at the last Congress, I need not make any apology. The subject is so interesting that I require no long perface to introduce you to it. The philology of the Indian languages, nay, the Aryan or General Philology will be incomplete without a knowledge of the History and Philology of the Vernaculars at this day spoken. The past languages are like the fossils and crystals that are long formed and settled down in the history of the development of the human tongue. The living vernaculars whether Aryan, Semitic, Dravidian or others, whether of India and the East or of the West are the current stratification and formation, aggregation or segregation of words and thoughts that we can see with our own eyes and test and touch with our own instruments of research and study. As in geology and other physical sciences we go up from the present to the distant past, so we can do the same in Philology here. Western India has been from the earliest times a busy field of the actions, re-actions and inter-actions of many an ethnic and linguistic force in the continent.

Waves after waves of nations and races have swept over its face with their peculiar social and political formations, languages, creeds, and culture, as varied and multifarious as themselves. In this

6

paper we have nothing to do with pre-Aryan or non-Aryan waves of colonization or forces that formed and and influenced them. The Vedas and the Avesta give us the picture of life and language of the Indo-Iranians, either in the Airyana Vaejo or the Hafta Hendu, the Elttarh Kuravah or the Sapta Sinthus, the highlands of the Hindu-Kush or the fertile plains of the Punjaub. They were followed at varying intervals by numerous other races, and principally among them those that are collectively named and described as the S'akas or Scythians or the Indo-Scythians. The current of the spread of nations took the course first of a concentric enlargement all round from Brahmâvarta to Brahmarshidesa and then literally eastwards and southwards to Madhyadesh and Aryâvartta according to Manu. The Paurânic extent further south and including the whole of India in Bharata Khanda was perhaps of a subsequent date. The Vedas represent the first stage of Aryan colonization of Upper India. The Râmâyana takes us further inwards, but even then we find colonies or Ásramas of Rishis on the Bengal side, here and there, and a few more in Central and Southern India, as those of Bhâradvâja on the Ganges, of Valmiki on Chitrakûta, of Agastya and Lopâ-Mûdrâ southwards. In the Mahâbhârata there is a further advance and it is then that we alight upon Gujerat with the Yâdava Colony of Krishna. The Skanda-Purânâ in its Prabhâsa Nagara and other Khandas aquaints us with Gujerat under its name of Kusâvarta, (âvartta and its monarchs). But the Province became *Saurashtra* or the good country later on. At first it as well as Sindhu, Sau Vira &c. were under a ban, and the Konkan was wrested by Parasurâma according to the Purânas, from the Sea. All these epic and paurânic accounts of some of the later Avtâras, or incarnations are illustrative of the ethnic spread of the Aryan races over India and their general colonization of the continent. The *Sankalpa*—that is made daily almost prefacing every moral or religious act of his—repeated by an Aryan gives us an idea of how this took place. While naming the time of the desired act it also specifies the place and in the description of the latter it gives in detail the several early geographical divisions and appellations in an inverse order. The earliest state of the country was of *Aranyas* (Forests) and Gujerat of the valley of the Saraswati and Sabhramati and Mahi was still Arbudâranya. South of it was Naimishâranya between the Mahi and the Narmada; further south was Dandakâranya recognized in the modern Dàngas. There was a Champakâranya in Kattywar. The next stage was of *Kshettras* or plantations as Kûmarikâ Kshettra (Gujerat), Prabhâsa Kshettra &c. We can here see an analogy in the colonization of America and Australia within historical times. Then we come to *A'varttas* or circles as in Brahmâvartta, Kusâvartta, and Aryâvarta, and *Desas* or Countries as Brahmarshidesa, Madhyadesa, Anarttadesa &c. Latterly we have *Khandas* and *Dvipas* or Continents and Islands, nine and seven each, of the Purânas and historical times. We have further divi-

sions of *Mandalas, Vishayas, Pathakas,* i. e. provinces,
divisions and districts. The terms, *tirtha* or the bank
of a river or a lake and *Asrama*, a hermitage, are to
be relegated to the *Aranya* period.

These are then descriptive of the Aryan Colonization. But the descents or eruptions, from time to
time of the Scythian hordes, were invasions rather
than colonies. We see an analogy of this in the Gallic
i. e., Celtic, Teutonic, Gothic, and the like invasions
of the Hellenic or the Italio-Romanic regions. They
are to be distinguished from the Latin and the Greek
Colonies that resembled the Indo-Aryan colonizing of
old, and the Indo-European colonizing of the present
day. We have above taken Scythic as a generic appellation. Some of the principal of these races with which
Western India and the subject of our paper have to
do anything are the Kâthis, the Gûrjaras, the Mâlvas,
the Châvdas and the Solunkis known also as Chalûkyas,
Chaulûkyas or Châlûkyas and perhaps the Râthods or
the Râshtra-Kûtas. Elsewhere we shall show how
the Kâthis migrated from place to place and settled
and gave name to the Province of Kattywar.*
These Kâthis who are also identified by some scholars
with the Kathas of the Sutras and the Upanishadas,
were confronted by Alexander the Great in the fourth
century before Christ, while in the early Aryan
Colonization, the course taken was south or south-
east along the river systems of Upper India (*tirthas*) and

* Vide my paper on Baroda Antiquities and Gujerat
History.

mountain chains or forests (*aranyas*), the course adopted
later on with regard to Western India by some was by
the Punjaub, Cutch and the north-west of Surâstra
and then along the south-west and south sea-shore, and
by others it was by Central India, Rajputana and across
Malwa and thence crossing the Nerbudda and the Tapti
to the tableland of the Deckan and thence in a deflection along the Konkan coast into South and Central
Gujcrat. Both these first met at Pâtan in N. Gujerat
with the Châvdas and Solunkis and then intermingling
spread all over the Province and Peninsula of Gujerat,
Cutch and Kattywar. While the Châvdas shooted off
west-ward, the other races deflected east-wards, the
Râthods and Solunkis going first to the Deckan and
Malwa, and the Kâthis to Malwa and next through
Soreth and Scinde to Kattywar. While the two
streams were moving as above, others took a middle
course right through N. W. and S. Rajputana and
entering Gujerat through the northern passes of Mt.
Abu came and settled in the Nerbudda and Tapti
vallies in S. Gujerat*, other parts of the country being
already occupied by the Valabhis. And it was there
that they confronted the Râthods and the Solunkis. These

---

* Cf. also General Cunningham's Ancient Geography of
India Vol. 1, with regard to Guzzar or Guzaristan, the Chinese
Hosalo Capital of Northern Arachosia p. 39, the Ozola of Ptolemy
p. 40, also Gujarat in the Punjaub, anciently Hairat p. 179 and
Gujara, a Province of Western India, Capital Balmer in the Seventh
Century p. 312 identified with Western Rajputana p. 313. Refer
again to Dr. Buhler's remarks about the Gurjara race, Ind. Ant;
Vol. XVII. pp. 192 et seq.

southern invaders finding the Gûrjars a formidable
barrier to their conquest north-ward had them uppermost
in their mind, while they thought of the whole Province
and their people, which and whom they therefore named
Gurjarâstra and Gurjars respectively, terms which are
are now represented in Gujerat and Gujeratis. Their
language therefore was known as Gujerati as that of
the province to the south was known as Marathi from
the country and people of Mahârâstra. We have the
analogy of thus designating the country from the
powerful race opposing the course of a conquering force
in the name given to the whole Province of Kathiawad
from the Kâthis that proved hard nuts to crack to the
Maratha invaders of the Province, the Peishwas and
the Gaekwads. Thus principally these five or seven
races have populated Western India with an admixture of the early or the contemporary Brahmin
settlers from the regions of Ahichatra, Kanyâ-kûbja
and Rajputana like the Nâgaras, Udichas, Pragvatas,
Srimalis &c.

It is therefore that the dialects of these races are
likely to be grouped to-gether. It is therefore that Gujerati and the dialects spoken in Cutch, Kathiawar,
Malwa and Rajputana are more closely allied and re-
lated to those of Upper India than to those of S. India.
Punjaubi and Scindi have been kept quite aloof like
Bengali and Uriya on the other side and Pushtu, Ne-
palese and Kashmirian and the minor dialects on further North, North-East and North-West. The real
languages of hard historic, ethnic and linguistic fights

are Hindi, Gujerati and Marathi, representing Upper India of the Doab and its vicinity, Western India connected with the bee-hive of nations in the Punjaub and the Central and Southern India respectively. While the later history kept up the political status of Hindi and Marathi, the genius of Gujerati was diverted into another channel, mercantile or commercial.

It is on account of the causes and forces enumerated above that the Gujerati poets and authors could write works and poems in their native tongue as also in the sister tongues, Hindi &c. A poet of the last quarter of the eighteenth and the first of the nineteenth century has written poems not only in Gujerati and Hindi but in Marathi, Marwadi, Sindhi and Punjaubi as well. It is therefore that Gujerati is richer in forms, words and phrases than any other vernacular of India. While the other vernaculars have preserved single forms of words and terminations, Gujerati has multiple ones. It shakes hands on the south with Marathi, on the east and the north with Hindi and on the west and the north-west with Sindhi and Punjaubi. It is therefore also that I include not only Cutch and Kattywad but Rajputana and Malva in the area influenced by Gujerati. Haranti, Mewadi, Marwadi, Malvi and the minor dialects are therefore rather branch dialects of Gujerati than of Hindi—I mean Urdu also—and as much as Cutchi and Jadeji and Charani are of the same Gujerati. I have travelled over some parts of Rajputana, I have received information of linguistic forms in Malva from those who have travelled there, and I have collected a good number of Haranti songs and writings as also of the Cutchi Jadeji and Charni-songs—and on a comparison of them I am led to this conclusion. The subject is so vast that only a separate treatment can fully satisfy the requirements of the above conclusion. But any scholar can satisfy himself with a look at those collections with me which will be separately published later on with a descriptive paper. I am also led to this conclusion about the affiliation of these dialects with Gujerati rather than with Hindi on philological and other grounds. While the Sanskrit verbs have got two Padas, the Parasmaipada and Atmanipada, some of the modern varnaculars have preserved the one or the other and some both, but imperfectly. The case in point can be illustrated by taking the forms of the verb "to be" in them. Marathi has *"ahe"* for *"is"*—the Atmanipada of *"as"* *to be* while Gujerati has *"asai"** *"achhai"* *"chai"* *"achhi"* *"chhi"* *"chhe"* softened down to *"chha"* and *"cha"* at various stages of its existence

---

* The forms given are no myths. They are actually found in that order in time in works of different periods. The earliest *"asa-i"* is obtained from classical Sanskrit *"asti"* first by the separation of the consonants "s" and "t", as is usual in Gujerati that disjoins conjunct consonants of Sanskrit and then by the ellision of the consonant "t" as is the case with the mediæval Pakritas. *"Asai"* I am told has left an ancestor which would be exactly *"asati"*, in Vedic *"asati"* for *"syat"* as an equivalent of *"bhavet"* Gujerati *"havi"* of old and *"hoya"* of the present day. For this Vedic *"asati"*, I have the authority of some of my European friends and Orientalists.

and these are Parasmaipadi. Hindi has also **Paras-maipadi** forms derived from Sanskrit *"bhu"*, to be.

This shows a close intimacy and relation between Gujerati and Hindi rather than between the former and Marathi. Now the forms of the same word "to be" will assist us further in showing the closer relation of Gujerati and the dialects mentioned above than of the latter and Hindi. While Gujerati has got the forms derived, as we have seen above, from the Sanskrit root *"as"* to be, Hindi has got the same from the Sanskrit root *"bhu"*, to be. Haranti, Chârani and the allied dialects also have forms for the verb from Sanskrit root *"as"* like Gujerati and not *"bhu"* like Hindi This establishes the same family for Gujerati and those dialects. The speakers of the two set of dialects also are of the same races like the Rajputs, Brahmins and Banias of the Provinces of Gujerat, Malva and Rajputana. The group of Kattywad states is a continuation of the Rajputana states and the Province of Malwa is but a sister to that of Gujerat. The super-imposing of the Mahomedan and Maratha influences since the Mahomedan and Maratha periods of history makes all the apparent difference of our time. The public and official records of Rajputana are kept in Urdu and Persian even now and the local dialects have therefore no written literature in Rajputana as is the case with Cutchi in Cutch through a Gujerati influence. The Maratha States of Indore and Gwaliar &c. have similarly supplanted the local dialects partly by their Marathi as the old Gaikwadi

7

did the same with Gujerati in Baroda Territory. But the scholar has not to read his lessons from the courts of Princes but he has to study the language of the people from their own lips, their huts and hovels, ordinary life and pleasure-resorts.

Again the great Rajput poetess Mirabai of Mewad was a writer of the sweetest lays in Gujarati—some of the most favourite songs, to this day, of Gujerat ladies. The marital songs called *banadas* also of the Nâgaras savour of some of these Rajputana dialects. It is thus that their connection with Gujerati is established and the extent and area of the language enlarged. Under these circumstances the *Prithiraj Rasau* of Chanda Bardai would be called, and classed as, a Gujerati work rather than a Hindi one. But as the question requires more light, I cannot afford to be decisive on the point. Having thus determined the area of the language and its dialects, we can next glance over its constituents or rather the constituents of these neovernaculars of Western India. The Rajputana, Cutch and Malwa dialects are in the traditional or unwritten stage. Even Sindhi and Punjaubi have not advanced far in that direction. Sindhi is thoroughly crushed down as far as I know of it. It has lost its character and the one in use is derived from the Moslem conquerors of the unfortunate Province which has ever been the foot-ball of all that chose to invade the continent or a part of India. It is the rise of the Sikh religion and their Grantha and the character that it is written in, that has saved Punjaubi from a like catastrophe. But it has not been cultivated as much as its Southern and Eastern sisters are. Then it is Gujerati that remains to be examined by us.

We have seen how Gujerat* was the field of conquering and settling races. The province possessed advantages that were possessed by few others of the continent. With a fruitful soil it was known as the Garden of India and the Golden Chersonese. It was veritably a *Saurashtra* or Good Country with an ample and well-indented sea-board having good sea-ports. Its commercial advantages and aptitude were unmatched especially with its large rivers like the

---

* The Statistical Atlas of the Bombay Presidency for 1889, published under Government orders by the Director of Land Records and Agricultural Statistics, Bombay, gives the population of the Bombay Presidency including Sindh and excluding the native states to be 16,454,414 and the area as 113,191 sq. miles. The feudatory or native states including Baroda have an area of 82,328 sq. miles or 42.1 p. c. of the gross area of the Presidency and a population of 9,121,560. The Hindus are 13,204,968 or 80.31 p. c. of the total population, the Mahomedans 3,021,131 or 18.36 p. c. (in the Presidency proper less than 8 p. c. and in Sindh 78 p. c.) and the Parsis chiefly in Gujerat and Bombay City 72,065 or .044 p. c. while the aboriginal races found in the Puncha Mahalas, Surat, Thana, Khandeish and Nasik Divisions are 476,638 or 3.6 p. c. (vide p. 3) of the total population. 47.11 p. c. speak Marathi, 18.86 p. c. Gujerati, 12.77 p. c. Kanarese, 12.47 p. c. Sindhi, 5.30 p. c. Hindustani. Marathi is spoken throughout the Deccan, Konkan, North Karnatic, but little in Gujerat. Gujerati is slightly more diffused as it is the commercial tongue of the chief trading classes, of the Parsis, Mahomedans as well as of Hindus. Sindhi and Canarese are entirely localized in

Mahi and the Nerbudda. Its mountain chains abound-
ed and abound in minerals and its forests in vast sup-
plies of good timber. Its mild and mellow climate
had not the entremes of cold and heat of Upper India.
A broad plain extended between Mt. Abu and the
southernmost confines of Gujerat and from the hills
of the Puncha Mahals to the westernmost shores,
broken here and there by some spurs of hills as
Satrunjaya, Girnar and Barda or a dense knot of jungle

their respective geographical divisions. (ibid). According to the
census of 1882 A. D. the Presidency of Bombay extends between
13·55′ to 28·32′ n. latitudes and 66·43′ to 76·28′ east longitudes.
The aggregate area there given is 123,860 sq. miles. (Vide p. 3
Vol. I). With regard to the advantages possessed by Gujerat
over the other parts of the Presidency the paragraph about it on
pp. 13-4 can probably be compared with what is given here. The
area of Gujerat proper is 10,860 sq. miles (cf. Census ibid p. 6)
i. e. 8.19 p. c. of the entire area. It is roughly speaking $\frac{1}{3}$ of the
Karnatic, $\frac{1}{4}$ of the Deccan and one-fifth of Sindh and nearly equal
to that of Konkan. (Ib. pp. 6-7). With regard to population Gujerat is the densest. It has 281 persons per square mile. The
total number of persons enumerated at the time of the census
in 1882, was 16,454,414 in the Presidency. " Gujerat is as large
as the State of Vermont " but its population is larger and stands
about half way between that of Sanoni and Wallachia (cf. pp. 8-9).

For population according to religion &c. cf. ch. III. pp. 45
et seq. Census 1882 Bombay, and according to language &c. ch.
III. pp. 106-16. ibid. The limits of Gujerat are defined between
the Daman river and the confines of Rajputana. " Here Marwar
takes its place *though there is at least in the Western Rajpu-*
tana States very little difference between the two, except in
pronunciation and a few verbal clauses."

like the Gir. Nature had showered all the bounties
upon the land and the people were largely benefited
by them. The Gujeratis, by whom I understand not
only the Hindus, but the Parsis, Mahomedans and
Christians as well, traded with distant China and
Further India and the East Indies as well as with the
Red-Sea and Arabian Sea-board and the East African
Coast, carrying their sweet language, honest industry
and affable manners wherever they went.

Wm. Marsden Esq. writing in one of the Volumes
of the Royal Asiatic Researches of Bengal "On the
traces of the Hindu language and literature, extant
among the Malayans" remarks that "It has borrowed
many words from Sanskrit. Only some metaphysical

The italics are mine and they are worthy of note. In Cutch
the language though more Gujerati than anything else has a strong
Sindhi element in it and is often returned as a distinct language.
In the eastern part of the division there appears a dialect which
the natives call Malvi probably a sort of Hindi. Owing to the
enterprize of merchants from Gujerat and to the use of the same
language by the Parsis as well as the Hindu traders, it has become the commercial tongue of the seaports and is found all over
the Presidency. In the extreme South the particular tribe of quasi-
Hindus called the Lamers returned their language in many cases
as Gujerati but generally as Hindi. So it is supposed that they
wandered like so many others of this sort of tribe, from the plains
of North-Western India through Gujerat to the South (p. 113
ibid). With these may be compared the deductions of this paper
which are arrived at on independent grounds. Table I for general
area and population, III and II, for the latter according to religions
and IX according to the mother-tongues also should be referred to
in Vol. II. of the Bombay Census pp. 11-3 to 71 and 38 to 41.

terms are borrowed from Arabic, from Koran, this being the religious book of the people who speak the language. As regards their letters they have rejected aspirants which are found in Sanskrit as will be found in the following examples which indicate other differences :—

सुक S. सुख	बुदी S. बुद्धि.
सुक्चेथ S. सुखचित्त.	लोब S. लोभ.
दुक S. दुःख	जाग G. जागवुं.
बागी S. भाग पाडवा.	(?) पुत्री
बांस S. वंश.	रत S. रथ.
बासा S. भाषा.	पर्णेम G. पूनेम.
बिचार S. विचार.	चुरी G. चोरववुं.
बीजी S. बीज.	

"If the communication must necessarily be supposed to have its origin in Commerce, I should be inclined to consider the people of Gujerat notwithstanding the distance, as the instructor of the Malayas. Their resort Malacca is particularly noticed by Dr. Barrus and other authentic authorities. And the Hindu Bhasa has been preserved with more purity in that than in any other maritime province of Bharat Khand."

A Sanskrit writer from the Deccan, the author of *Vishvagunadarsha** or the Mirror of the Virtues

* Cf. the passage quoted below:—

वि॰ सक्षाघं सखे स एष सर्वसंपदामास्पदतया त्रिदशालयस्या-
देशइव गुर्जरदेश श्रक्षुणी सुखी करोति । अत्रहि ।

(and Faults) of the World, also was struck with the sweetness of the language, the trade enterprize of the people and the beauty of Gujerat ladies. Even in India itself, you find this interesting people beyond the natural limits of the extensive province. You will meet with Nâgara Colonies in the United Provinces, the Central Provinces and in the Deccan. You will come across the Khedâvâla Brahmins so far south as Mad-

सकर्पूरस्वादुक्रमुकनववीटी रसलस
न्मुखाः सर्वश्लाघाः पद विविधदिव्यांबरधराः ।
लसद्रत्नाकल्पाघुमघुमितदेहाश्चघुसृणै
र्युवानो मादन्ते युवतिभिरमी तुल्यरतिभिः ॥ २५

अत्र वधूनामनादृशं सौन्दर्यं ।
तत्तत्स्वर्णेसवर्णेमंगकंमिदं ताम्रोमृदुश्वाधरः
पाणी प्राप्तनवप्रवाल सरणी बाणीसुधाधारिणी ।
वक्त्रं वारिजमित्रमुत्पलदलश्रीसूचने लोचने ।
केनां गुर्जरसुभ्रुवामवयवा यूनां न मोहावहाः ॥ २६

कृ० सत्यमेवं तथापि न ते स्मरवस्तूपभोग चतुराः ।
तथाहि ।

ब्राडामारव्यतिकरवती विद्युदामाः कुशांगीः
क्रीडायोग्येप्यहसमये गेह एव त्यजंतः ।
निःसांसक्ता निरूपममणि श्रेणि वाणिज्यलाभे
बभ्रम्यन्ते बहुदिन परिमाप्य देशांतरेषु १७ ॥

वि० सएवपुरूषाणां गुण विशेषएव न तु दोषः
देशेदेशे किमपि कुतुकादद्धुतंलोकमानाः

ras where a whole street is known as the Gujjar Peth. The Marvadis are called the Jews of India. But looking to their commercial enterprize and trade instincts and upon Gujerati as the commercial language of India and of the East, I will call the Gujeratis the English of India.

The natives write their *hundis* or Bills of Exchange in the Gujerati or Bodia or bald characters without the vowel marks or strokes. Wherever they go they preserve their own vernacular, whether you go to the Nagars anywhere in India or to the Khedavals at Madras, or the Bhatias, Luvanas, Boras, Memons or Parsis in China, Siam, Africa or Arabia. Of course the English language is sharing the honour with the vernacular as it has done with other languages and dialects in other parts of the world.

With so wide an extent and range, with so many interests and races combined to-gether, the language should necessarily be a very rich and composite one, that it is. Gujerat has proved to be the America of India for colonization in its past history, and we have noted above some of the streams.* In the early History

संपादौनं द्रविणमतुलं सद्य भूयोप्यपाव्य ।
संयुज्यंते सुचिर विरहोत्कंठिताभि: **सतीभि:**
सौरुयं धन्या: किमपिदधते सर्व संपत्समृद्धा:

and so on in the same strain in the 4 verses that occur thereafter (Vide pp. 8-9 of the Bombay Edition). The passages in black type deserve attention.

* For further information refer to my letters on the Unpublished Literature of Gujerat published in the *Advocate of*

of Gujerat we have also seen the conflicts of the Jain, Buddha and Brahminical religions as also the deadly wars of the Hindu and Mahomedan faiths and the conversions following in their train.

This Province has also afforded a safe home to the Zoroastrians from Persia, the ancestors of the Modern Parsis who immigrated to it in the 7th and 8th century when the language was just assuming its present form. The Exodus of the Parsis also is believed to be twofold and by two routes by certain scholars: one by the Afghanistan route and the other by the sea-route from the port of Ormuzd to Diu in Kathiawar or Sanjan in Gujerat. Christianity also has had its conversions under the Portuguese as also under the English. Thus this has been a province of many races, creeds, castes and denominations and orders of society. The language was sure to be influenced by these forces. You will find the Parsi speaking it differently from the Brahmin, the Borah from the Bania, and the Kutchi and Kathiawadi from the Gujerati proper and the Rajput, the Charan, the Bhat and the Malavi and other races from one another. This incident therefore cannot raise these dialects into separate and independent languages.

India in 1887 and lately as an Appendix to my edition of *Mughdhavbodha Auktika* or a grammar for beginners of the Gujerati language written in V. S. 1450 (A. D. 1396) in my Prachina Gujerati Sahitya Ratnamala or the Garland of Gems of old Gujerati Literature Series.

8

Thus the Gujerati language appears to have been formed by four separate streams of dialects, (1) the Brahminic of the early Brahmin Settlers, (2) the Bardic, Charanic, Jadeji, Kathi, Rajputi or, give whatever name ycu choose to it, of the martial races that came later on and settled there, (3) the Jainic of the Jain converts of the people and of the later commercial interests, and (4) the Parsi and miscellaneous of the foreigners like the Parsis and converts to the Mahomedan or Christian faith. The Gujerati Literature is also similarly constituted of similar four streams which may as well be distinguished by those names. There are again localisms or provincialisms. And each town or city or district and community would call its own language correct and perfect and the rest incorrect and poor. And angry discussions on the point are not of unfrequent occurrence. The dialect that we have termed Brahminic above has nothing peculiarly Brahminic about it nor its Literature but we have given it the name from one of its earliest speakers. From their universal contact with every other race and community of the land, their language has become that of the country- They have also largely influenced the literature that I have above named after them and they are the leading writers and thinkers in it. The Brahmins with the concentrated civilization of centuries, as Dr. Sir William Hunter calls it, have and will have that position in the History of Gujerat and India. And the Nagar Communities that inherit all that is finest, noblest, and best of them, form the cream and flower of the nation. With these pioneers in the field the dialect showed surely slow affinities to the Vedic and the Classical Sanskrit and the earlier and the later of the Literary and Dramatic Prakritas. Gujerati belongs rather to the Sauraseni than to the Gaudian or the Maharashtri one because the earliest settlers had more to do with the Saurasena and neighbouring districts than with the Eastern or South Eastern

The second stream of dialect that we have termed Bardic inherits all the peculiarities of the Rajput tongues of Rajputana, Malwa and the still Northern homes of the races among which it is current. The same is the case with their literature. Bhats, Charans and other martial or minstrel classes, sing and compose poetry of heroism and chivalry and chronicles and annals in that dialect that is universally understood and appreciated throughout the Provinces of Gujerat, Rajputana and Malwa.

The Jainic stream traces its source and connection further west with Maghadhi—the sacred language of the Jainas, and the Jain monks or Sadhus are the writers of liturgical, anti-Brahminic and scientific works in the dialect. They command a very vast literature, ancient and modern, that is not yet opened fully to the general view.

The last stream embraces the channels of other races of Gujerat and the Parsis are from early times, the most prominent members of them. It is their numerous writings that have given rise to the terms the

Parsi Gujerati language and literature. The Borahs and others have no literature of their own in the dialect.

Of these four, the last three are the most conservative of branches, being sectional and confined to their own channels. While the first and the main stream, which we may very well call Gujerati, is broader and deeper, being constantly in flow and over-flow, overstepping its banks and borders, and is ever advancing. And yet it is all the four to-gether that can instruct us in the correct history and philology of the language and give us a correct key to those of the Indian Language System.

We have thus seen the position of these important and interesting tongues. Gujerati is a language of races that have gone the round of the whole of Historic India before settling in India. It is a language that had to do with the sacred languages and literatures of the early Aryas as with those of the later Brahmins, Buddhists, Jainas, and Parsis. It shakes hands with Marathi on the South and the North-East, with Urdu—Hindi on the N. E. and N. and N. W., with Punjaubi further North and with Sindhi further North-West. Situated as Gujerat is like Italy or Greece in the centre, its language and literature have imbibed the best elements of its neighbours. It is filed off in a sweetness and fluency peculiarly Italic. Its preservation of sounds and vowels and consonants is fuller and richer than that of any other, such that it would do credit to any tongue. Where in the matter of any form or peculiarity others fail, Gujerati does not run short. From Mr. Marsden's note above quoted we have seen its far-reaching effects in the Indian Archipelego. We who are already familiar with the proverb among us that "He who goes to Java does not return and if he does he brings enough for his generations after generations to enjoy" (જે જાય જાવે, તે કદી ન આવે, અને આવે તો પરિયાનાં પરિ- યાં આવે તેટલું ખાવે.) do not wonder at it.

Besides these facts it is the earliest of the vernaculars of modern India and I have the authority of Mr. Beames for it. (Vide his Comparative Grammar Vol. I. pp. 187-8). He remarks :—

" Gujerati is older in form than Scindi, and is in fact little more than an archaic dialect of the language brought by the Chalukyas, into the peninsula of Kathiawad and there isolated off from other Hindu dialects and thus gradually developed into a separate language, retaining antique forms, which have dropt out of use in the parent speech. Its grammatical formations are consequently more complicated than those of Hindi and in respect of the preparation of the stem it exhibits special peculiarities. Nouns ending in consonants i. e. mute a in this language have more than one form but the oblique form is universally applied. In some cases the case particles are affixed to the direct or nominative form, in others to the oblique ; the accusative and dative (which are only two different branches of one case, the objective) and the genitive affix their case particles to the direct form ; the instrumental, locative and ablative use both the direct and oblique forms. Thus હેવને, હેવના, હેવથી, હેવમાં. The oblique form is the same as the nominative but there is also an oblique case in *e* of which more will be said in a subsequent section." Barring his view of the antiquity of the Gujerati language and its preservation of older forms, I cannot endorse Mr. Beames' other views about the origin of the language. The peculiarities of the language enlarged upon by him should have led him to assume for it an independent origin and rise as I have proposed above while discussing the relations of Gujerati and the dialects I have pointed out where the divergence occurs in the language. Parasmaipada and Atmanepada divide Marathi on one side and Gujerati and Hindi on the other and the " *as* " and " *bhú* " forms for the verb " to be " in their turn.

Hindi, especially its Eastern phase, is Gaudian while Gujerati is Sauraseni, Marathi being perhaps Maharashtri. Of course these divisions are not very sharp. As we rise higher up in the stream of time, the branching off of languages gets thinner and we get the 3 or 5 Prakrits of Vararuchi. And still earlier perhaps we have only Pali and Maghadi, combining higher up in the Vedic Sanskrit. Even the fountain-head of the Indian Languages is believed by scholars not to be one language but a cluster of dialects like the early Greek. But this, as we have seen in the case of Gujerati, cannot make them different languages. It was the distribution of the Aryan race and its admixture with foreign elements that led to the divergence of Sanscrit into the earlier and the later Prakrits and then of the last into the modern vernaculars with their dialects.

The greater the political complications and the more intricate the ethnic admixtures, the larger the linguistic divergence and development. Thus historically, ethnically as well as philologically, Gujerati and Hindi are two separate streams. Perhaps Mr. Beames had not the materials at his disposal, here so largely drawn upon, so that he was led to the conclusion above quoted. We have now got a historical evidence of the existence of the Gujerati language in the eighth century of the Christian Era, near about the time of your Pusya (Pandu-Puspa) of Ujani of 713 A. D. mentioned by Mr. Grierson. It is a short line at the foot of the image of Ganapati at Patan in N. Gujerat, and it runs thus.

"संवत् ८०२ वर्षे चैत्र सूदि २ शुक्रे
अणहिलवाड ३ पाटाणि वनराज
राउनि उमा माहेश्वर स्थापनाछरू "

It can be translated thus :—

"In the year of Samvat 802 Chaitra, bright half 2nd, Friday, is the foundation of Uma-Maheswara of Ráv (King) Vanaraja in Anhilvada Pátan."

'Chhe' has all the elements of antiquity about it. In "Chhai" we have an old form of "Chhe" as noticed before. It may also have been "achhai", its a having combined with the preceding "a" under the rules of euphony. This form has the authority of the author of Mugdhavabodha (V. S. 1450) and, if I remember aright, of Hemchandra (Circa 1150 A. D.) and even of Vararuchi in his *Prakrita Prakasha*. Case in apposition terminations of Patan and Anhilwada, also point to the same direction and the existence of a contemporary poet about the time mentioned by Mr. Grierson remove all doubt as to its genuineness. We have already shown the connection of Malva and Gujerat linguistically and so we may take him as well as the author of the Khuman Rasau of the Ninth Century of Mewar, and KedarKavi (A. D. 1150) and Chand Bardai (A. D. 1159) and the Bard Jagnaik his contemporary of Bundelkhanda, as also Sarang Dhar (A. D. 1300) all mentioned by Mr. Grierson* to be poets of this language of Gujerat, Rajputana, and Malwa. Kavi Narsinha Mehta, a Nagara poet hailing from Junaghud, is sometimes called the Chaucer of Gujerati poetry. He flourished in the fifteenth century of the Christian Era. Him I class as a mediæval poet of Gujerat. The period before his I style as of Ancient Gujerati Language and Literature. Or if we take the period from the Vanraj Inscription and Puspa Kavi to Kavi Premanand, as that of Mediæval Gujerati the period before the former may be styled Ancient Gujerati and the period with and after the latter as Modern Gujerati.

Undoubtedly we have no works extant of Gujerati before the time of Vanaraja, although we can safely hold the language of the Asoka Edicts at Girnar of the 3rd century before Christ as the language of the country. But the language was not advanced far enough from its earlier Prakrita form to be called

---

* Vide Ibid pp. 5 to 9.

Gujerati. The form "*asti*" has not progressed to the Gujerati stage. "*Bhavati*" also has not assumed the form *thai* Guj or "*hai*." Hindi.* Even the 3rd person singular termination "*ti*" of the present tense is not changed into the Prakrit "*ei*" or vernacular "*ai*" or "*e*".

The language§ of the Nasik, Karle and Junnar Caves of the Andhras and the Kshetrapas as well as private individuals was also of the people that wrote them. Here although there is a less frequent use of verbal forms, "ti"§§ has not yet been mellowed into "i" &c. But the genitive terminations "sa" and "na" changed to "nâ" sometimes are losing their Sanskrit rigidity and they are being used with vowels as well as consonants and the latter indifferently for the singular as well as the plural. These Inscriptions fall before the 3rd Century of the Christian era. I would class the legends on the Kshettrapa and Gupta Coins also with these. Although "ssa"–double "sa"–appears in the Kan-

---

* Cf. pp. 93 to 126 Archœological Survey of Western India, Kathiawad and Kutch Vol. III. by Dr. Burgess, 1876.

§ Ref. Tablet II. p. 99 Ib. Edict IX. p. 115 Edict XI. p. 11 Edict XIV p. 125.

§§ Vide Edict IV. Ib. p. 101, Edict VI. p. 108, Edict VIII p. 111, Edict XI p. 118, although there is the form *Hoti* also with it there as in Edict XII p. 119. Vide Edict V p. 106, Edict VII p. 110, Edict X p. 117, Edict XII p. 119.

Ref. Dr. Burgess's Buddhist Cave Temples, Archœological Survey Vol. IV pp. 82 et. seq. Cf. also Vol. V pp. 60 et seq. Cf. also Dr. Bhagwanlal's Nasik and Pandu Lena Cave Inscriptions en. pass. Cf. Dr. Burgess's Elora Cave Temples, Archœological Survey Vol. V p. 75.

9

heri Inscription of Gotami-putra SiriYana, Satakarní, sometimes there is "sa" single too with it, as above and as in the Nanghat Inscription. Although the Classical Sanscrit idiom of participial forms instead of verbal forms is followed in the inscriptions of the age, yet the termination "ti" is not changed to "i" or "ai." Dr. Bhugwanlal's Inscription No. 14 naming Bheru-Kachha (Broach) and Ujjayini justifies us in connecting it and the Family Inscriptions with the Gujerati of the time as defined above by us. The language of the Inscriptions appears to be a descendant of the Asoka Edicts as a passing comparison would show and so we might for a similar reason characterize that language also to be an ancient form of Gujerati. The case in apposition forms of the Kshetrapa and Andhra Inscriptions and the Kshetrapa and Gupta coin legends may be compared with those we find in the Vanaraja Inscription quoted by me above. Thus these links of grammatical form connections make them of one piece. These periods were of constant wars, troubles, migrations and confusions until the time of Kurna Solunki I. as described elsewhere. And so the language was little likely to be in a written form and if it had assumed one such, it was still less likely to have preserved works in them. Mr. Grierson has noticed the case of Khuman Râsau which was to be recast over again.[*] Prithiraja Râsau also is said to have received a similar treatment for a similar reason. There is no hope of any ray

* Cf. Tod's Rajasthana Vol. I Annals of Mewar. Cf. VIII H. pp. 223-4.

lighting the dark chambers of the history of the Gujerati Language of the time. And we must rest content
with what we have already got.

After the Gujerati Inscription of Vanraja quoted
above, we come to the Grammar of Hemchandra in V.
S. 1168 or the 12th Century. Shastri Vrijlal Kalidas
quotes some of the couplets cited by Hemchandra in his
grammar of the *Apabhransa* language, in his History of
the Gujerati language, 1866, p. 42. There we see the Sans-
krit-Prakrit genitive termination "sa" changed to "ha"
and the verbal termination " ti " changed to " i."

झोली तुट्टवि किं न मूऊ किन हूऊ झारह पुंज ।
घरि घरि भिक्ख भमाडीइ जिम मंकडु तिम मुंज ॥
कातीकरवत कापतां वहिलउ आवइ छेह ।
नारी वेघ्या टलवलइ ना जीवइ ता देह ॥

§ This is followed by a Vishnudasa, author of
Soma Parvan of the Mahabharata in V. S. 1300.

Then I find a colophon in Gujerati in a Ms. in a
Jain Bhandâr at Cambay. It is in the Mss of Bhavan
Sundri Katha of Vijayasinha Suri in Mâghadhi.
It is also noticed in Jour. Bo. Br. R. A. S. Vol. XVI
N. XLI p. 39. It runs thus :—

संवत् १३६५ रत्ना देवीये मूल्ये ल्येइ साधुने ओरावी.

In Samvat 1365 Ratnadevi bought it (the manuscript ?) and presented it to a Jain *Sadhu.*

While the Grammar is dated V. S. 1168 (A. C.

---

§ Cf. also the language of the Postscript in Dr. Buhler's Anhilwad Chalukya Grant N. 6, of V. S. 1287. Ind. Ant. 1877.

1112.), this date is V. S. 1365 (A. C. 1308). We come next to the Grammar of the Gujerati Language i. e. Mughdhavabodha Auktika of V. S. 1450 (A. C. 1394) which is in evidence of a sufficient advance and development of the language to be thus reduced into a systematic form. I do not know of any other vernacular, having such a grammar or any grammar at all. It would shortly be in the hands of all Orientalists, edited and published by me of late. I have come across a जिन कुशलसूरि स्तवन or Prayer of Jina Kusalasuri, written in V. S. 1481. (A. D. 1425.) and it satisfies all the rules of the Grammar of V. S. 1450 (A. D. 1394). The date of a ms. thereof is V. S. 1490 or A. D. 1434. And then a Ms. of the same worth at Ahmedabad is dated V. S. 1510 (A. D. 1444)*. As we approach the close of the fifteenth century the number of our finds of works in the language increases. V. S. 1507 (A. D. 1450) is the date of an inscription of Mandalika at Junaghud, Uparakot. V. S. 1509 or A. D. 1453 is that of the work of Sabha Silaguna Suri, by name Sanskrit Katha Kosa, containing citations of couplets from the Rasau of Prasanajit. V. S. 1510 is the year of Soma Sundara Suri's Updeshmâlâ in 5000 Granthas of which I have got a Ms. (A. D. 1454). V. S. 1512 (A. D. 1456) is the date of Kavi Padma Nâbha's Kanhadade Prabundha, discovered by Dr. Buhler and published by the late Navalram Luxmiram in the Gujerat School Paper. V. S. 1525 is the year of another Gujerati Inscription

* Vide Dr. Bhandarkar's report for search for Mss. 1883-84 p. 16.

and that is of Jayasinhadeva of Pâvâgadha. Unfortunately it is lost among the papers of my friend with other notes of mine that I had lent to Dr. Bhugwanlal (A. D. 1469). Kavi Narmadâshankar cites a passage in his introduction to his dictionary of the Gujerati language from a Ms. dated V. S. 1559 (A. D. 1473)§. V. S. 1541 (A. D. 1485) is the date of Kavi Bhima's Hari Lilâ Shodasha Kalâ and V. S. 1556 is that of the quotation of Kavi Narmadâshankar from Guj-Sinha's Rasa. (A. D. 1500). And this was the age of Kavi Narsinha Meheta alluded to before. Perhaps a Bardic poem, Ramchandra Khandana, containing older forms of " chhai" prevalent at the time also belongs to that century and period. Within a century of Narsinha, there were Kavi Bhalana, who has rendered Bana's Kadambari into Gujerati that my brother Mr. K. H. Dhruva B. A. has been editing, and his three sons who were also poets. There were many contemporaries of theirs of greater or lesser note. But this poet that I have been able to bring to light is the poet of the 16th Century and he has been followed as a model by Kavi Premanand, the greatest of Gujerati poets, whose son Vallabha also was a poet of the 17th and 18th Century, and by Kavi Dayaram the greatest of lyric poets in the Vernaculars of India already referred to. Thus like Narsinha Meheta, Premananda and Dayaram, Bhalana also marks an important epoch in the History of Gujerati Literature and with him closes the mediæval period of Gujerati

---

§   Vide Shashtri Vrijlal's History pp. 14-18.

History. These four poets and Miranbai named before, we will shortly notice further on as model poets of Gujerati. For the present let us be content with some of the Gujerati works which I append a list of. Thus we have in our past review seen that the antiquity of the Gujerati language can be dated so far back as the third century before Christ i. e. with the Asoka Edicts. And the period of ancient Gujerati extends between the Girnar Inscriptions and the date of the foundation of Anhilwad Patan. It is one of unwritten and arohaic literature. Then begins the mediæval period closing with Bhalana and his contemporaries. Here we see the stream swelling in its onward course till it falls into the beautiful cascades of the poetry of Narsinha and Bhalana. Although of the Parsi Gujerati Stream there is only the Syâvaskhasnâmâ of Mobed Rustaîn Peshutan Homjigar Surti before us, there is every likelihood of there being many more seeking light and publication. Although it is dated V. S. 1736 (A. D. 1680,) yet it can be relegated to the mediæval period of Bhalana and his contemporaries.

European as well as native scholars speak of the Vernaculars of India having no literature worthy of the name. The Vernaculars are no embryonic uncouth dialects as the fore-going dissertation might have convinced the scholars here assembled in the Congress. I refer the cavillers of the Vernaculars to my letters in the *Advocate of India* of 1887 already alluded to. We have not our collection in *Navanita* alone as in

Marathi. Let the curious but turn the pages of two Volumes of 'Kàvyadohana' by Mr. Dalpatram Kavi C. I. E., three Volumes of 'Brihat Kàvyadohana' by Mr. Itchharam Suryaram Desai, the 12 numbers of the Aprasiddha Gujerati Literature Monthly by Mr. Chaturbhai Sankerbhai of Nadiad, to the more than 16 Nos. of 'Prachina Kavya' of Rao Bahadoor Hargowandass Dwarkadass Kantawalla, Director of Vernacular Instruction, Baroda State, and Shastri Nathashankar Punjashankar and to other publications of Sâmal, Prémânand, Dayâram, and other poetical works by the press. Let them but pour over the collections of Kavi Narmadashankar, Mr. Navalram Luxmiram, over those of the Gujerat Vernacular Society at Ahmedabad, of the Cutch State and perhaps many other States, of Mr. Chatnrbhai at Nariad, of Shastri Nathashankar at Baroda, and Mr. Ichharam at Bombay. I append lists of some of them. I also append catalogues of Mss. my friends are in search of. H. H. the Maharaja Gaecwar of Baroda has sanctioned Rs. 12000 out of the Rs. 18000 that will be required to publish the hitherto unpublished works of 21 poets* that have

---

* Kavi Narmadashankar Lalshankar was born at Surat in V. S. 1889 first Bhadurva Suda 10th, Saturday, 24th of August (A. D. 1833). He died on Thursday the 25th of February A. D. 1886 at Bombay. His career as a writer commenced with 1850-51 A. D. and as a poet in 1855 A. D. He is the author of several original works and has edited a few. He wrote the first dictionary in the Gujerati Language. He also attempted to supply works to Gujerati in every branch of literature—about Grammar, Prosody, Rhetoric and a Glossary of Classical Antiquities. He was the S. Johnson of Gujerat and Raja Rammohunrai of Gujerati prose.

lived in H. H.'s territory. The Ràmâyana, the Mâhâ-bhârata and the Bhâgvata have been left out in the counting which would otherwise have cost double that sum in addition and yet this is but a small fraction of Gujerati literature. Gujerati is a language of songs and poetry—the Italian of Western India. It is a language of more than a century of poets. One of the recent numbers of a Bombay Gujerati Magazine, by name "Âryadnyân Vardhaka' gives a list of some of the poets–which is not intended to be complete.

The collections of Gujerati poetry published here-upto are 2 Vol. of the 'Kâvyadohana' under the direction of the Educational Department of Bombay compiled by one of the first living poets of Gujerat, Kavi Dalpatram Dayabhai who has been honoured with a C. I. E. by the British Government. These being out of print, they were followed by the 'Kâvya Sankshepa' compiled by the same gentleman. The Educational Department had got another leading poet, since dead, Kavi Narmadashankar to edit the 'Nalâkhyâna' of Kavi Premananda. But in this as well as in the 'Kâvya Sankshepa', the official expurgator and perhaps the Christian and Missionary members of the Book Committee have been instrumental in mutilating the poems and cutting out the best pieces out of them, simply because they contained a name of Krishna or so, as god or that the passages were love-pieces or *shringara*. I doubt if they would be allowed to do anything of the kind with Shakespeare or Milton, Homer, or Virgil, Dante or Tasso, Byron or Shelley,

Moliere, Cavendish, or Goethe, Wordsworth or Tennyson, Edda or Emerson in Europe. But besides these, Kavi Narmadashankar has given us excellent and critical editions of the 'Dasamaskandha Bhâgvat' of Kavi Premanand and the Poems of Kavi Dayaram. Kavi Dulpatram Durlabhram of Broach and Mr. Navalram Luxmiram have given two more editions of the same Kavi Premanand. But the critical editions did not take such a systematic and extensive form till we had the monthly 'Aprasiddha Gujerati Pustaka' of Mr. Chaturbhai and the 'Prachin Kâvya' Quarterly of Rao Bahadoor Hargovandass and Shastri Nathashankar. Among selections comes the 'Kâvya Nimajjan' of a Shastri of the Surat Mission High School. And the enterprising Editor of the *Gujerati* has given us 3 large Volumes of the popular, not critical, editions of the Gujerati poets. The two Volumes of 'Kâvyadohana' of Kavi Dalpatram C. I. E. contain selections from 90 poets, of which those from 88 are in the first volume and 12 in the second, 10 of these being of the old ones and 2 others. Of these 15 belong to Ahmedabad, 12 being of the City proper and 3 of the Suburbs (2 of Gomatipura and one of Rajpura), 3 come from Baroda and 3 from Junaghud. Each of these places viz. Bhavnagar, Cambay, Kaira, Torana, Gadhada and Muli claims 2 and Udepur in Rajputana, Vijapur in North Gujerat, Randeir, Amreli in Kathiawad, Savli, Godhra, Dakor, Umreth, Dabhoi, Vartal near Nariad, Sojintra near Petlad, Vehelal and Dholka near Ahmedabad, Hansalpur (Paṭun) in RevaKantha and Sandhesar one

10

each, as also Kuntalpur, Lalichosad, Vasavad, Pihij near Petlad, and Kadi, while places of 37 are unknown.

The same again according to caste are distributed as follows :—6 Vadnagara Nagars, 2 Sathodra Nagars, 1 Prasnora, 1 Audich Sahasra Brahmin, 2 Audich Tolakias, 2 Modha Chaturvedis, 2 Bhat Mevadas, 1 Trivedi Mewada, 1 Rajput, 4 Bhats, 1 Bania, 3 Sanyasins, 3 Miscellaneous Sadhus, 11 Jain Yatis, 1 Mochi or shoe-maker, 2 Lewa Kunbis, 1 Gandharva or musician, 6 Swami Narayan Sadhus, 1 Soni or goldsmith, 1 Sarasvit Brahmin, 2 Rayakval Brahmins, 1 Sri Goda Malavai Brahmin, 2 other Brahmins, 1 Joshi or astrologer, 1 Bhavsar or dyer and 31 unspecified. Thus of the 90, more than one third the number are unspecified, 10 or one ninth are Nagars, 14 or 15 i. e. one sixth are other Brahmins, there is only 1 Rajput and 1 Bania and there are two Kunbis or cultivators and 4 Bhats or bards. Of the artizen classes there are 4, one musician, one goldsmith, one dyer, one shoe-maker. The goldsmith is a Vedantist i. e. Akho Bhagat. His poetry as also of the shoe-maker is not quite commonplace. The rest are of the mendicant or monkish class. The same 90 according to their creeds and religions are 3 Vaishnavas, 4 Devi Bhaktas, 11 Sadhus, Sanyasin and Vedantists, 11 Jain Yatis and 61 Saivas and Smartas &c.

The 'Kâvya Nimajjana' gives only 10 poets—9 of them past and one present, i. e., Kavi Narmad who also is since dead. Two of these are from Ahmedabad and the rest are from Wadhwan and Ahmedabad, Dabhoi, Surat, Junaghada, Baroda, Savli, Gathda, one each and one unspecified: 4 of these are Smartas, 2 Vaishnavas, 2 Vedantists and 1 Swami Narayanist. One of them is a Sathodra Nagar, 2 Vadnagra Nagars, 1 Srigod Malvi Brahmin, 1 Srimali Brahmin, 1 Modha Chaturvedi, 1 Goldsmith, 1 Bard and 1 unspecified.

The monthly 'Aprasiddha Pustak' has got fifteen poets. Of them three are from Baroda and one each from Junagadh, Patan, Vaso near Sojitra, Bavanpur, Sandhesar, and Dabhoi while six are unspecified. Three are Nagars—two Vadnagara and one Sathodra—one is a Bhat, one a Bania, three Brahmins and seven unspecified. Of these Bhalana, Laxmanadas, Narhar (a contemporary of Akho, Gopal and Botak), Vishnudas, Surbhat, Narayan, Baldeva and perhaps Ramkrisha are not included in the above-mentioned poets nor is the Ramayana in prose, a manuscript whereof with me is dated V. S. 1673 (1616 A. C.). The 'Brihat Kâvyadohana' Vol. 1 has got 43 poets—37 of them being included in the older Kâvyadohanas and 6 being new. Five of these are from Ahmedabad, 3 from Junaghud and one from each of these places, namely, Patan, Junaghud, Kuntiana, Dakor, Bhalej, Broach, Amod, Kapadvanja, Porana, Savli, Godhra, Udepura (Mewad), Girpur, Vadnagar, Dungarpur, Khangam, Baroda, Vashvad, Gadhda, Dholka, Dabhoi, Kaira, Dhandhuka, Vartal, Sandhesar, Sojitra, Pihig, Petlad, Muli, Umreth, Vehelal and 8 unspecified. Three of these are Vadnagar Nagars, 1 a Sathodaro, 1 a Rajput, 1 a Srigod Malvi, 1 a goldsmith, 1 a Chaturvedi Modha and one an Audich Tolakya. Vol. II. of the work contains

22 poets and all but four of them namely Ṭulsi, Dwar-
ko, Dhandas and Viravijaya are included in the first
volume and these 4 are included perhaps in the earlier Kavyadohanas. Vol. III. of the same work gives
21 poets. Of these all but Hariram, Gopaldass, Ratne-
sara, Premanand Swami, Manohar Swami, Haribhut,
Bapu, Sivanand and Govinddas are included in Vols.
I and II and all but the first and third and last of
these latter are either to be found in the earlier Kavyadohanas or the 'Aprasidha Gujerati Pustaka'. The
'Prachina Kâvya' also knows Ratneswara and the
Baroda list of 21 poets given in a note before includes
him and perhaps Bapu. The 'Prâchina Kâvya' has
published works of 8 poets viz: Kavi Premanand,
Narasinha, Bhalana, Dayaram, Samala, Ratneshvar,
Sivdas and Dhiro Bhagat. We know all but Sada-
shiva in the above collections. Of these Premanand is
not a Chaturvedi Modha as hitherto described but he
is a Chovisa Brahmin, Ratneswara is a Srimalli, Samal a SriGoda Malvai, Narsinha and Sivdas are
Vadnagaras, Dayaram a Sathodro, Dhiro Bhagat and
Bhalan are Brahmins of other castes. Among these the
earlier Kavya Dohanas give two poetesses, Miranbai
and Punjibai. To them Vol. I. of the latter adds 2
more viz. Krishnabai and Ranibai and the Baroda list
gives Radhabhai in addition.

Thus while the Navnit Collection that has run
through about 10 editions (1854–57–60–62–64–68–71
–73–78 and 82) has got 23 poets by the side of the
90 and more of the Gujerati Kavyadohanas. They are

Nâmdeva a tailor, Tukârâm a Sudra and contemporary of Sivaji, and the rest Brahmins i. e. Eknatha and his
daughter's son Mukteswara, Vâmana Pandit, Râma-
Dâsa Swâmi who was the Guru of Sivaji, Moropanth,
Sridhar Pandit, Amritraj, Mahipati &c., in the 17th and
18th Centuries. A comparison of the poets of the
two languages show, that while in Gujerati poetry
was distributed over all classes, it was confined to the
Brahmins only in Marathi. While the poets of Marathi flourished in the 17th and the 18th Century and
one or two in the 15th and the 16th, in Gujerati the
stream of poetry had been continuous from before the
11th Century and perhaps ever since the 8th Century. In
Marathi also there were poetesses Janâbâi, Nâgabâi,
Gonâbâi, but none of them has the fame of the Gujerati Mirânbâi, much less her popularity. While the
Marathi poetry is Sanskritic and learned as of Moropant, Vâman Pandit and Jnâneswara, the Gujerati
is popular and really vernacular. Tukâram is of the
class of Narsinha Mehta, Jnâneswara of Akho Bhagat
perhaps and Moropant and Vâman Pandit &c. of Premananda and Bhalana but the Gujaratis will appear
to far excel the Marathis in their description of life,
nature and sentiments, although they may not have
been in the artificial groove of the Sâhityakâra's Rule
of School.

But no, we cannot do injustice to our West India
Sister, the Marathi. The *Navnita* does not exhaust its
literature. The Marathas have their 'Kâvyetihâsa
Sangraha' and other periodicals. The ten volumes thereof

(1887) give, besides the Poems of Moropant, Râmadâs
Swâmi, Mukteshwar and Vâman Pandit, also the
letters and *Bakhars* or memoirs of their eminent political men of the 17th and 18th Centuries, and the
poems of different poets (Sanskrit and Marathi), 32
more in all. Even the addition of these does not come
to the Gujerati number which is more than double.
Again in the above analysis while we have works of
poetry and annals in the Maharastri we have got all
branches of literature from tales to songs, rituals to
medicine and *Shilpa* or engineering. There is prose, there
is poetry. There are translations. There are adapta-
tions as well as original compositions. Gujerati without its being the sacred language like Sanskrit of the
Brahmins, Pali of the Buddhists, Maghadhi of the
Jainas, or Hindi Brajbhasa of the Vaishnavas as also
without being the political or court language like Urdu-
Hindustani of the Moguls and Mahomedans and Marathi of the Marathas, has worked its way as a lan.
guage of the people or peoples as described above.
Now it has time to revive its past and bring about the
confluence of all its straggling streams and make itself
a powerful instrument of thought and expression. Unit.
ed we stand, divided we fall. Even the current Gujerati has its literary men. We have the two blind
poets Dalpatram and Guttulaljee. We had the best
prose writers in Navalram and Narmadashanker and
a worthy Nagar School of poets and writers is rising,
in our midst. Our Parsi friends are showing a good
start. What we want is more light, more education

which should be the anxious care of our princes and people.

Before concluding the paper it is but meet that I should subjoin a short account of five of our poets who mark the different Epochs in our Literature. They are, 1, Princess Miranbai (circa 14th century), 2. Bhakta or the Great Devotee Narsinha Mehta (15th century), 3. Kavi Bhalana (16th century), 4. Kavi Premananda (17th and 18th centuries) and 5. Kavi Dayaram (18th and 19th centuries). With the exception of the 3rd all the others have their lives written in the language. Kavi Dayarama is the author of Mirancharitra or the Life of Miran.* Kavi Premananda has written on many an incident in Narsinha Meheta's life ; e. g. 1 *Mameru*, 2 *Hundi*, 3 *Narsinha Meheta-na Chokarano Vivaha*, 4 *Narsinha Mehta-na Bapanu-Sradha*, 5 *Haramala*—(1. the Pregnancy or *Simanta* Ceremony of his daughter Kuwarbai, 2. the Honoring of the Bill of the poet by the God Krishna of Dvarka, 3. the Marriage of the poet's son Samaldass, 4. the *Shradha* or obsequial ceremony of the poet's father and 5. the giving of the *Har* or Garland by the God Damodar at Junaghudh to the poet when he was hard-pressed for it by the king Mandalika &c.) Kavi Premananda has found his biographer, critic and commentator of some of his difficult works in his own son Vallabha. These works are *Premananda Katha* or the life of Premananda, 2. *Premananda Prasansa* or a eulogy of Premananda where the merits of the poet are described, 3 *Premananda*

---

* Vide Kavi Narmadas edition pp. 176-8.

Ninda or the censure of Premananda where his faults
are pointed out only turned to virtues, 4 *Vallabha–
Shamal–samvadno patra* or a letter of controversy between Vallabha and Poet Samal about the comparative merits of the latter and Kavi Premananda and
5. 6. 7. Tikas or Commentaries on some of the poet's
works viz. the *Draupadi Harana*, the *Nalakhyan* and
the *Dasama*. This Vullabha flourished in the 18th century of the Christian era. Kavi Dayaram has found
the best biographer in Kavi Narmada who has published a critical edition of his works. Kavi Narmada
has also written the *Kavi Charitra* giving the lives of
most of the Gujerat poets. Rao Bahadur Hargovandass, I myself and one Narayan Bharati Yasvanta
Bharti at Pattan have carried on research about the
time &c. of Bhalana. Unlike other poets he gives no
dates in his works. He was the author of *Kadambari**
as already mentioned, of *Sapta Sati*,§ a version of the
celebrated *Chandi Patha*, of *Ram Bala Charitra*§§ or
the Doings of the infant Rama, the *Dasmaskandha* **

---

* *Kadamberi*, G. V. S. Ms. whereof is dated V. S. 1672.
(A. C. 1616) No. 1461 of the Society's Catalogue (Vide Shastri
Vrajlal's History pp. 65-6) and the *Nalakhyana* are not published.

§ *Sapta Sati* is published in the Prachina Kavya Series as
Vol. III. No. 3 which see.

§§ *Rama Bala Charitra* also is unpublished but I have
noticed it in the *Buddhi Prakasha* and published extracts therefrom. I presented a copy of it to the G. V. Society which unfortunately is now missing.

** *Dasmaskandha* the G. V. S. Ms. whereof is dated V. S.
1755 A. C. 1699 no. 1479 of the catalogue has extracts from it
published in the Aprasidha Gujerati Pustaka and the Brihat
Kavyadohans under names of its different parts which see.

or a version of the 10th Canto of the *Srimad Bhagvata,*
5, of *Harsamvada*[*] or an Interview between Hara—
Siva—and Parvati attired as a Bhildi or Bhil woman,
and 6, of *Nalakhyan* and probably a few more. Gosâmi
Narayan Bhârti in the account of the poet given in
the Prachina Kavya *Sapta Sati* places the Poet, on
the strength of certain letters and papers said to have
been found from the Poet's place, in the 14th–15th
Century. A son of Bhalana, Visamadasa, according to
that authority has written the *Uttara Kanda* of the
Ramayana in which he gives the date of its completion
to be V. S. 1575 (A. C. 1519), the ms. whereof is
dated V. S. 1869. I have got a manuscript of another
work, probably of the same Visamadasa, in 7 Kadvas
or Cantos (the earlier ones being lost), the ms. date
of which is V. S. 1670 (A. D. 1614) from Pâtana.
Another son of Bhalana, Udhavdasa has written five
Kandas of the Ramayana, the 6th being written by
one Bhima Kavi of Karnapura near Modhera in V. S.
1687 (A. D. 1631). A third son of Bhalana, by name
Chaturbhuja, has translated into Gujerati the *Modhera
Purana* about the Modha Brahmins from Sanskrit. He
also does not give the name of his place or the date
of the composition.§ The writer of the life gives another name of Bhalana as Purushottama. From the

---

[*] *Harasamvad* is also called *Bhildi Samvad* or *Shiva Bhildi
Samvad.* The G. V. S. Ms is no. 1506 in the catalogue. It is
published in the Aprasidha Gujerati Pustaka and the Brihat Kavya-
dohana Vol. I.

§ Vide Sapta Sati. Kavi Charitra pp. 13 &l. s.

11

above date of Visamadasa' *Uttara Kanda* as also on philological grounds, I place Bhalana in the 16th century and after Kavi Narsinha Mehta. The ms. of *Kadambari* of the Poet above alluded to of V. S. 1672, as also the ms. of *Padmanabha Charitra* of his son (V. S. 1670) both give "chhi" as forms of "chhe" (is) which is later than "chhai" and "achhai" used by Kavi Narsinha Mehta and earlier writers and speakers. "Chhi" is later than "achhai" even. The question may be kept open till we get more light on the same. This poet has proved to be a beacon in the dark sea between Narsinha Mehta and Premananda. He has been a model and mirror to the Poets, to Premananda and Dayaram with regard to their style, subject, metres, figures and several homely terms and expressions. Kavi Dayaram has gone so far as to adopt bodily as his own, a piece from Bhalana's *Dasamaskandha*. The poet also serves us as a land-mark to divide the earlier from the Modern Gujerati. There lived other poets also in the same century as his contemporaries. I have already mentioned the three sons of the poet. The other poets were Tulsi (V. S. 1614, A. D. 1553), Sivánanda (V. S. 1657, A. D. 1601) Sivadása (V. S. 1673, A. D. 1617), Devidás (V. S. 1618, A. D. 1562), Lucksmidass (V. S. 1640, A. D. 1584), Narhara (V. S. 1677, A. D. 1621, to 1709 V. S. 1653 A. D.) and Baldeva (V. S. 1609 A. D. 1553). Here I have given them, taking the Vikrama Era as the standard and the period between V. S. 1600 to 1700.

Now we come to Miranbai. She was a princess of

Midala in Marwad and daughter of Jayamull Rathod.
She was given in marriage to the Rana of Chittore
in Mewad. She was attached more to thoughts about
God Krishna and divine love than to those of life or
any love to her royal consort. Many legends are current about her devotion. She passed her time in the
service of the god and sâdhus. Many attempts were
made to turn her from her path but they were all
fruitless. The Rana at last grew jealous and once ran
up with a drawn sword to her palace to slay her
and her love with whom she was reported to be flirting
and dancing. The Rana to his surprise found no human
being there as the person was no other than the God
Krishna and he retired greatly abashed. He thereafter sent a cup of poison which she, Socrates-like
drank away, but the god turned it into nectar and so
the poison could take no effect upon her. After that
she went to reside at Dwarka on her return
from a pilgrimage to Vrindavana and the Jumna.
The Rana repented afterwards and sent messages and
men to call her back from Dwarka. Then she was
told at last that the Rana had left off food pending
her return. She went to the image of her god to ask
permission to return. The god Hari smiled and pressed,
her to his heart, where she disappeared. This is the
life of a poetess and a Hindu and a Vaishnava and with-
al a Princess.* Let us see what Col. Todd has to say
about Miranbai. " Kumbho " he informs us "married
a daughter of the Rano of Mairta, the first? of the

* Cf. Dayaram Kavi's Miran Charitra.

clans of Marwar. Meera Baee was the most celebrated princess of her time for beauty and romantic piety.
Her compositions were numerous, though better known
to the worshippers of the Hindu Apollo than to ribald
bards. Some of the hymns and odes to the deity are
preserved and admired. Whether she imbibed her
poetic piety from her husband or whether from her
he caught the sympathy which produced the *Sequel
to the Songs of Govind* we cannot determine." We have
seen above on the authority of Kavi Dayaram that
the latter was the case. For a warrior constantly engaged in war cannot afford to be devoted to romantic
or poetic piety and infuse the same into his queen. The
life and nature of Kumbho also account for his jealousy
and rash acts depicted above. "Her history is a ro-
mance" continues Col. Todd "and her excess of devotion at every shrine of the favorite deity with the
fair of Hind from the Yamuna to the "world's end"
gave rise to many tales of scandal. Kumbho mixed
gallantry with his warlike pursuits. It carried off the
daughter of the chief prince of Zalawar who had been
betrothed to the prince of Mundore. This renewed
the old feud and the Rahtore made many attempts to
redeem his affianced bride. His humiliation was un-
supportable, when through the purified atmosphere of
the periodical rains, the tower of Kumbhomer became
visible from the Castle Mundore and the light radiated
from the chamber of the fair through the gloom of a
night in Bhaddon to the Hall where he brooded over
his sorrows. " According to Col. Todd, Kumbho ascend-

ed the throne in V. S. 1475, A. C. 1419. He defeated the combined forces of Gujerat and Malwa in V. S. 1496 (A. C. 1440) which had invaded Mewar. "Kumbho" Col. Todd tells us " met them on the plains of Malwa bordering on his own state and at the head of 10,000 horse and foot, 1400 elephants, gave them an entire defeat carrying captive to Chitoor, Mahomed, the Khilji Sovereign of Malwa "* and " Abul Fazel relates this victory and dilates upon Kumbho's greatness of soul in letting his enemy at liberty, not only without ransom but with gifts."§

Kumbho occupied the throne for half a century. He was assassinated by his son Ooda in S. 1526 (A. D. 1469). " He composed a Tika or Appendix to the Divine Melodies in praise of Krishma " (Gita Govinda.)

One quotation more from Col. Todd about Kumbho and we take leave of him. " Kumbho Rano was also a poet but on a far more elevated strain than the troubadour princes, his neighbours, who contented themselves with rehearsing their own prowess or celebrating their ladies' beauty." " We can pass no judgment on these inspirations of the Royal Bard as we are ignorant whether they are preserved in the records of the house, a point, his descendent who is deeply skilled in such lore might probably answer." I remember to have seen the work and it is perhaps no. 1584 ms. dated V. S. 1643 (A. C. 1587) of the catalogue of the Gujerat Vernacular Society's collections. This

---

*· Cf. Todd. Ibid p. 221.

§ Ibid p. 222.

work, Kumbho R̄no might have composed after his wars with Gujerat and Malwa and probably after the disappearance of Miranbai, when he was in a mood of comparative repose and rest and repentance for his behaviour towards his queen and disappreciation of her romantic piety. This, as also the disappearance of Miranbai, then would fall between V. S. 1496 and 1525, the latter taking place first in Sī ka V. S, 1500. Then the time of Miranbai falls between V. S 1475 and 1500, that is, about the close of the 11th century. Among her contemporary writings there are 1. the Grammar Mugdhavabodha, V. S. 1450, A. C. 1394, 2. a work on medicine found and quoted by Shastri Vrijlal in his history pp. 60-1 which he supposes as of date V. S. 1400 but which is perhaps too early, 3. a. Vedia Brahmin's work on rituals also quoted and named by the Shastri pp. 59-60 as of the Vikrama year 1481, A. C. 1425, and 4. Jain Kusal Suri Stavana of the same year and perhaps many more, not known to us. On philological grounds we can name Surabhata and Narayana of the *Aprasiddha Gujerati Pustaka* among her contemporaries.

Besides the odes and hymns (Garbis and Padas) of Miranbai mentioned by Col. Todd above, a friend of mine has got 50 garbis and 200 padas and Shastri Nathashankara of the Prachina Kavya mentions *Krishna Swami Akhyana* and *Dridha Bhukti Akhyana* among her works.

Our next poet is Narsinha Mehta. Accounts of his life have been written by several, Kavi Narmada, Rao

Bahadur Hargowandass and Mr. Ichharam of the Brihata Kavya Dohana Vol. II. being among them. I also have been able to give information about him and his family from his collateral descendants, the Majmudars of Amreli. He belonged to a family of poets who were originally natives of Mangrole on the south coast of Kattyawad. He and his uncle Parvata Meheta, also a Vaishnava, of whom one of his descendents Trikamdass has written *Parvat Pachisi*, repaired and settled at Junaghad. The Chandasania king, Mandalika ruled there at the time (V. S. 1489 to 1529— A. C. 1433 to 1473), who was defeated by Sultan Mahomed Beguda of Ahmedabad and converted to Mahomedanism. There is still seen his tomb at Ahmedabad in an obscure corner of a sweetmeat seller's shop. The poet was a Bhakta and a Vaishnava of the time of Miranbai of romantic or poetic piety. He was a Vadnagara Nagar Brahman. His religion was not a favourite at court as of Miranbai with the Rana, as well as with his caste.

He was derided, ridiculed and persecuted by both the powers, for a caste in India is also a power in the land. The poems of Kavi Premananda about this poet tell us in all their charm how this was done and how the God Krishna under various forms and in several manners came to his help. The family was originally known as Pandiyas, (contraction of Pandita), while at Mangrole and they came to be known as Vaishnavas in the time of Narsinha and Parvat Mehta. They are also known by their official title at present as the

Majmudars. This has been a family of poets. Narsinha
Mehta was a poet. Fifth in descent from his uncle
Parvata Mehta, Sârangadhara was a poet. Fifth from
Sârangadhara's brother Sadafala Trikumdas, author of
the *Parvata Pachisi*, was a poet. So were also brothers Rangildasa and Revashankar*, (mentioned in
the earlier Kavyadohanas and the Brihat Kavya Dohanas, which see), were poets. Rughnathrai, their brother or cousin, also was a poet and one of his grand-
sons Jayasukhrai, still living, is one as well. He is
fifteenth in descent from Parvata Mehta. The son,
Shamaldass, of Narsinha died in the lifetime of the

---

* This poet was the 12th in descent from Narsinha Mehta's
uncle Parvata Mehta and he was a son of Trikumdasa, author of
the *Parvata Pachisi*. He knew Persian and Sanskrit well. He
lived in the time of Major (afterwards Col.) Walker, V. S. 1864
A. D. 1808. He was a minister of Junaghad State in the time
of and after Ranchodji Diwan of Tawarika-i-Soreth fame. Rangildas
was an elder brother of the poet. They were seven brothers and
the poet was the youngest of them. They had a sister by name
Deva. The other brothers too were in high positions in that
State as well as in Baroda. Manohardas was a private Karbhari
or agent in the time of the Nawab Hamad Khanji and he had
greater influence at court than Amarji Diwan, father of Ranchodji. Dewan Gavaridass and Rangildass were the Majmudars
of the Gaikwad. Rasikadasa was a Sibandi Vakil. Kasidass was
taking out farms and Manecklal was busy settling and enlarging
Dhari Division of the Gaikwad. Revashankar displaced Ranchodji Diwan and came to power. This family came originally
from Aurangabad in the Deccan and they took service first under
Pilaji Gaikwad. Revashankar left three sons and their descendents are still in existence.

poet leaving no issue. So we have no direct descendants of Miranbai and Narsinha Mehta nor of Kavi
Dayaram who died a bachelor and therefore childless.
We have seen that with the other two poets the case
was different. The Nâgars are said to have emigrated
to Junaghad in the year 404—it is not known of what
era. Perhaps it was the Vikrama or the Kshatrapa
era. For we find Nâgars in the Vullabhi period as
donors of some grants (आनंदकर विनिर्गताय cf. Dr. Buhler's Valabhi grants *en passant*).

To this period we may ascribe the foundation of
Anandapura, already mentioned as situated on the
Maiwati or the Soormat river, not far from Junaghara,
almost midway between Mangrole and other Nâgar
towns of Soreth. So also of Vadnagar south-east of that
Anandpura and 2 or 3 miles north-west of Kodinar discussed and settled in this paper and that on the Baroda
Antiquities and Gujerat History, although Visalnagar
or Visnagara close to it or Visna on the Rami River
eastward may be of the time of king Visaldeva Solunki
Vaghelo in the 13th Century A. C. The Nâgars and
their places are divided into two groups of *Bargam*
or 12 villages each, the Gujerat *Bargam* and the
Kathyawar *Bargam.* They have a common board but
no intermarriage—although the strict rule is being re-
laxed of late in these times of railways and free com-
munications. The Kathyawad *Bargams* are Junaghud
(including Vasavud, Gondal and Mahuva), Bhavnagar,
Nagar, meaning Jam or Navanagar, Bhuj, Una, Patan
12

(meaning Veraval or Somnath Patan, and not the one in Gujerat), Mangrole, Khambalia, Vadhawan, Limdi and Saidhar. Of these Mangrole was the first residence of the family of our poet and Junaghad the next. His son Samaldasa is said to have been married to a daughter of Madan, the minister of Vadnagar, according to Kavi Premananda. This Vadnagar can only be in Kathyawad and not in Gujerat according to the Bârgâm rule.

Similarly the poet's daughter Kunverbai was given in marriage at Valum near Visnagar. Mr. Hargovandas identifies it with the town of that name near Visnagar in Gujerat as he does Vadnagar of Gujerat also for the son. But that also cannot be right under the Bârgâm rule. The Baroda Gheer Appeal Appendix XIV Map gives Valum on the sea-coast where the river of Visna to the N. N. E. of it falls into the sea west of Diu. It is named Vailuna Bunder in Captains Slight and Pollen's Map C (Appendix XV) of 1856. The map of Baroda Territory hereto appended also calls it Velum Bunder. This seems to be Valum if Rao Bahadur Hargovandas's tradition be correct. But Kavi Premananda gives the place as Una which seems to be correct as it is included in the list of the Kathiawad Bârgâm. According to Mr. Ichharam, the poet had to leave Mangrole as he had not the means to give her a dowry in marriage from. The Mehta about that time first went to Dwarka. He fasted, before going there, for seven days at Prabhasa Patan. He returned therefore after making necessary arrangements and married Kunvarbai at Una. This also would support the Kathyawar and Premananda tradition and not the Gujerat or Valum or Unja tradition. The poet was born in V. S. 1469–71 (A. C. 1413–15.) He was married at the age of 18 or 19 i. e. in V. S. 1488 (A. C. 1432) and he got Harmala in V. S. 1512, A. C. 1556. These are the only fixed dates connected with the life of the poet. He is said to have written 125000 *padas* or odes. His principal whole works are *Chaturi Bal-Lila* and *Dana Lila* of Krishna, *Govinda Gaman, Surata Sangrama, Sahasra Padi Ras &c.* The sweetness of his poetry is equalled and sometimes excelled only by Dayaram's. The pathos and ease are all his own, so also a halo of romantic devotion about it. The odes and songs of Miranbai are favourites with Gujerat ladies, while the *Padas* and *Prabhatias* or the odes and matins of Narsinha Mehta are popular with everybody. His popularity is shared only by Dayaram and no one else. They are the national poets of the people while Bhalana and Premananda, though higher and abler, are not so popular. They are great literary geniuses of Gujerat and the latter can aspire to a seat by the side of Milton, Kalidasa and Shakespeare. Kavi Dayaram has been rightly called the Byron of Gujerat.

Kavi Premanand was a native of Baroda and he has written some poems also while residing at Surat and Nandarbar in Khandesh. The year of his birth is placed between V. S. 1692 and 1700 (A. C. 1630 to 1644). He died about V. S. 1790 (A. C. 1734) at a very old age, surely before V. S. 1796 (A.

C. 1740). He was a Chovisâ Brahmin. His father's
name was Krishnaram and his grandfather's Jayadeva.
His son was Vallabha whom we already know. He
had a second son by name Jivana. His greatest work
is *Dasama-skandha* which he did not live to finish. His
other equally famous and popular works are the
Mameru, Sudama Charitra, Nalakhyana and *Okha
Harana*. His earliest work is perhaps dated V. S.
1720, the full-moon night of Sarad or autumn (A.
C. 1664) and has 600 lines written in a day. He
wrote *Narsinha Mehtana Chhokarano Vivaha* in 2
days. Thus we see how fast the poet composed and
how his poetic faculty continued unimpaired from his
early years to a green old age. From V. S. 1720 to 1790,
a period of 70 years, is not a short one. And it was
natural that he wrote many works remarkable for
their sweetness and beauty. For his flights of fancy,
soarings of imagination, merry turns of humour, mild
satire, brilliant descriptions, quick and flashing wit,
appreciation and description of the human heart and
its passions, the ordinary life as well as nature, the
pictures of which are quite life-like, faithful and natural, he has no equal perhaps among the Vernacular
poets of the whole of India. His transitions from one
subject and sentiment or *rasa* to another are so pleasant and imperceptible as to stamp him a great poet.
His *Dasama* can very well be put in comparison with
Milton's Paradise Lost and his *Nalakhyana, Sudamo*
and *Mameroo* with any of Dante's or Goethe's works.
He is the author of some dramas also. And even with-

out them his descriptions of life, persons, and actions are quite dramatic like Chaucer's as his contemporary Samal's are rather Spencerian. This puts him in the same class with Shakespeare. Whatever subject or episode from the Ramayana, the Mahabharata or the Puranas he has touched, has improved in his hand and with his pen.

The following is a list of some of his other works. I. Poems—1 *Karan Charitra Mahakarya*, 2 *Bhisma Champu*, 3. *Jayadevakhyan-GitaGovinda*, 4. the *Ten Skandas* of the *Bhagvata* (of which the 6th, 7th, 8th, 9th—*Vamana Katha*, probably written at Nandarbar and the 10th are published), 5 *Sabbaparva* 6 *Subhadra Harana*, 7. *Viratparva*, 8. *Markandeya Purana*, 9. *Babhruwahanakhyan*, 10. *Vallabhakhyana*, 11. *Dangavakhyan*, 12. *Revakhyana*, 13. *Vallabha-no-zaghdo*, 14. *Ramayana* (V. S. 1741, A. C. 1685), 15. *Chandrahasakhyana* (V. S. 1727, A. C. 1671), 16. *Dana Lila*, 17. *Narsinha Mehta ni Hundi* (V. S. 1754, A. C. 1698), 18. *Rishyashringakhyana* (V. S. 1729 A. C. 1673) 19. *Madalsakhyana*, 20. *Sudhanvakhyana*, 21. *Abhimaniu-akhyana*, 22. *Bhramara pachisi* and those without the poet's name, 23. *Ashtavakrakhyana*, 24. *Haramala*, 25. *Suka Janaka Samvada* 26 *Vraja Vela*; and II. Dramas—*Mityaropadarsaka Nataka*, *Panchali Prasad Nataka* and *Dusta Bharya Nataka*. These 29 with the *Skandhas* of the *Bhagvata* counted separately and the *Okha-harana*, *Sudama*, the *Mamera*, the *Nala-khyana*, *Narsinha Mehta ni Hundi*, *Narsinha Mehtana Chokrano Vivaha* and *Narsinha Mehtana bap nu Shraddha* and

Lakhshmana Haran, already referred to before, make up in all nearly 50 works by the author. and yet we may find many more. The lists given by Messrs Kavi Narmada and Navalram may be profitably compared here. No poet either of the past or the present, the East or the West, as far as I know, had any such long tenure of literary life—70 years and an existence close upon a century. He stands alone giant-like in the midst of a number of poets. His was the Augustan age of the Gujerati Literature and yet there was no crowned head as its patron. It was the sovereign people that appreciated and patronized the poet and his works.

Among the Contemporaries of Narsinha Mehta were Bhima Kavi, author of *Hari Lila Shodasa Kala,* V. S. 1541 (A. C. 1485) and Padmanabha, author of the *Kanhadade Prabandha* V. S. 1512 (A. C. 1456) and a few more while among those of Premanand, there was a large host of them. They were 1. Tulsidasa (V. S. 1732, A. C. 1676), 2. Jag-jivan Sanyasi (V. S. 1772, A. C. 1716), 3. Akho Bhakta, a Vedantist goldsmith (V. S. 1705, A. C. 1649,) 4. Samal Bhat, the great story-teller in verse and an equally voluminous writer (V. S. 1785, A. C. 1729), 5. Vallabhabhut, the great ode writer in honour of Devi Bahuchara (V. S. 1790, A. C. 1734), 6. Dvarko Bhagat (V. S. 1800, A. C. 1744), 7. Jivram-bhat also of the same year, 8. Vinaya Vijaya (V. S. 1738, A. C. 1882), 9. Ratno (V. S. 1795, A. C. 1739), 10. Jivan (V. S. 1800, A. C. 1744), 11. Udaya Rutna

(V. S. 1763, A. C. 1707), 12. Dhandas (V. S. 1783, A. C. 1727), 13. Viravyaya (V. S. 1793, A. C. 1737) and many more—in all not less than 40 or 50.

We now come down to Dayaram. He was a Sa-, thodra Nagar of Dabhoi. He led an exactly Byronian life. While Premanand's movements extended as far as Nundurbar and Surat only, and while Miranbai's pilgrimages lay between the Jumna and Vrindavana on one side and to Dwarka on the other and Narsinha Mehta perhaps did not go out in Soreth beyond Dwarka and not at all out of the peninsula, Dayaram travelled over the whole of India more than once. It is therefore that we find his facility in writing in the several vernaculars, Sindhi, Punjabi, Marwadi, Marathi and Hindi. He wrote Braj and Urdu or Hindi and Hindustani as the very native of Upper India and the Duab could write. His contemporaries also were numerous. Chief of them were Dhiro, (V. S. 1884, A. C. 1828), Kalidas, (V. S. 1817, A. C. 1761), Pritam (V. S. 1838, A. C. 1782), Revashankar (V. S. 1875, A. C. 1819) and Krishnarama Maharaja with whom he is said to have held a controversy at Ahmedabad (V. S. 1895, A. C. 1839). He had all the tastes, accomplishments, merits and demerits of his contemporary, the English Poet, Lord Byron. He was born in V. S. 1823 or 1833, A. C. 1767 or 1777. He lived to a very old age and died in V. S. 1908, A. C. 1852. He wrote some of his works at Dabhoi, Chanod and Broach. He visited Dakor, Kasi, Jagannath, Rameswara &c. in his seven years' tour. He visited Mathura thrice. His

poems collected and edited by Kavi Narmadashanker
extend over more than 600 royal octavo pages. And
the rich legacy that he has left to Gujerati will ever
be cherished and treasured up by the province and
the people.

Now we draw to a close. We have found
that Ahmedabad has given the largest number
of poets and yet we have none of them among these
epoch-makers. Among their contemporaries we have
named Akho Bhakta and Samala who are the best
representatives of that matter-of-fact city. The former has hammered down some of the prejudices of
his time and town without mercy, sparing nobody, flat-
tering nobody, and given us gold trinkets of pure
thought. The latter is the retailer of troubadour
stories of Bhoja and Vikrama and his didactic verses
have passed into pithy sayings of worldly wisdom and
advice. But with all their powers and performance
they have not come up to Bhalana, Premanand, Narsinha, Dayaram and Miranbai who received their poetic
inspirations in the earlier towns of Patan, Baroda (Surat), Junaghad, Dabhoi (Broach) and Cheetore. As
we have repeatedly said, Premananda is our Shakespeare or Milton and Samal is our Spencer or at the most
Chaucer. But the former unquestionably stands first.
Their quarrel for pre-eminence is also as old as the
times of Samal and Vallabha, Premanand's son. It
was repeated in our time in a controversy between
Kavi Dalpatram C. I. E. who espoused the cause of
Samal and R. S. Mahipatram C. I. E. and others who

supported ·Premananda in the *Buddhi Prakash* and the *Gujerat Shala Patra*. In going over the extensive ground of my subject I have perhaps too much tried the patience of my hearers, for which I beg their pardon. But I will deem the time well spent if I succeed in inducing the Orientalists of the West to study such a philologically and historically interesting and important language as Gujerati with its extensive literature and eminent poets, unsurpassed by any other vernacular of India.

13

The Antiquities and Archæological Finds of Baroda Territory,* India, and the Light shed by them on Gujerat History.

I have to congratulate myself for the selection of this subject, on account of the many facilities afforded me under the enlightened administration of the State and the Prince, I represent here in the Congress. Ever since the memorable Resolution of the Bombay Government, General Department, Archæology, No. 3549, dated 26th November 1875, on the motion of Mr. Burgess, the then Archæological Surveyor and Reporter to the Government, Baroda has been taking means to preserve and collect such monuments and relics. The Madhavrao-Melville administration was a bright epoch heralding the advent and accession of the present rule and succeeding the clouds and confu-

---

* The area of Baroda Territory is 8,569 sq. miles, 24 miles in excess of British Gujerat and 24 sq. miles less than that of Mahi Kantha and Rewa Kantha put to-gether and 2000 sq. miles more than Cutch State. Wales approaches Baroda in extent, Belgium is greater by about 3000 and Denmark by about 6000 sq. miles (in population the latter only by 400 of Souls). While Greece has double its area, it has two thirds of Baroda Gujerat population. While Sweden and Norway have an area of 293,848 sq. miles its population is 6,270,266. While the population of Baroda Territory is 1,951,015 Hindus (against 2,247,794 in British Gujerat), 174,236 Mahomedans (295,751 B. G.), 46,716 Jains (65,378 B. G.), 7,934 Parsis (16,448 B. G.), 338 Christians (3349 B. G.) and 27 others (356 B. G.). Of the Hindus there are at least 138,506 Brahmins.

sion of the past. The eminent Minister of the State as also the distinguished Agent to the Governor General spared no pains in this behalf, so early as January 27, 1876. Eight copies of the Resolution were circulated to the Subhas or Officers presiding over the several divisions of the State, calling upon them to collect all information they could. (Cf. Memo No. 280, Political Department). The result of this was that several copper-plate grants and coins were brought to light, and we have the early harvest in the eleven Chalukya land-grants of my friend Dr. Buhler. While digging the foundations of the New Central Jail, the offices of the State and of the Baroda College, several coins were found. Those from the first 2 places were sent by the then Minister, Raja Sir T. Madhavrao, to the first Prince of Travancore for inspection and decipherment. There were 12 silver coins, six from each of the places and six gold coins found at Anhilpura, while ploughing in a field. (Cf. No. 2947 Baroda 9-4-78). Prince Rama Varma reported thus on the 23rd of the month ; the gold coins are somewhat common.

...The silver coins are by far the most interesting. I have been able to identify them in Prinsep's *Indian Antiquities*. All the six pieces found in the Jail diggings are of one series and the six of the Public Office diggings of another of Saurastra (Gujrat) coins....... The P. O. coins correspond with figures 13–14–15 in Plate XXVII Vol. I, Prinsep's *Ind. Ant.* The Jail coins correspond with several figures in Plate XXXVII Vol. II. Prinsep's *I. A.*............Both kinds of silver coins are illustrated in Plate XV of H. H. Wilson's *Antiquities and Coins of Affganistan.* Wilson calls them "Sassanian coins". Figures 13–15 Mr. Prinsep has termed the Gadhais or ass money and he has attributed them to the Indo Sassanian Dynasty in Saurastra. (Vide I. A. Vol. I. P. 341)." Prince Rama Varma appends legends (B) of some of the silver coins from the jail diggings.*

Later on two packets of 63 pieces from the Public Office diggings and 138 pieces from the Central Jail diggings were sent to General Cunningham, (cf. Diwan's letter to Agent No. 3896 dated 17–6–78 and latter's reply), who gives the results of his inspection of them in his letter of the 14th of August 1878 in two memoranda that I append to this paper. The Central Jail findings cover coins of the five early kings or Satrapas of Saurastra "hitherto erroneously called Shah Kings, for there is not a single Shah amongst them, the whole of the names being either *Sinh* or *Sen*" and the Kings are Rudra Dama (23), Damajata Sri (13), Rudra Sinh (40–bearing dates 100–101–102–103–104–107–114–115), Jina Dama (4–dates 120, 124),

---

* राज्ञ क्षत्रपस्स रुद्रसाहस, स्वामी जिन दामा पुत्रस्स

2
राज्ञ क्षत्रपस्स अगदाम्न राज्ञ क्षत्रवस्स रुद्रसाह पुत्रस्स

3
राज्ञ क्षत्रपस्य विजय साहस राज्ञो महा क्षत्रपस्स दामा साहसपुत्रस्स

4
राज्ञो माहा क्षत्रपस्स अयाम्न राज्ञो महा क्षत्रपस्स रुद्र साह पुत्रस्स

Rudra Sena (34–dates 121-125-127-130-131-133-134 -137). Of the other finds he describes, six small thick silver coins as *drammas*-no doubt the direct descendants of the Greek drachmas. " Their types however were borrowed from the Sassanian coins of Persia. They are the same as Gadhais or ass coins generally found in Northern India" from about 700 or 800 A. D. to 1000 A. D.

These were no ordinary finds or results. One of the coins forwarded and presented to the Royal Asiatic Society, Bengal, and deciphered by Dr. Rajendralal Mitra (2-9-78) had the only legible letters on it " Ra jna-ma-ha Kri-tri-ma-Sa-Rudra–Shaha-pu " " of the son of the universally elected King Rudra Shah." " Rudra Shah " Dr. Rajendralal Mitra adds " had two sons Visvashah and Atridaman ; both of them successively became king and the coin must belong to one of them. There are no such words as Dama Jat Shri on the coins"

Thus the interesting finds had engaged Scholars in the far south, east, north and west, such as Prince Rama Varma, Dr. Rajendralal Mitra, General Cunningham and Dr. Buhler. These were followed by notes and reports on the architectural and archœological buildings in the territory by Captain Walker Scott (No. 125 of 19-9-79) and Captain, now Lieutenant Colonel, Jackson (No. 60 dated 25th March 1880.). The Subhas of Nowsari and Amreli also submitted their reports dated 24-4-80 and 24-11-87 respectively. Five more coins found about the Central Jail were sent to the Bombay Branch of the Royal Asiatic Society also in 1886 that were described by Dr. Bhagawanlal Indrajit, (Page 325 of Vol. II. of the Society's Journal, 1876), as *Gadhaias*. In 1881 were found two *Tamra Pattras* or copper-plate grants in Nowsari district—and I was invited to decipher them by the Revenue Commissioner and now ex-minister of the State, Kazi Shahabuddin and I have published them (Nos. VIII and IX of my series of Gujrat grants) in *Zeitsschrift* II, Heft Leipzig, 1886. Several other plates were also found in the Baroda Territory, five of which are lying with the Bombay Society. Dr. Bhagwanlal has edited some of them and Dr. Bhandarkar is engaged on others.

Apart from these general efforts there have been special ones also. The State has secured the services of Dr. Burgess who has prepared a beautifully got-up volume of the antiquities at Dabboi* and he is engaged to prepare similar Volumes for Patan, Modheyea &c. At the suggestion of our Survey and Settlement Commissioner, Mr. Elliot, in 1886, His Highness's Government appointed a special man to collect copies of inscriptions and information about them, and other matters of note and history and the results of Mr. Kripashankar Jhinabhai, the man appointed for the purpose, are left with me to prepare a manual therefrom. These contain 147 stone inscriptions &c. which will be described further on. These I have been able to supplement by my own researches and collections, especially since I began to act as a District Judge

---

* A copy of this has been presented to His August Majesty the King of Norway and Sweden with this paper.

iu the Amreli Division of the State. Of course I cannot enter fully into a description of the whole but
with the materials at my command, I shall be able
to score fresh results and present them to-day.

Thus with a continually active work done in this
province by a succession of ministers and the eminent
ruler, the State has been able to bring to light many
an important record of history. Of course, all the results have not as yet been published, as these matters
everywhere move rather tardily. But for all that we
are not a whit worse off so long as we can be sure of
sterling work in the field. The example of Baroda has
now been very worthily followed by Bhownagar and
Junaghur and they, especially the former, are now
masters of very good collections. The *Sodha Sangraha*
of my friend Mr. Vajeshankar G. Ozá of the Bhownagar
Ministry is a useful addition to the archœological literature of Gujerat and Mr. Campbell of the *Bombay
Gazeteers*, another friend of mine, has also brought
Junaghur to the front of late, by his find of *Buddhist
Stupa* of Lakha Medi in a beautiful valley of
Girnar. We cannot at the same time ignore the services of the Divan of the place, Mr. Haridas V. Desai,
to whose appreciation of the subject, we owe the careful guarding and protection of the celebrated edicts of
Asoka and the latter inscriptions by their side. I
have been able with the assistance of Pandit Girja-
shankar Shamalji to obtain *fac similes* of the former
which I present to-day to the Patron of the Congress
among other things. Through some inadvertance, I

have left behind the impression of the VIII. Edict,
which I hope to supply later on. Besides these states,
Vala, or the modern representative of Valabhi, also
has started a Jubilee Museum but it requires to be
put on a better footing still. And we have a larger
museum of such collections at Rajkote, but the un-
timely and calamitous death of Col. Watson has de-
prived us of its further development. I mention these
efforts as associated with those of the Baroda State
because of the peculiar relations that it bears to the
other states in Kattywar in conjunction with the British, as succeeding the Peishwas. It is the work
of this whole that we have before us and I propose
at other times and on other occasions to enter into
details of the same. My recent visits to Girnar, Sana
and Vala as well as Palitana were of too short an
extention to put me in complete possession of the
materials. But I wish to submit the result of my in-
quiries from the materials above detailed as also from
52 silver and 6 copper coins from the Baroda State collections and from a loan of 13 coins from Pandit Girja-
shankar Shamalji, also with my own collection of 59
coins—28 silver ones, 28 copper and 3 lead ones of different sorts, not to mention a great number of about
850 copper coins that I found at Monpur near Vala
or ancient Valabhi. Some of these coins I present to
the Patron of the Congress from my own collection
and others may I lay at the disposal of you, learned
gentlemen, for inspection and decipherment. Besides
the collection of State coins above-mentioned there is

14

a large one of nearly over 800 of different kinds, me-
tals and periods, that are lying with the Chief En-
gineer of the State, Mr. Reynolds, who is in charge of
arranging the museum in progress at Baroda. But
several of them being of the class above described
and a larger number of them being of the Mahomedan period, I have neither noticed them here nor have
I brought them over for the inspection of my colleagues
of this August Congress.

Besides the coins, grants and inscriptions, there are
other relics of interest found out in Kattywar, especially that are of great importance for the moral and
material history of the country and the people. I
have not been long in Kattywar nor have I been able
to move out much, being as District and Sessions
Judge fixed to my station with no vacation, nor at the
same time could I devote a sufficient degree of attention to what could I get at already. Otherwise I should
have been able to tell a longer and more valuable
story about them. Here I produce some of the larger
bricks that were used for building purposes in the
Valabhi period and a little after it, that are now a
matter of the past in Gujrat life of after-times. The
size, the material, the weight, and the strength and sta-
bility of them are noteworthy. You have now nothing
of their like in the buildings that you would meet with
from one end of the land to the other. Even in parts
where stones and rocks abound and where they form
the principal building materials they form the principal articles in the construction of the Buddhistic Stupas
almost all over India.

I have picked these up from the *timbas* or mounds
of earth that were once the sites of flourishing towns,
cities or villages about and near Amreli.

I have made the selections from Amreli and the
village of Daida, Radhia, Mangavapal &c. I saw them
about the caves of Sana and in the temples of Kunta,
at Bhimchas and Rukmini on an eminence at Talsi
Sáma in the heart of the dense Gir Forest, as also at
Vala where I saw excavations of some of the buildings,
not to mention other places. In old Karnavati, perhaps
at Patan and near Bhagva Dandi, places of the earlier
Gujrat Chalukyas of the North as well as the South,
they are reported to be met with at times. But on
this side of the 12th century they have disappeared.
In the Mahomedan times their appearance is not due
to any new construction of them but these materials
have been drawn upon from the earlier ruins. I saw
such a work going on at Bhimchas in May last, when I
visited the place and the Majmudar's Well near Randhia
is built out of the bricks from the *Aimbo*, now waste
close by. At Vala the bricks taken out crumble to pieces
because of the saltish earth of the bed of soil on which
it appears to have been built while at Amreli several
buildings of the old Mahomedan Syeds bristle with
these records of the past. A *Murshid* or *Guru* or
teacher of H. H. Khanderao began the building of a
mosque from out of them, but he did not live to finish it,
which still stands in its unfinished state as a skeleton of
past building materials. The local traditions speak of
Amreli as Kanakavati of old and the neighbouring

Mangavapal as Trambavati. I beg to draw the attention of the antiquarians to these relics other than coins and copper plates, grants and inscriptions of the antiquities of the place which we can approximately fix as falling on the other side of the 10th and 11th centuries, and earlier still.

Side by side with the above relics, we meet with another important index of the kind also. The thick piece of pottery I submit, belongs to an age that is past and gone. It is more than 3 times the thickness of its present kinds. The colour on either side of it has not suffered from time and long burial. The thinner pieces that accompany the same are remarkable for their glaze and colour that look fresh still. The descendents of this latter pottery can at once be distinguished from their having the colour only on one side and the glaze too being not so shining. There is also an earthen hold on which a door would hinge on the threshold corners. This tells us the absence of iron chains, hinges, clasps, and their like of a later age.

These records of a by-gone life and civilization lie buried with the ornaments, especially of ladies of the times. You have the *Cowrie* which has now become the favourite decoration of *Banajara* women. But still more interesting are the *Churis* and bangles made out of conch-shells of different sizes, patterns and workmanship. The inner folds and rims and indentations of the conch-shell have supplied the materials to make these ornaments. And any one can satisfy himself from a look at conches that have been picked up from the same beds. These are the *Sankhbharanas* or *Sankha* or conch-shell ornaments that added to the beauty of Mahâsweta of Bâna in his *Kadambari*. The sermons in stone that we read here are too important to be lost sight of and I will present to you a page from the lectures in trees, I mean the two fossils that I have presented to the August Patron of our Congress. I found them in a fossiliferous bed which was of a thickness of more than 6 feet. Two feet above them are met with the *Sankhabharana* pieces and some Kshattrapa coins, one of which I saw with the Kathi Girasia Vasta Vala Surga Vala of Samadhiála, about 25 miles S. E. of Amreli. The bed of fossils and these relics lie near about his estate. One of the fossils is the trunk of a tree and the other contains leaves of the *Jamoodo*, *Peepul* or *Banian* trees as well as *Khakhara(Gutteria Longifollio, Ficus Religions* and *Ficus Indical* as well as *Butea Pronodosa*). Animal and human fossils are also to be met with there. Lately a set of fossils of two cranes reclining on the bank was unearthed by that friend of mine. Even this bed which extends over several miles with another of salt earth and the adjoining ones of rocks &c. have to tell some tales in the History, I believe, of the Valabhi Kingdom which I propose to work out at some future date in a séparate paper. The above pickings have been obtained from a region extending between Vala and Monpur in the east, Zar and Samadhiala in the south or south east and Daida and Radhia in the north.

I have not as yet ascertained if these limits can be

extended further; at least they end in the south or south east where they have been described to have been found as above. My enquiries in the western direction extend to Mangavapal and the adjoining Sulio Timbo and Valishas and we can find light further north and west still. We cannot close this chapter without noticing another ornament made out of the Conch-shells, namely, the necklace beads whereof with the pendant I have picked up from about Zar which with Amreli is as old as the Valabhi Kingdom that we shall see further on. Yes, these Conch-Shell ornaments with the cowries have ere long been out of fashion and they are used only among the wandering aboriginal races. Bullock cars in Kattywar near about Amreli are to this day decked with trinkets made out of them and the cowries for horses, cows and bullocks in wider areas are not entirely out of fashion. These humble things have no interest at the first sight but we have seen above what light they can shed upon the history and life of the past times.

Gujerat has ever been rich in its Historical Records which have not all been exhumed and exhausted yet. A wider search and inquiry would bring us light that will clear many passages in our History as well as Literature. I invite the attention of my colleagues to these lines and strata of research as well. The native states of Gujerat, Cutch, and Kattywar, would do well to institute a search and collection of these things. The Museums in India have yet to learn a good deal from those of Europe and they can very profitably do that. It is only the British Government that can set a bright example to them by having such museums in Bombay, Calcutta, and Madras, as also in each of the divisional and subdivisional centres. It is hoped that H. H. the Gaikwar of Baroda, with his two visits to and sojourns in Europe, will be the first of the reformers in making his museum as complete as possible. After this cursory glance over the mute records of the Past, and perhaps the Gupta and Valabhi records of Gujerât and Saurâs'tra history, life, and civilization, let us go to the speaking ones, I mean, the eloquent coins, inscriptions, and copper-plate grants. I subjoin a statement of 172 of them. Of these 134 are of Mr. Kripâs'ankar's collections under State employ. To these I have added 13 more from his other notes; and those that follow are from my own collections and editions. Some of these last are published in the *Buddhi Prakas'a,* the *Zeitschrift* and the *Indian Antiquary,* and a few of them still unpublished. Most of the first 147 also are unpublished.

Very shortly I shall be bringing out a complete ous Volume of the whole under the direction of the Baroda Government.

Of the 147 Baroda State collections 135 are stone inscriptions, 7 of which are Pras'astis*, 19 Pâliyâs§ and

---

* Nos. 16 (G. S. 850), 17 (V. S. 1448–1442), 18–19 (V. S. 1273 Bhimadeva II), 108 (V. S. 1208–1680?), 118 (V. S. 1518–1537), 119 (V. S. 1518).

§ Nos. 2 and 3 (V. S. 1114, 1246), 4–5–6–7 (V. S. 1358), 8–9 (V. S. 1258), 12 (V. S. 1104), 15 (V. S. 1484), 23 (V. S. 1850), 27 (V. S. 1582), 30 (V. S. 1582), Grave 34 (A. D. 1844), 43–45 (V. S. 1720), 46 (V. S. 1850), 97 (V. S. 1733), 137 (V. S. 1163).

the rest are on images× (14), Pâdukâs (5), Pillars (3), on
a wooden Palli (1), and on a seat (1), and miscellaneous
the rest. And there are 12 Copper plate grants.+ Of
these grants and inscriptions, one comes from Dohad,
(Panch Mahals), 1 from Amreli, 2 from Sugâlâ, 9 from
Adi Pushkara near Kodinar, 1 from Cambay, 4 from
Prabhâs, 9 from Dwârkâ, 2 from Kodinâr, 5 from Mt.
Abu, 28 from Pattan, 1 from Dhinâki, 1 from Sindhaj,
15 from Bet Sankhodhar, 1 from Nariad, 21 from Sid-
dhapura, 2 from Dhrasana, 1 from Monpur, 1 from
Venipur, 5 from Unjhâ, 1 from Tobar Sim, 3 from
Nowsari, Kadi-Visnagar, 1 from Bahucharji, 1 from
Zar, 3 from Petlâd, 5 from Sunâk, 1 from Vâgodrâ,
1 from Mesânâ, 10 from Karnâli, 2 from Dethali, 1
from Junadpur, 2 from Sidhavâi, 1 from Bhinmal, 2
from Degam Sampgamv. Of the above 147 Inscrip-

× Images &c: Nos. 10 (V. S. 1660), 29 (V. S. 1452), 67.
Pillar, 70 (V. S. 1388), 20. Pillar (V. S. 1601), 28 Pillar, (Kshatrapa
S. 210), 58 (V. S. 1662), 59 (V. S. 1664), 60 (V. S. 1709), 61
Pâdukâ (V. S. 1387), 62 (V. S. 1510), 63 (V. S. 1349), 64–65
seat (V. S. 1664), 73 (V. S. 1361), 74 (V. S. 802), 76 Pâdukâ
(V. S. 1856), 78 (V. S. 752), 79 (V. S. 802), 82 (V. S. 1527),
Pâdukâ 83 (V. S. 1671), 95 Pâdukâ (V. S. 1862), 103 Pâdukâ
of image (V. S. 1140), 143 wooden Palli (V. S. 1687 and 1326).

+ Copper plates: Nos. 24 (V. S. 794 Jâinka-deva), 25 (V.
S. 941 Sarvajid-varmâ), 47 (G. S. 252 Sri-Dharasena), 49 and 50
(S'. S'. 836 Indra-râja IV.), 55 (V. S. 1030 Mulrâja I.), 66 (V.
S. 1326), 80 (V. S. 802 Vanarâja), 84 (V. S. 1051 Mularâja I.),
88 (V. S. 1148 Karnadeva I.), 111 (V. S. 1256 Bhimadeva II.),
112 (Forgery ? Y. S'. 2663 ? Sudhanvâ ?), and 133 (Cambay
Copperplate).

tions 54 are in the Gujerati Language and the rest
are in Sanskrit. Two are dated in Yudhishthira S'aka
(years 2663 and 4899 or 4799), two in Valabhi, rather
Gupta, Samvat (years 252 and 850), 21 in S'áli-
váhan S'aka (years 1447-1623-1733-1727-1722-1733
-1714-1692-1728-1645-1746-1785-1596-1705-1704—
1384-1750-1689-1732-1808-1728- 1657 the earliest
year being 1384, i. e. A. C. 1462, and the latest 1808 i. e.
A. C. 1886), one in Kshatrapa era (year 210 of Rudrasena), 2 in Hezira Sana (1196 and 1199), 2 in Christian era (years 1844 and 1887), and the rest in the
Vikrama era, the earliest of these being dated 752,
794 and 802 and the latest being dated 1943.

From the above we can see at a glance the distribution of inscriptions and eras in Gujerat, and especially in the Baroda Territory. I cannot take up the very
valuable time of the Congress with a detailed notice
of each. Some of these tell the tale that we already
know. And so I would select a few of them.*

Pras'asti No. 16, dated G. S. 850, has been recently
edited by Mr. Vajeshankar G. Ozá and Dr. Buhler, in
the *Vienna Oriental Journal*, Vol. III. No. 1, pp. 1ff.
which therefore need not be enlarged upon. No. 17 is
dated V. S. 1442 and 1448, recording the building of a
well &c., by Queen Yumuná, daughter of a Yádava
Prince Bhima and his queen Mánikyadevi, and wife
of a Rashtrodha Prince Bharma. We have no further

---

* They are Nos. 10, 11, 15, 20, 22, 23, 32, 33 to 46, 54, 56,
66, 68, 69, 72, 81, 89, 90, 91. 92, 94, 95 to 100, 110. 117, 120 to
123, 128, 130, 138, 140 to 141 and 174.

information about them, except the interest, that attaches to the appellation Rashtrodha, as a predecessor to *Ràthoda* of our times. No. 19 records the construction of Meghadhvani Mandapa of Somes'vara in V. S. 1273, by King Bhimdeva II. It brings to light the Inscription of the king and his connection with the celebrated temple of Somanâtha. No. 111 of the same monarch has already been published by me in the *Indian Antiquary.* It is No. 2 of my series. The Nânâka Pras'astis also are similarly published as Nos. III. and IV, in the Journal. I had no facsimiles of them at the time I edited them, which I have recently obtained from Kodinâr. The need for it was suggested to me by Mr. Henry Cousens of the Archœological Survey, and an inquiry into them has brought to light some new points, that I cannot but notice here. The Varangad mentioned at the foot of the second Prasasti is a place North of Kodinâr, a few miles from it, and the native place of Nânâka, who is styled Visala-nagarîya, that is Visanagar near the same Vadanagar which is now desolate.

The two Prasastis are engraved on one stone Pâliyâ. It is in the temple of Siva, a field's distance to the south of Kodinâr. It is on the left side, near the door, fixed in the ground by itself. There is a tradition about it that when the Moslem Syeds of Kodinâr were desecrating the temples of Somanâtha, and those about the place for their excellent stones and images they brought this also to Kodinâr, but it is not known from where. But its original home appears to be

Prabhâsa or its vicinity. The Syeds brought it
to the place about which it lies when at night the
Atits of the Matha or Monastary of the place sur-
prised the Syeds and got possession of the stone
about the time of Holi Holidays. The powerful leader
of the Atits was on terms of intimacy with the Syeds,
who therefore could not speak against the violence
done to them, and the booty continued to be there
since that time. The Bávás of the place spread mir-
aculous stories about the stone, that it used to give a
pound and a quarter of weight of gold every day, but
it is more than its weight for us in the history of
the period. The stone was brought there under the
above circumstances about a century ago. The stone
is breast high. Some part of it both at the top and the
foot is blank. The two Prasastis are written without
a break. There is no division in the middle of them.
This place is 12 *Kos* or 24 miles from Prabhâsa. The
inscription itself specifies its *locale* Sarasvatî Ságara
Sangama, the meeting of the Sarasvatî and the Sâgara
or the sea (cf. the opening salutation in No. III. also
vv. 3-4 Ibid. Prabhâsa, Khanda has the following
verse descriptive of the place—

हिरण्या व्रजिनीन्यंकु (लंकु)

कपिला च सरस्वती।

प्रभासे यादव श्रेष्ठ

पंच स्रोता सरस्वती. ॥

At Prabhâsa, Oh best of Yadavas, the Sarasvatî is
five-streamed viz. Hiranyâ, Vrajini, Nyankû, Kapilâ,

and Sarasvatî. The modern Soory in map is Vrajinî. The Hiranyâ is still marked by that name as also the Sarasvatî. The three unite near Prabhâsa Patton where it goes by the name of Triveni.

The Kapilâ is described as Demka in the map, which meets the sea, eastward of Verawal near Danibara. In the map, the Nyanku is named Singavado. This meets the Kapilâ, near Mûla Dwârkâ. We have seen the meeting of the Kapilâ to the sea. Varangar, as described above, is the place north of Kodinâr. There is a well near it. called Solankîvâv. The Rajputs living there are called (named) Kâradiâs as distinguished from Girâsiâs i. e. they are without any Girâs or state of their own. There are Solankis among them, and these can be no other than a colony from Gujrat,. a military colony settled there by King Visaladeva on his further conquest of the Province. The close of the reign of Bhîmdeva II., whom we have seen above, putting up the Meghadhvani Mandapa, was one of confusion and usurpation, as witness that of Jayanta Sinha of Dr. Buhler's Grant. King Tribhuvanpâla, that ruled for a short time, was perhaps a weak Prince; and it was thus that the grandson of Lavana-Prasâda, who was getting powerful at the Court, as we know from Dr. Buhler's several Grants, recording donations to Institutions, connected with his family, came to power. And the province of Kattywar, well nigh lost, must have been re-conquered by Visaladeva and he must have settled these soldiers militant of war, in the ancestors of the Kâradiâs of our time, and those of peace in Nânâka of the place. There are Solanki Giràsiàs also in Soreth within 14 Koses of Kodinàr, though none, at Vadanagara itself. These must have lost the lands in the rise of the Syeds in the general pillage of the 15th and 16th centuries, and afterwards. Probably Vîsaladeva might have given the name of Varanagar to the place, in commemoration of his settlement of the country, as reminding him of the Vadanagar of Gujrat. He also, then, was the founder of the Visnagar twin village with the Vadanagar aforesaid, which he founded in contrast with that founded in Gujrat, by a namesake of his from Rajputânâ. Thus the Nagar of V. 7 No. III., and Anandapura of V. 1 No. IV. can be our new Vadanagar and not the one in Gujrat.* This Vadnagar occurs in the map of Captain Pollcufex of the province of Kattywar of the year 1856 A. C.§ The Map of Gujrat and Kattywar Territories of the Gaicwar (Baroda State),§§ copy of which I hereto append, also mentions the place as Vadanagar. Then the town Gunjà might be sought near it. Or, perhaps, it was possible, that the Nagara and Anandpura of the verses, referred to the Gujrat town, and Nànàka's family also was a colony from Gujrat, but an earlier one, and it was therefore, that he was selected

---

* There is an Anandapura on the river Maimatec falling into the sea near the Matha of Mula Dwarka No. IV. of Kodina, and Vadanagar aforesaid. (Vide maps appendices I. XIII. Of the Baroda Geer Appeal).

§ The original thereof was prepared by Captain Slight in A. C. 1821.

§§ It is omitted in this reprint, as it is too well known to Indian readers.　　　　　　　　　　　　　　　　　H. H. D.

by the King to do the rites for him. Then Gunjâ might go with it to the other Province. As there is a sprinkling of the Solunkis Kâradiâs and Girâsiâs, so there is a large number of Vadanagara Nâgars also about Pattan, Veraval, Mangrole, Una, Delvâdâ &c. And these might be of the Brahampuri of this Nânâka. Mr. Fleet's No. 176 published in the *Indian Antiquary* of June last (9 V.) also speaks of a Nâgara Mâdhava son of Parâsara from Prasamapura (can it be Anandpura?), and a Bhrahampuri may be a village, as also a number of houses, where Brahmans or Brâhmanas are settled, under gift of it to them.

The present Vadanagar above specified has been re-built on an old *Timbo*. Visnagar is desolate now. But the *Timbos* of the two places are within 2 or 3 miles of each other. Both have marks of the old forts there. The Dehjada of the Kodinar Purganah of the year 1825, which forms Appendix III. pp. 138 *et seq.* to the Gir appeal of the Baroda State, mentions the two villages under the head of Vadanagar, where Visnagara is described as a hamlet.

Thus we have been able to fix the places of Nânâka, as mentioned by the Prabandhakâras as Visnagara, and of the inscribing of the stone, as Vadanagar: and of the inscription, as Triveni, near Prabhâsa, beyond doubt and dispute. And these Vadanagar and Visnagar have nothing to do, so far as the present inscriptions go with those of Gujrat and the older ones. This question has a bearing on another question in the History of the Gujerat poet Narsai Mehta, which we have noticed in its proper place.

At Triveni, pilgrims perform Srâddhas, and offer *Pindas* or oblations to the manes–and it was for that permanent benefit to the manes of himself, when dead, that King Vîsaladeva settled Nânâka, who is eulogized in these Prasastis for his work. I have not been able to ascertain the locality of the foundations of this Nânâka which I hope to do some other time.

Now again to our other Inscriptions. No. 108 is the celebrated one trom Vadanagar in my No. I of the series frequently referred to, relied on and quoted for the longer reign of King Siddhrâja Jayasinha about which differences exist between me and my friend Dr. Buhler (q. v. *Ind. Ant*; also *Vienna Oriental Journal*). More light is needed still on the question. But I might notice that Mr. Kripashankar also gives its date as V. S. 1208 like myself. I visited the place 3 or 4 years ago but it was in a hurry, and the facsimiles, I took thereof, were not complete, and even these are not with me at present, for I have presented them to the Gujerat Vernacular Society at Ahmedabad. Better and very accurate facsimiles only can solve this question.* Nos. 118 and 119, both dated V. S. 1518 and the former also S. S. 1324 (the earliest date in the era in the present collections, are of the period,—why his own,—of Râjâdhirâja Mahamud. They are at Degam Sampagam. There is another Sanskrit Inscription of the Great Mahamud at Dada

---

* It has since been settled by my friend in his able edition of the Inscription, in favour of the old dates as contended by Dr. Buhler. H. H. D.

Hari's well near Ahmedabad dated V. S. 1556 (No. 160) of the accompanying statement. There is a fourth Inscription of the said ruler at a rice-frier's shop at Dahod, in a very mutilated state, which I saw in 1880, when I went there for the Chabbua Tank Inscription of King Jayasinha Siddharája, No. 1,–in my series in the *Indian Antiquary.* It is dated V. S. 1545 and also S. S. 1410 *Vaisàkha Sudi* 13, Tuesday (*Vide* No. 161 of the statement). Inscriptions Nos. 163 and 164 at the Cambay step-well of the Maihiras, dated V. S. 1529, *Bhàdarvà Sudi* 8 and *Vadi* 11 (?), Thursday and Monday respectively, and one more at the Borsad step-well, dated V. S. 1553 *Sravan Vadi* 13 Sunday, No. 170 of the present collections. No other Mahomedan Sultan of Ahmedabad has got so many Sanskrit Inscriptions, either of himself or of his time. The Neriad Well Inscription, of Sultan Mudafar or Muzafurshah of Ahmedabad, is dated V. S. 1572 *Vaisàkha Sudi* 13 (*Vide* No. 145 of the statement) which I have already edited for the *Buddhi Prakasa* Vol. XXX., pp. 85 to 88 and 102 to 106. I have found lately another Inscription of the same Sultan Mujafar at a dilapidated well (*var*) near Vaisadà, about 5 or 6 miles east of Amreli. It is dated 1577 V. S. *Jeth, Sudi* 9. It tells us that the Minister of the Sultan was of the Nàgar caste, Maham Sri Ràmaji, Maham Sri Dhàriga. But both the Inscriptions are written in the vernacular dialect. There is another step-well at Devalià, a few miles S. E. of Amreli, which is built in the Mahomedan or Saracenic style of the Architecture at Ahmedabad. It had also an Inscription, but it has disappeared of late. These wells and others in the villages near about, are attributed to the said agency, to a Brahmin of Marwad by the tradition. The people might have mistook the Minister of the Sultan of Gujerat as regards his caste and native place. No. 75 bearing date V. S. 1425 *Vaisakha Sudi* 11th, Friday, is the earliest Inscription of the time of the family. It is of the time of Sultan Ahmed, founder of Ahmedabad, under the Nandikes'wara or the bull of S'iva at Pattan in Golvád and in Sálvivád. In this notice I have left out the Inscriptions of the time of the Emperors Akbar and Aurangzebe*, as also of the earlier Gaikwads (q. v.), that do not throw much light on the known History of Gujerat.

The other stone Inscriptions are on *Páliás* or stone images of Rajput warriors &c., who might have fallen in the field. Some of them are in Gujeráti and they are useful for the study of its past forms. They are also useful in knowing the spread and existence of Chávdás &c. in the several places and times. Among copperplate grants, No. 24 is the same perhaps that Dr. Bhandarkar has edited for the *Indian Antiquary*. It is dated V. S. 794. Nos. 25 and 112 are very important, if they be genuine. They are in possession of the S'ankaráchárya at Dwarka. The *S'áradá Matha* at Dwarka

---

* One of this Emperor's Inscriptions (No. 113 in our statement) is also dated in Y. S. 4799 (नंदांकादि युगोन्मित) and its V. S. is 1755.

16

is one of the four Sees founded by the great Vedantist reformer and philosopher, the great S'ankaráchárya. These copperplates have been subjects of several angry *Sabhas* between the owner and the S'ankaráchárya from the Deccan Mula Bagal, Sadánand Tirtha, and also of actions and suits in Baroda and British Territories, as well as between them and the former, and the Gûglis of the celebrated temple at Dwarka. The former is dated V. S. 941. It has been made in favour of the Head of the Matha or See at Dwarka Nrisinhás'rama by one who styles himself Gurjara Mandaládhiswara Saûravajidvarmâ. His minister is named Mahîpálavarmâ. It names Pattan Manadala which can be the portion of the country about Veraval or Prabhas Pattan.

Kus'asthalî is Dwârikâ, and Gomatî the Gomatî there. This Edict was passed on the Head of the Matha above mentioned having vanquished the Jain heretics, while on his tours. The occurrence of the words S'ri-Ambe, and the royal seal at the top, are said to be unusual. The other grant is said to have been made by King Sudhanvâ in favour of the Great S'ankaráchâryâ at the time of his founding the four Mathas. And it is dated Y. S. 2663. (?3663?) The characters of the grant, and the form, size, and thickness &c. of the plate, lead one to doubt its genuineness, as also do the occurrence of salutation to Mahâkâlî at the time, and the like minor points. I was shown by the present holder of the see several letters from the celebrated Ranchhodji, Diwan of Junagad, author of the *Tawarikh-i-*

Soratha, requesting a loan of the copperplates &c. for his work, when they were lent to him. Questions regarding these are, surely, unsettled. Still, as I cannot discuss the subject in this greatly crowded paper, I reserve it for another occasion, and content myself with subjoining a Pâttavali of the Dwârikâ Matha.

But I cannot close, in all justice, this subject without noticing shortly the appended Vans'âvali. Some of its letters having been worn out, it was published (प्रकाशिता) anew in V. S. 1846, at the command of the then living Madhusûdanâs'ramaswâmi by Nilcantha S'âstri, the son of Ranchod S'âstri of the Modha caste at Dwâramâtî, on the Gomatî, in the presence of the image of Krishna. It gives a succession of the holders of the seat since the time of S'ankarâchârya, and his disciple and representative elect at Dwârikâ, Mandana Mis'ra or Sures'varâchârya. It gives the date of the birth of the great S'ankarâchârya, as Yûdhishthira S'aka 2631, on the 5th of *Vais'akha S'udi.* He was invested with the sacred thread in Y. S'. 2636 *Chaitra S'ukla* 9th, and he entered the fourth stage, viz. that of *Sanyasa,* in Y. S'. 2639 *Karttika S'udi* 11th. On the 2nd of *Falgun, S'uda* Y. S'. 2640 he received the *upades'a* from S'rî Govinda Bhagvat-Pâdâchârya. From that time to Y. S'. 2646 *Jyeshtha Vadi Amavasya* he was occupied in the composition of the 16 Bhâshyas, viz. those on the Vedânta Sû-tras the Bhagavad Gîtâ and the Upanishadas &c. There were also the Pratishthas of Srî Nârâyana as well as the Jyotirmatha. On the Y. S'. 2647 *Karttika S'udi* 8th was the *Prachara* or the spread of the Brahma Vidyâ in

company of Bâdaiâyanâchârya, and the living together
with Sanandana. On the *Margshirsh Vadi* 3rd of the
same year was the commencement of the discussion
with Mandanamis'ra. On the 4th of *Chaitra S'udi*, the
following year, was his victory over Mandanamis'ra.
On the sixth of the month was the *Kala Prasanga*
with Sarasvatî who was defeated on the 1st of the Vad
of the month. And as she was rising up to the sky, she
was brought down by the *Mantra* called *Chintamani*.
While she was again flying away through fear of
widowhood on the 9th of *Falguna S'udi*, she was again
brought down and settled at S'ringapurî. A Matha
was founded there and she was established there on
the 9th of *Chaitra S'udi* Y. S'. 2649. Mandanamis'ra
adopted the best of âs'ramas, *Sanyasa*, and style as
Suresvarâchárya. On the 10th of *Margsirsha S'udi* Y.
S'. 2649, King Sudhanvâ became a S'ishya or follower.
From the 3rd of *Vais'akha S'udi* Y. S'. 2650, was the
commencement of the Digvijaya. Trotaka and Hastâmalaka were respectively met on the *S'ravana S'udi* 7th
Y. S'. 2653 and *As'vina S'udi* 11th, Y. S'. 2654.
Hastâmalaka Áchárya was established on the seat
of S'ringapura on the 15th of *Pausha* Y. S'. 2654. From
the 15th of *Bhadrapada* Y. S'. 2655 to *Amavasya*
of *Pausha* of Y. S'. 2662, was a continuous Digvijaya,
and the defeat of the 99 sects *viz.* of the Baudhas,
Kâpâlikâs, Saivas, Vaishnavas &c. Sudhanvâ and
other kings were asked to be favourable, and the pristine
Varnas and As'ramas were established over again.
The greatness of the whole Yoga was published, and

the people were satisfied. Thus India or the continent of Bharata was regenerated. From that day forward was the residence at S'âradâpîtha. On the 15th of *Karttika* Y. S'. 2663, the great man went to Kailâsa; and the copperplate No. 112, noticed above, therefore, is the last* act under him i. e. on the 15th of *As'vina.* And thus was the glorious life of 32 years nobly and bravely closed. This Vans'âvali and copper-plates, as well as the age of the great teacher will form a separate paper by itself.

No. 47 of our statement is a very important grant. It is dated G. S. 252. From it we learn that Amreli and Zara are as old as the date thereof, and the Kingdom of the *Valabhis* extended to these places. I have appended maps of Dhâri, Amreli, Okhâmandal, and Dâmanagar Divisions, separately, to illustrate some of the many places, occurring in this paper, or the statement, and its other appendices†. Alongside with this, I may refer to another Valabhi grant; and that is of King S'ilâditya I. (No. 157 of our statement) from Bhâdaran, near Baroda, bearing date G. S. 291, *Ashadha S'udi* 3. I obtained a rubbing of the former, as late as June last, and I have but the copy of the 2nd plate of the latter. These will be separately published, later on.

Grants Nos. 49 and 50 have been edited in the *Zeitschrift* (Leipzic) as already observed, and they require no remark. Nos. 55 and 84 are of King Mûlarâja. The former is dated V. S. 1030 and the latter 1051. The for-

---

* It has already been noted that the year is *Chaitrâdi.*

† Omitted in this reprint.

mcr records a grant of land (1 plough) in the Village of Pâliâ Gambhûtâ, on the 5th of *Bhadrapada S'uda*; and by the latter, the King grants Varnâka-Grâma in Satyapura Pathaka, on the 5th of *Magha*.

Grant No. 66 dated V. S. 1326 *Magha S'uda* 13, is obviously a forgery. It is in the Gujerati language, which speaks of its being quite recent, abounding in foreign words, not possible to exist in the language of the time. With regard to No. 80 also, a doubt has been expressed by Dr. Burgess, in his Correspondence with me on the same· I myself have not seen the plate itself, and the facsimile I got, was not very well executed. The owner, besides, does not wish to part with it, even for a few hours, outside his house. No. 133 is the Cambay Copper-plate, noticed in the *Zeitschrift* (Leipzic) by me. It was only one part. I could not find its trace when I visited the place in 1881.

Grant No. 88 is a very interesting grant, and it belongs to King Kar'nadeva. It is dated 15th of *Vais'akha*, V. S. 1148, Monday, the penultimate year of his reign. He grants 4 ploughs of land at Sunâka in Pattan sub-division of Kadi District. It is dated from Anhilapâtaka. It does not give any geneology. He styles himself Trailokyamalla S'rî Karna Deva. This gives one *terminus ad quo* for the age of his son's rule, i. e. it cannot be earlier than the time assigned to him.

Inscription No. 57 of the statement is a fragment, dated V. S. 1234, *Falguna S'udi* 2, Saturday, which alludes to King Ajaya in vv. 61 and 62, and Bhim-

deva in v. 63. No. 116 is another Inscription of the
same king, and that at S'rí Kâles'vara Mahâdeva at
Unjhâ. It bears V. S. 1231 *Chaitra* V. 11, Thursday.
The copy I have with me in the collection is very imperfect. But here we have *termini-ad-qua* of the reign
of the monarch.

In the statement hereto appended, I have added
Nos. 148 to 172, that I myself have had to do with.
Some of these, I have noticed above. No. 149 is a
Karnâvati fragment, that I have presented to the
Bomday Branch of the Royal Asiatic Society. I have
renoticed it in the *Buddhi Prakash* Vol. XXVII. pp.
174 to 176.

There remains now the copperplate grant of king
Kîrttirâja of the family of Bârpa, and grandfather
of Trilochana Pâla (No. 158) of No. 9 of my series.
(Vide No. 157). It is dated S'. S'. 940. The name of the
father of this monarch that I have read as Gongirâja
(2) Agnirâja or (3)Goggirâja is now settled by this grant
as Goggirâja. Lines 8 and 9 in our grant run thus :—

तस्यापत्यं समजनिदलत्कीर्ति भख्यातवंशः
श्रीमान्विद्याविनयनिलयो गोग्गिनामा नरेन्द्रः
यद्दोर्द्दण्डापहत कमला विप्रयोगोपतप्त
शंके सौरिः सलिल शयनास (*sic.* सं) गमगींचकार.

The present Grant also gives the same origin of
the founder of the Chalukya race as,

धातुः संध्या विधिविरचिता—दञ्जलेर्जायतेस्म
स्फारतेजो दिशिदिदिशि किरन् कोऽपि चौलुक्यनामा

यष्टे यस्मिन्नसमसमरत्रासलोलैस्तदार्नो
शंके सिन्धोः पयसि वसतिः कल्पिता. दानवेन्द्रैः

In that family, the next verse tells us, was born
Nimbârka,–and from him was born Bârappa, who is
eulogized in the verse following. His son Goggirâja is
described as above. He had a son by name Kirtti Nripa,
who too was warlike (रणरस निवासः). This inscription
also settles, by the identification of the names, that
this Goggirâja was the same as the Goggirâja of the
Grant of Seunachandra II. dated S'. S'. 991. His
daughter Nâyiyalla Devî, the other grant tells us, was
the Chief Queen of Vaddiga.*

In my No. 81 it is said of Goggirâja that
he strengthened his position by securing the alliance
and support of the rising family of the Yâdavas of
Chanod, and the verse quoted in the note speaks of
him as a *Samanta*. But the verse from this grant of
Kîrttirâja shows that the two families were not on the
best terms possible in the times of the father and the
son, while the verse speaks of the withdrawal and
retirement of S'auri meaning the Yâdava Prince. It
does not speak of the giving of Princess Nâyiyalla
Devî, which can be inferred from the continuance of
the wars even in the time of Kîrttirâja who was the

* Cf. Verse चालुक्यान्वय मंडलीकलतिका श्री गोगिराजानका दुत्पन्ना
दुहितात्र या द्रुणवती घाम्ना कुल द्योतिता—स्त्री रत्नंनतवेषसामकटितं साम-
न्त रत्नायसा श्री नाइयल देवि नाम सुभगा श्री पट्टराझी सदा. The
verse is too confused to decide who was her husband, whether Vaddiga or Tesuka. Dr. Bhagwanlal takes the latter, perhaps rightly.

abode of martial sentiment. He also appears to have
dealt a defeat on the enemy who fled,—Tesuka of the
Yâdava grant of S'. S'. 99 being curtly dismissed. This
was the King that Kîrttirâja perhaps defeated. Tesu-
kas' successor is now reduced to a *Mandalikaship,*
while, before, Goggirâja was described as *Mandalika.*
Perhaps Tesuka died in prison. And the *Vidveshi
Va lhujana* was the sister of Kîrttirâja himself.
This family had an ally in the Râshtra Kûtta
Kundarâja who had a son, by name Amritarâja, and
from him was Samburâja, who was a feudatory of Kir-
ttirâja. He has got a Mathikâ established in Palâsá,
Chandrikâ or Palsânâ in Nowsari District of the
Baroda State. Thereupon S'ri Mahâmandales'vara issues
this grant. The grant of Trilochanapâla also tells us
of the warlike life of this King and of his son Vatsarâja. In their reigns the dynasty was in the height
of its power. But the wave again turns. The grant
of Seuna Chandra II. tells us that Tesuka's son Billama
married the daughter of King Jayasinha and sister of
Ahavamalla, and the family again rose to power. King
Seuna Chandra is again said to raise the Kingdom, as
the Boar Incarnation of Vishnu did the earth. This
was by the year S'. S'. 991 and perhaps the sun of the
Kingdom of Kîrttirâja was already set after Trilo-
chanpâla between that year and S'. S'. 972.

Thus we have seen by the light of these two Barp family
grants of S'. S'. 940 and 972 and the Nasika Yádava Grant
of S'. S'. 991, what great changes have occurred in South
Gujerat, and the portions of the Deccan adjoining it.
17

The Râshtra Kûtas of Gujerat fell, and on their ruins
rose the Chaulukyas of Barp, the Senapati of Chalukya
Tailapadeva. In course of time, the Râshtra Kûtas descended of Kundarâja became their allies, while they
i. e. the Chaulukyas, got their enemies in the
Yâdava house of Nasik. Goggirâja had to give his
daughter Nâyiyalla Devî, who became chief queen of
Tesuka who came to be *Mandalika*. Wars continued.
Tesuka's power again declined. Bhillama was reduced
to *Mandalikaship* and Kîrttirâja became a King (*Nripa*)
or Mahamandles'vara. Bhillama married the daughter
of Chalukya Jayasinha and sister of Ahavamalla and
again got the better of his enemies. Vatsarâja, son
of Kîrttirâja, also had a life of war and troubles. Bhillama's son Sena succeeded at last and we hear no
more of Trilochanapâla's successors. The Râshtra
Kûtas were gone. The Châlukyas too and the Yâdavas
also did not survive long. The Châlukyas of Gujerat
(Pattan) and the Yâdavas of Devagiri were moving
like two powerful waves which were again swallowed
up by volcanic eruptions of the Moslem power at the
close of the Thirteenth Century.

A word more about the statement and we take
leave of it. Mandalika's inscription of V. S. 1507, *Magha*
5 Thursday is of great moment in the History and Philology of the Gujerati language that it is written in (No.
171). No. 172 is an Inscription dated V. S. 1473 from
the same place, namely, Junaghad. The former is from
Uparkot, the latter from Dâmodara Kunda.

After the above, the Baroda Territory abounds in

its numerous finds of gold, silver, copper and lead-coins.
Herewith I append a statement of some coins, 3 of which
are of lead, 34 of copper, and the rest silver. There is
a beautiful coin of Syâmotika's son Chashtana, and 2 very
old coins of the As'oka character and type. The three
lead coins, my friend Dr. Buhler tells me are also as
or more ancient. In Kattywar all old coins are known
by the names of *Gadhaias* or ass money as General
Cunningham translates the word. But these are also
locally distinguished as *Morlis* or peacock coins that
are the Kshatrapa or the Gupta coins, a very appro-
priate term for them, as the fan-tailed and winged
peacocks on the latter show. Even the altar mark, and
the sun and the moon in the former, can very naturally be compared by ordinary people to a peacock;
and the *Gadhaias* proper are the so-called Sassanian
coins. I also append a photograph of some of the
coins taken for me by my friend Mr. D. P. Derasai
of the Training College at Rajkote. The coins in the
middle are the copper coins from Neriad and of the
Mahomedan period. Throughout the Baroda Territory
especially the *Gaddhaias* are found in the largest
quantity and then the *Khshatrapas* and the least of
all the *Gupta* coins. The smallest *Gupta* copper coins
of Kumara Gupta in my present Collection are the
only unique ones of them. The Gupta coins are of
the fan-tailed peacock type. Some of the *Khshatrapa*
coins bear date also, and especially some of those of
Swami Rudrasena, the 26th King, whose dates on a
few of the recently found coins from near about Valabhi

are S'. S'. 294, while others have figures showing the
Century for hundreds, tens or the units with the rest
gone off. The find of the earlier Khshatrapa coins, of
the five coins noted above, takes back the History of
Baroda to a very early age, and the extent of the
Khshatrapa rule to that part too. Now remains the
only curious silver coin with a blank on one side and
श्री विष्णु engraved on the other. Before taking leave of
the subject, I have much pleasure in presenting for
inspection to the Congress a lead seal coming from our
State, as a loan from my friend Major Snell, Assistant Agent to the Governor General at Amreli. It has on
one side of it the peacock and on the other some
characters which look very much like the early Guptas.
Major Snell got it from a river in Upper Burmah.
If the seal proves to be a Gupta* one it would no
doubt be of great value. Yes, these coins, copperplates, inscriptions, *pattavali* and relics of ornaments
and arts, of buildings and pottery, do not exhaust the
whole list of Baroda antiquities. The Territory comprised in the Baroda State, as will be seen from the
maps† accompanying, are the seats of the old Kingdoms of Gujerat, West, South, North or East. Okhá-

* I have lately read the inscription containing the name
Budha Gupta, probably one of the late Guptas of Eastern Bengal.
(1893.)

† The maps have been omitted from this reprint as they are
too well known to our Indian readers. Copies of them and of a
photograph of coins have been left at Stockholm and Christiania
with Congress collections for European Scholars.

mandal is the early home of the Chávadás. Their
next emigration was to the southern sea-coast strip of
territory called Nagher, about the Kodinar Sub-
Division of Amreli, and somewhere grazing the skirts
of Dhári too. The Kshatrapas, Guptas and Valabhis
had their sway over other parts of the Amreli Division and the territories of our feudatory princes also.
We find the Kshatrapas again at Baroda and in the
vicinity. The early Chálukyas of Dr. Bhagavánlal
Indrajit too may be relegated to that region. The
old Kingdom of the Gurjaras touched some part of the
Central or Baroda Division and also of the Southern
or Nowsari Division, while the Gujerat Ráshtrakútas
and the Chaulukyas of Bárpa's family ruled over almost the whole of the Southern Division of Baroda
State. The Chávadás first, in part, and the Solunkis
next, ruled over the whole of the Northern Division or
the Kadi District. While the Native States such as
the Baroda Rájya and its Feudatories own the old.
Rajput Territory, to the British has passed the territory comprised in the Mahomedan Kingdom, ruled over
by the Viceroys of the Dehli Emperors, or of the
Sultans of Ahmedabad, or of the Peishwas, as also bits
of territories of the Kingdom of Gurjaras, Ráshtra
kútas, and Chálukyas in the Broach and Surat collec-
torates and of the Valabhis and Kshatrapas in the Kaira
Collectorate. It is, therefore, that the former are richer
in antiquarian remains than the latter.

Then, apart from the above records of history and
antiquity, there are important traditions also. I propose

to refer to two of them among many. The one is as per
Geneological Tree of the Kâthis, that I append to this
paper. I got it from Bâbrâ and it is said to have
been prepared at the instance, and under the direction
of the Kâthi Chief of Bagasarâ. It tells us quite another story from what we learn from the Kattywar
Gazetteer. This is a branch which demands a separate
treatment by itself. But here I propose to run over
some of the peculiarities of this Vaas'âvalî.

It begins with the first Demiurge, Adi Náráyana,
and his lotus, and through them, it passes to Brahmâ
and the Sun. The Solar Descent must have arisen
from their worship of the Sun. The Sun or *Sûrya* is
named here Karana, and not Manu, but from the con-
text they appear to be the same. The Geneology counts
among them–Ikshvâku, Sagara, Dilîpa Bhagîratha,
Raghu, Das'aratha, Râma, &c. of the Solar race. There is
not a trace of the Kâshtha or Stick Theory of Production
by the Hero Karan of Mahâbhârata. This name has
been preserved in Karana, Son of Sûrya. The founders
of the cities of S'râvasti Champu also have been included
in the list. The myths of the destruction of the sons
of Sagara, and their regeneration, by the waters of
the Ganges, brought from the sky by Bhagîratha, also
are given. Râma, it is said, was called an incarnation
of God, as he freed the gods from the terror of Râvana.
Atithi we are informed was a son of Kus'a, that Lava
adopted, from whom is the further race. Then we
pass to Agnivarna of Poet Kâlidâsa, and come to Sa-
dhoda, perhaps S'uddhodana, father of the Great Bud-

dha, who is falsely called Bâgala here. Then we arrive at the foundation of Valabhipura by Sumitra, who was also called Valabhi. His grandson Varaketa, (Viraketu?), born of Padma Nâginî, daughter of the Nâga-Pundarîka. This is perhaps illustrative of their early Serpent Worship, a twin child of the Sun Worship. His great-grandson was Mâno from whom are the Mânavas who ruled at Kasi or Benares. He gave away the city to the Brâhmanas, and repaired to Gokula, where he fought one Somes'vara, defeated him, and there founded his Kingdom. Fifteenth in descent from Mâno was Kânadeva alias Jeta Vâlâ, who founded Jetpur. His son Ebhal I. took Talâjâ from the demon Tâla. Eighth from him was Ebhal III. He flourished when 3000 years of Kaliyaga had elapsed i. e. in the last quarter of the Second Century before Christ. He left Gokula and came and founded a Kingdom at Mándavaghada (Mandu) in Mâlavâ. Perhaps an eruption of foreign invaders made him leave Gokula.

These were perhaps the early Scythian invaders. This is mythically explained away by his vow of Ganges water bath, and the miracles of the Ganges, obtained through prayers, by his *suttee* queen Somâbâi, who afterwards was known as *Somal.* Fourth from him was Ebhal IV., who emigrated to the South from Mandavagadha, and commenced to rule at Vâlâ. Can he be our Senapati Bhatarka? He is said to have conquered the Kingdom from the Kolis who ruled there. Can they be the Maitrakas—Maiharas of latter times and the Mers of our day, who are aboriginal, and who latterly attached themselves to the Jethvâs and Chundásatmás ?

I pass over the traditions about him and Ebhaï VII., twelveth in descent from the last, about their giving away numberless girls in marriage, as being of no very great historical value. His son was Selàit (S'ilâditya). Thus there is an attempt to connect the rulers of Valabhi also with the race. A brother of Selàit Châmparâja is said to have founded his Gadi at Jetpur, where a gate is still called Châmparâja Bàri or Châmparâja's Gate. Selait's son was Dhâna and there is a tradition about his giving six of his 9 sons to the Padshah as a price of the head of a Charana's son. The Padishâh did not kill them, but, after exhibiting the eyes of deer, showed that he had done so and then he returned the boys to their father. The Kathis since that time do not chase or kill the deer. From the sons of this Dhâna here branched off several races and principalities. From the fourth son Vanâra were the Ahirs. This is perhaps to connect the latter with the Kâthis. From Bâlavana, the eighth son, are said to be similarly the Avasura Châranas. Veravalji is said to have gone to Padar (Dhâvara) in Scinde. His son Valomji married Rupâi the daughter of Patgar Kâthi, and turned a Kâthi from a Rajput that he was upto this time, and went and lived in Pawar. But there, he was pursued by the army of the Jam; and so he came to Than, northward of Soreth, in the Fourteenth Century of the Christian Era. The Jam followed him there also. This terrified Valomji. The

Sun-god appeared to him in a dream, and told him that a certain horse would appear to him, and that would be the sign of victory. It did appear the next day and the Kâthîs routed the army of the Jâm. In celebration of it, they built a temple of the Sun-god at Than, which is resorted to, till this day. This Valoji was a son of Vâlamji, and he lived in A. C. 1400. His brothers were Khumân and Châmprâj, from whom were the races of Khumâns and Khâchars respectively. Tenth from Valoji was Devâit, who ruled at Sisâng Chândali, and who conquered Chital and Devaliyâ and founded his titular Goddess there at Devagâm. Then, we see the Race branching off and spreading all round gradually at Jetpur, Mohota, Dadavà, Luni, Kâthamâ, Bâbarâ, Sânthadi. The great grandson Mâncho of Bhâyo, nephew to Devâit noticed above, migrated from Devagâm and Devaliâ to Bagasrâ, and displaced the Bâbariâs that ruled there. (These probably were the descendents of Barbaraka conquered by King Jayasinha Siddharâja). This was in V. S. 1581, (A. C. 1525).

Then we come to the Kâthîs of Dared, Devalâ, and Pipariâ, Monvel, and Lunghi (?). Fifth from Mancho, was Deso who flourished in V. S. 1764, A. C. 1708, and who assisted Nabab Bahâdurkhânji, the elder, and defeated Jâm Tamâchi, who thereupon gave him the title of Kâthad Jâm, and honoured him with grants of the insignia of royalty. Grandson of Deso was Harsur Valo, who became a follower of the Bhagat of Chalâlâ now the Guru of the whole

18

Kâthî race. Then the tree further branches off into
the not minor, but other sub-branches, till we see the
Kâthis throughout the province, and where we found
them now.

The beginning portions of the *Vansavali* being
mythical, as also the succeeding one of Bardic Tradition, we may not rely on it much for dates and their
account of high lineage. But it is not uninteresting
to note its zig-zag progress from the early home of
the Indian Aryas, of the children of Vavasvata to
Kâsî, Gokula, Maadanaghada Soreth, thence to Pavad
in Scinde, again to Thân, North of Soreth, and their
final spread and settlement in the Province to
which they have given the name of Kâthiâvâd. Here
we see waves of a moving powerful people, surging one
way and the other, advancing, and receding, receding
and advancing, with their Nâga Cult, their Sun-worship,
and their love of a horse and a free lance, and war and
plunder. No ordinary light, then, is shed by this
Vansavali. It will also assist us in the determination
of important or vexed questions in the History of
Gujerat.

We are to draw upon their analogy,—I mean
with respect to the movement of the Châvadâs, and
their overthrow by the Solunkis of Bhuvada and
Mûlarája, and with regard to the determination of the
basis of operation of these Solunkis viz. Kalyânî.
There are, besides the above records, several traditions
and names of places, associated with them, which
remain like the things left behind on a barren sandy

shore, after the tide has gone far, and ebbed away, never more to return. There is no question, I believe, as regards the parts where the Châvadâs originally lived. They first appeared in Okhâmandal, then in Nâgher, and last near the *Run* of Zinzuvâdâ, at Panchâsara. They are traced higher up in Cutch and Scinde. They have probably followed the same route as the Scythians, Sassanians, and the Arabs, in early times, and the Jethawâs, Chudâsamâs, Kâthis and the Jâms &c. in later. The population of India from the earliest pre-historic-times has been formed, stream by stream, and layer by layer, by successive waves and consecutive stratification of races after races. The instances of the Kâthis and Gujaras are matters of history, and my friend Dr. Buhler suggests to me the case of the Mâlavas also. To form the bee-hive of nations of India, the Punjab and the North Western Indian Frontier, the Highlands of the Kâshmirian Himâlayas and the Hindu Koosh have poured forth these powerful races, that after several wanderings and vicissitudes have settled in the countries to which they have given their names. Kus'âvarta or Saurâshtra, Anartta and Avanti, became Kâthiawâd, Gujerat and Mâlavâ respectively. To these, the Kâthis, who were in Upper India, and on the confines of Scinde, and the Punjâb, in the time of Alexander the Great, were the first to come and the Gurjaras and Malavas followed them. We have to this day Gurjaras in the Punjab and Upper India, as also the Malavas. The Kâthis of Kâthiâwâd also speak of their brethren in the Punjâb, but they are much changed from them :—they do not know that they themselves have rather changed. Gurjaras have left Georgia—Gurjeestan—Gujerat (in the Punjab) and the Gurjar Kingdoms of North-Western and Southern Rajputana of Bâlmer or rather Bhinnamâla &c.; so have the Mâlavas. Similar occurrences have taken place with regard to the Châvadâs, Solunkis and Râthods of our History, Sanscritized into Chapotkatas, Chalukyas—Chaulukyas—Châlukyas, and the Râshtrakûtas. Of these the Châvadâs or, as they are sometimes called, the Chauras were the least known to history and power. It was the writers of and about the Solunkis that raised Jayasikhari and Vanarâja into heroes and great Kings. But their power seldom extended in Gujerat beyond the Saras'vata Mandala which Mûlarâja conquered for them. Mûlarâja's expedition to Cutch might have been a retreat before the pressing columns of the General Bârp of Tailapadeva or it may have been also to root out the Châvadâs from their earlier home. So also his expedition into Káthiáwár. This too may have the other object of putting down Graha Ripu, that looted the pilgrims, who remind us of the habits of the Châvadás, who were thence nicknamed Chauras or free-booters. The free-booter lives of Surapâl and Vanarâja also, and their sallying out from Káthiávád, perhaps from the Ghcer, show their character and force. Another object of Mûlaraja was perhaps to demolish the nest of these free-booters. The alliance of Graha Ripu and of the Ruler of Cutch also point to the same unity of interest in the two homes of the Chávadás. We shall see further on that the Solunkis were perhaps pressing on them and routing them at every turn from earlier times.

The smallness of the Chávadás' Kingdom is also proved from the fact that the regions of the Sàbhramatì, the Mahi and the Narmadâ &c. had to be conquered by the Solunkis. After the wave of Mahomed's expedetion had passed over Gujerat, the country was settling down, and Karana cleared the banks of the first river, and his queen Mayanaladevi and his son Jayasinha Siddharaja covered the land with monuments of peace, while the latter and his successor Kumârapâla extended the dominion all round. There is a tradition in Okhâmandal that originally there lived at Pàtâla on the bank of the Indus, S'akas, and Nâgas or Scythians. In about the First Century these Scythians who were no other than the Chávadás came into this Country after several migrations—one of which connects them with Sàkyasinha or the great Buddha of Kapilavastu—and they put down the pirates of Okhâmandal. The Bhàts or Bards also say that the Chávadás were the first that put down the pirates.

The first invader of Okhâmandal was Okherâjji Chávado. He was driven away from Kàthiàwâd, says a local tradition. He ruled for some days, and his son Bhuvadaraja succeeded him, who was followed by Jayaseu, the founder of Chávadâ Pàdar. He having no son built a pond near Mûla-Vàsaria to perpetuate his memory His father ascended the throne. The pond 'was called Chavadasar. He ruled for 21 years

His son Mangalji had a short reign. He was followed by his son and grandson Mangaladeva and Jagdeva respectively. The latter had two sons. Kanaksen, founder of Kanakapuri (Kanakavati, Amreli) and the latter fell.

In Okhaman lal there is one more tradition that originally these Chàvadàs were Yavanas and they can be no other than their modern representatives the Vàghers. The use of the term Yavanas is well known. It is not restricted by the ordinary people at all to the Greeks or Western foreigners. The Chàvadàs were also extirpated or put down in their turn; and there gather around them the traditions of the Assyrian invader, Sukkur Belim and the Vadhels and the Heroles. There figures the name of Veravalji in connection with a colony of the Chàvadàs referring to Southern Kathiawad and settling there. He wrested the towns of Somanatha Patan from the hands of the Rajputs of the place, making a war on them, and strengthening his position there. He thence went to Aramabhada, north-east of Dwarika and founded his Gaddi there. His son was Vikamsi, who was succeeded by 9 Rànàs that ruled for 120 years in all. Tenth from Vikamsi, Somganaji became a very powerful Rana and famous. He ruled long. He extended his dominion 40 miles east of Dwarika as far as Khamabhalia. He committed great forays all round. He increased his wealth as well as power. His son was Bhimaji that looted Moslem pilgrims going to Mecca, that brought down upon him the Sultan of Ahmedabad and what followed is given in the Kathiawad Gazetteer.

This is about the Chàvadà Branch in Okhamandal.

But there was a Sorath branch of them also. After the fall of Valabhi, tradition tells us that Jasaraj Chavado ruled at Deva Patan, and he perhaps was a feudatory the Kingbom of Valabhi. After him Jayshikhari retired to Panchasara and founded a kingdom there. As the migration from Okhamandal was not through a peaceful colonization of Soreth, so was not that perhaps of Soreth to North Gujerat. Hard pressed by a foreign enemy the Chavadas must have been constrained to leave the fertile Nagher for the desert confines of Zinzuwâdâ. Bhuvad Solunki was his enemy, he of Kalyana. This Bhuvad is either a common name in the vernacular (*Bhu-bhata* a warrior of the world), or a contraction of Bhuvana ditya a name of no common occurrence among the Châlukyas. He perhaps was a soldier of fortune. The western Châlukya Kingdom was in the height of its power in the 7th and the 8th Centuries. It was throwing out branches on all side and there was one ruling already in Gujerat not afar off from Jambusara and Navasari, as we learn from some of the grants edited by Dr. Bhagavanlal. This could not have continued long in the countries where the Râshtrakûtas and the Gujaras were great powers in Broach, Surat and Navasari Divisions and so these could have been pushed higher up to the Baroda and Kaira Divisions, the territories of old of the Kshatrapas and Guptas and later of the Valabhis. We have not many grants and inscriptions of the Branch as they, perhaps, had not thoroughly settled down. But they were drifting all about in migrations and hardening to a soldier's life. It was perhaps one of these incursions of theirs that brought down the Kingdom of Valabhi; and if it was already gone, it was they at least that pushed the Chàvadàs further north. And so it was not one Bhuvad who displaced the Chavadas but there were several of the name. They have left their trace in a Kallyanapura and Bhuvad in Okhâmandal also.* Similarly there are Dvandva Sarovara and Bhuvad-no-Timbo in the Kodinar division as well.† There is a Bhuwad Timbi in the Dezadas of Pattan and Sutrapada Puruganahs of Junaghad‡, and Bhowawad.§ We have seen in a note before that the Solunkis had driven away the Chavadas from Soreth into Okhamandal, where, after sometime, some of them built Chavada Pádar. One of these Chavadas did this before the name of Bhuvad also came there, which accounts for the village Bhoovada or Bhuvada and Kalyana that they got from the conquerors of their places. Thus we have marked the two migratory races in conflict from place to place.

Now let us see where Kalyanî is. It cannot

---

* Compare similarly the names Chavadakei Chavada Padar &c. confirming the presence of the Chavadas there.

† I find on Colonel Lester's map (Appendix 1 to Baroda Gheer appeal) a Bhooa Timbi and 2 Bhoovavaras on the river Maimati falling into the Sea near the Matha of Muladwarika. I see similarly the same places marked in the same spots in the map Appendix XIII with the only difference there, that Bhuva Timba of Appendix I is given erroneously as Bhuva Timbi in Appendix IV.

‡ Vide Appendix XIV. 146 Baroda Geer Appeal.

§ Vide the following page of the same.

be Kalyâna near Bombay or in the Deccan that Sir A. K. Forbes supposed it to be in the Râsamâlâ. The Jain Chronicles of the race connect them with Gujerat, but they are the Chálukyas or Chalukyás of the Deckan. The name is Chaulukyás of one and Chalukyas of another. For the names are written differently. We see that the Chaulukyas of Bárp took up that denomination, although they were decidedly from the South, and connected with the Chalukya or Chálukya family of Tailapadeva. While the Yádava grant of Seunachandra describes and names one of their Kings Goggirâja as a Chálukya, and not Chaulukya: similarly their Kanyâkubja connection need not disturb us. For, we have seen that the Chaulukyás of Bárp traced their connection with the city through a Râstrakûta Kanyaka or princess. that Brahmadeva asked the founder of the family, Chalukya, to marry, when he asked the god as to what he should do. And the race of the Châlukyâs was descended of that union (cf. vv. 6–7 of no. 5 of my series in the *Indian Antiquary*). And I have, in the Edition of the paper on the grant, discussed the identity of the several ramifications of the race. Consequently the Chálukyas of Gujerat, Bhuvad and Mûlarája need not be sought for anywhere about Kanouje ; Kalyânî was nearer at home. It was neither in the far north, nor in the distant south. There is a place named Kelanpura a mile or two from Baroda, which is in the midst of the parts about which the Grants of the earlier Gujerat Châlukyâs concern themselves. We are assured of the

19

antiquity of the vicinity of Baroda from the coins of the five early Kshatrapa Kings. And so the early metropolis of the Solunkis of Gujerat was on the same site as Baroda, or near that of their Modern successors, in their Kingdom, the Gaikwars. It is south of Gujerat, in Lâta Des'a, at least south of Pattan. It is not very far from the latter, and the Sâras'vata Mandala, over which the Châvadâs ruled, and which Mûlarâja conquered. We can now understand the expeditions of the first successors of Vanarâja as described in the Râsamâlâ. They could not be against the rulers still further south. Probably between Bhuvad and Râji, the Kingdom had waned in power and extent, and perhaps Râji had remained for a time in Kâttywâd, at Somanâth Pàtana, where also these Solunkis had territory on the expulsion of the Châvadâs as described before. That also accounts for the *Bhuvad that* or *Bhuvad no Timbo* or *Timbi* and *Dvandva Sarovara* after the name of one of the King's generals Dvandva.* They mean a settled rule and conquest of the territory. So, differing from my friend, Dr. Buhler, on this head also, as I do from Mr. Forbes and Mr. Elphinstone,

---

* Cf. also Chandapura or Chandapadra—Chandode, a terminus of the Baroda–Dabhoi Railway line, from Chanda, another General of Bhuvad like Dvandva. The traditions about Visaldeva's birth at Dabhoi and his other connections and traditions point to the same predilections of the Pattan Chaulukyas for their earlier home. The Temple of Vâghanâtha (Sans. Vyâghra-natha) Mahâdeva the patron–god of the Vâghelâs and the underground way leading to and opening on the Nerbudda and called Visaladeva ni Bàri point to the same thing.　　　　　　　　　　H. H. D. 1893.

I fix upon Kelanpura near Baroda as the capital Kalyâni of the Solunkis. I have answered at least the principal objections of Dr. Buhler i. e. those about the name &c. His refutation of Merutunga does not at all affect my change. Now as regards the *Kuladevatâ.* These Solunkis had either conquered or overthrown the Valabhis, or they had succeeded to their power and portion, and in either case they adopted their titles as well as their coat of arms. With respect to the former, a comparison of the copperplate grants of the two dynasties leaves no doubt about it. The Valabhis too had their Bull, which the Solunkis adopted. It was not because they were S'aivas that they had the Bull and because the Southerners were Vaishnavas that they had the Boar. For, both the Valabhis as well as the Solunkis were very accommodative of all denominations of views and faith. Then the importation of the Udichyas too need not disturb us. A race would not necessarily bring their own countrymen. The Pàla kings of Bengal imported the Brahmins from the Doab and Upper India, with which they had nothing to do. In like manner, Kanouje country being traditionally connected with their race origin, that country was considered more sacred, and its Brahmins more learned, and so they were indented for and imported into the land. Mûlarâja either could not trust his newly conquered subjects or they had no learned Brahmins among them. Under the encroaching approach of the power of the rising Châlukya Tailapadeva, his own portion was so insecure in his own Kalyâni that he had to leave to seek fresh fields and pastures new and so he could not fall back upon the Brahmins of his own past realms. Now the presence of the Châlukya Rajputs in the Kanouje Districts according to the North-West Province Gazetteer does not at all militate against my position at one period of their history. They like the Gurjaras, Mâlavâs, Kâthîs, and Châvadâs were not in the places where they are found at present, but they were in Upper India, and some of them might have been left there as in the case of the other races. We do not know of any Solunki Kingdom at Kanouje at all. And this gives the last blow to the theory. We see then what light the Antiquities of Baroda throw upon the question.

My recent researches near about Amreli, point to a Buddhistic *stupa* where Vali-Shah's *timbo* stands between the rivers Vadi and Thebi to the W. N. W. of Amreli. I have not as yet been able to sink any shafts and make any excavations there, as the place at present is a Mahomedan graveyard of the old Syed Masters of Amreli. The tomb of Vali-Shah is quite close to it. This *timbo* is opposite to, i. e. east of, S'ûlio *Timbo* and south-west of Gohilwâd *timbo* and south of the Syeds' Rozo containing an inscription dated A. H. 1069 (A. C. 1653) as per following couplet in Roman Characters.

Aj Sale Binaje
Rize Sha Kabir Alf
1000

Sitin e Fisah aj Hiz
  60   9
Arate Gid.

There is on Vali-Shah's *Timbo* a square pillar
5ft. 6in. high on a square platform six feet square. A
succession of consecutive platforms growing larger and
larger descend one after another. The whole forms a
circle with a radius 80ft. to 82 ft. with a frontage
towards the south, extending thirty or thirty-two feet
beyond the last circumference. The square platform
over which the Pillar stands is 1 ft. above the top of
the mound. The superficial area of the Pillar is 2 ft.
3 in. square. It is surmounted by a cone that is 1 ft.
1 in. in height. There are three niches on the south
face of the Pillar representing as it were the two
eyes and the mouth there. There are also 2 more
niches one on each side, namely, the east and the
west, representative, as it were, of the ears. There is
no such thing on the north face of it. The top cone
perhaps represents the head and the entire Pillar
the sitting posture in Padmâsana of Buddha Sthavira
in *dhyana* or meditation, on the square platform, as if
under a *Bodhi* tree. A Lim tree forms the canopy
over the Pillar at present. *Kerda, Kihjada, Babul,
Aval* and *Lim trees* also are sprinkled all about it over
the mound. The west face of the surface of the mound,
on which the square platform and the pillar over it,
stand are 24 ft. above the level of the surface of the
road, leading to *Peepul-Lug*, the road on the East side
being *Yarundi*—wards. The position of the sides or
faces of the Pillar is 17 degrees out of the cardinal

directions. The S. W. corner therefore is due S. W.
S. The deflection of the south face is towards the
east, and the angle forming the cardinal east to west
line with the southern face of the pillar is 1 yd.

The Rozâ above noticed contains sepulchres of the
Mevâtis that accompanied Emperor Shah Jehan in
his expedition over these parts. *Gadhais* are found
there. But they are in Mehebub Miâ's premises to
the north of it from where we got some of our pickings, herein before described, as also about Vali-Shâh's
Timbo. The sepulchre outside the Rozâ and about the
timbo of Vali-Shâh are of Mevâtis and Sâdats (Syeds).
Vali-Shâh was a boy of 12, who went up to Futtehpur,
S. W. of Amreli, where the army of Futtekhan of
Junaghad was encamped. They had come to put
down the Kâthîs of Oghadmâtro, and the Syeds of
Amreli. These were not at home, and those that were
present, were old men, infants and ladies, in Amreli.
In order to save them and their honor Vali-Shâ went up
to the enemies camp and murdered Futtehkhan. But he
too was cut to pieces by the invader's guards. This
is said to be in V. S. 1825: and that Vali-Shâh was buried here, and that circumstance gave its name to the
Timbo.

During the rains the rivers wash the side of that
and the adjoining *timbas,* and gold, silver, and copper
coins are exposed to view. The Kolis live by the pro-
fession of finding them out, and selling them in the
Bazar for their metal. This extra-mural part of the
town of Amreli as also its intra-mural western half con-

taining Junokot, Juno Bazar aud Juni Amreli made up the Amreli of ancient history. S. W of it on the other side of the river near its bank is Navrang Khan's pillar bearing date V. S. 1650 in the Gujerati Inscription on it, mentioning the quarter and Mahajana of Amreli.

So these finds of coins &c., inscriptions, and traditions, joined with the Zar copperplate Grants, and the probable Stûpa take Amreli back to the Kshatrapa, Gupta and Valabhi periods. The probable Stûpa pillar is built in bricks and chunam as also its square platform. The surrounding gradation of stairs are built of stone bricks and chunam but they are greatly worn out and gone off. To the N. W. and S. of them, the washing of the rivers and, that during the monsoon, is considerable. To the west of it is the high road leading to Mângvâpâl on one side, Varudi on the other, and Pipul-Lug, Daidâ, Râmdhiâ and Gondal, straight between them, and so the wear there also is not little. The description given here may very profitably be compared with that of the Stûpa discovered by Dr. Bhagavânlâl in the Buruda Rajas fort in his Sopara and Paduna (pp. 21-2 &c.).

Thus we have seen the Antiquities of Baroda Territory to consist of Stûpas and like monuments, coins, copperplates, and like relics of arts, and ornaments, inscriptions and traditions, tales and *Vans'a valis* which are likely to amply repay the labour and search bestowed upon them. We have also said what light they have shed on some of the important chapters of Gujerat history. Would that I could have done

greater justice to this vast subject. But let it be put
off to some other time. I conclude this rather lengthy
paper with thanking this August Assembly for the
patient hearing they have accorded to it.

The Eighth International Congress of Orientalists at Stockholm and Christiania, and the Sanskrit Idylls about it.*

The Eighth Congress of Orientalists has come and gone, and many and better heads have spoken and written about it. It is here proposed to give the Sanskrit Idylls that convey an Indian Brahmin's view on the subject. The first of them was recited at the closing meeting of the Congress at Stockholm on the 7th of September, while the second was recited at the closing meeting at Christiania on the 11th of that month. They congratulate the Congress and its Patron King, and thank the King of Norway and Sweden and his people for the reception accorded to the Congress. The third and the fourth are descriptive of the feasting and rejoicings, at the Congress . and the Falls at Trolhatta, the last place the Congress visited. In them will be found a curious weaving of Oriental imagery with Western thought.

IDYLL I.

Congratulatory verses addressed to the Eighth International Congress of Orientalists and its Patron King Oscar II.

(SANSCRIT TEXT.)

स्वभावसौरस्यविशालिनी सिता
गंभैषिणी प्रोज्वलहंसवाहनी । ·
निशान्धकारं भरते विलोक्य सा
दिशां नु चक्रे भ्रमतिं स्म भारती ॥ १ ॥

---

* Reprinted from Trubner's Record.

शकैस्तुरुष्कै र्यवनै र्नवै र्नवै—
रुद्धेजितं पश्चिमदेशमंडलं ।
सन्ध्यारुणं हा रुधिरं परिप्लुतं
तमालनीलं तिमिरं सुविस्तृतं ॥ २ ॥

मिस्लं तमिस्लाहतमत्र न द्युतिः
च्युतिः समन्तादथ श्रीसरोमके ।
चलाजले वृष्टिमुखे घने ऽम्बुदे
मृगांकलेखां किमुदेति शारदी ॥ ३ ॥

शर्मं रसं भाव्य सुदुर्लभं क्षमं
दिने दिने वृद्धिमितं सुमूर्च्छती ।
दिवः पपातात्र तया यदृच्छया
य उत्तरास्ते कुरवः ममाश्रिताः ॥ ४ ॥

स्वतंत्रतां श्रीः सकलाः कला बलं
क्रमेण तस्याः समुपागतं स्वकं ।
निशा प्रभाता गलितं तमो ऽरुण—
द्युतिः प्रसन्ना मिलिताश्च बन्धवः ॥ ५ ॥

सतिात्रैवर्षं मुनिमंडलं निजं
समाह्वयन्त्याश्रममाश्रमात्सती ।
सच्चोद्यता संप्रति चक्रवर्तिनी
विराजते विश्वमुखी सरस्वती ॥ ६ ॥

सरस्वतीश्री लब्धप्रसाद उर्वीपतिः कविः सुमतिः
सुयशा भयतादास्कर नृपतिः शरदां शतं जगति ॥ ७ ॥
जगत्त्रयोद्धृतं तेजः शारदासंभवं नवं ।
आचन्द्रार्कमिरिस्कन्दावर्त्ते श्रीसिन्धु-भारतं ॥ ८ ॥

ENGLISH TRANSLATION.

1. Bhâratî or the Goddess of Learning, white and naturally remarkable for sweetness, seeing Darkness in the (land of) Bharata (*i. e.* India) of night, desirous of Light wandered in all directions, riding (her) shining swan.

2. The western countries were harassed by the S'akas (Scythians), Turushkas (Turks), and every new succession of Yavanas (Barbarians). Alas! blood red as the evening sky spread all round! Darkness as black as the Tamâla trees extended far and wide.

3. Misra (Egypt) was smitten with Darkness. Here there was no Light but a fall all round in Greece and Rome. What (then) will the Autumnal Moon shine out of dense clouds constantly fleeting (about her face) big with rain ? (Never.)

4. Seeing that quiet and pleasure were unattainable (there), (and that) trouble was increasing day after day, (she) fainting away fell here from from the sky. (And) she repaired by chance to what are called the Uttara Kurus or the Northern Kurus.

5. Here Freedom, Fortune, all arts and sciences (and) strength—all that was hers came gradually to her. The night passed away. Darkness melted away. The morning Light smiled (and) she met her friends.

6. Now the virtuous (Bhâratî) inviting every three years her Munis from one Âs'rama or hermitage to another is now Chakravarttinî (Universal Empress or going in a circle) engaged (as she is) in a Satra (or long session of sacrifices) (and she who was Bhâratî, *i. e.* of

India now) shines as universal Sarâsvatî (*lit.* movi ng about the whole World).

7. May His illustrious Majesty King Oscar favoured of Learning and Fortune—a Poet, Prince and Philosopher—may He glory for a hundred years in (this) World !

8. May this new Light born of Learning, manifested here, glory as long as the Sun and the Moon, the Hills and the Seas, Scandinavia and India last !

METRICAL TRANSLATION.

On swan astride in search of Light,
The Goddess Bhârati, pure and white,
From clime to clime, from land to land,
Her course unwitting she did bend ;
When she observed the darksome night
Drop on the Land of Bharat as blight.

The Scythian swarm, the Turkish troop,
Each new Barbarian boldly swoop,—
On lands extending westward far,
She saw, all bathed in blood and war,—
Blood crimson as the evening sky
Thick gloom set shrouding low and high.

It smote the land of Egypt wise.
In Greece and Rome there was no rise,
But fall all round. How from the cloud,
Big-with the rain, that would flit, shroud
Her face, can shine and smile serene
The lovely Dian's dainty mien ?

Her Peace and Bliss for ever gone

And misery daily· growing, alone,
Was left to her ! ha ! Bhârati feels,
She falls from sky, she faints, she reels !
She here by chance alighted sheer,
On Lands as Northern Kurus we hear.

Her wealth, her freedom, arts, her strength,
To her returned, all all at length
The Darkness melted. Night was set.
Sweet smiled Aurora. Friends she met.
From hermitage to hermitage,
Every three years, invites her sage,

Devoted votaries, faultless She,
In sacrificial sessions' glee.
And She, that was up to this time,
The Goddess of old Bharata's clime,
Moves in her right imperial sway,
Sarasvatî, that all obey.

Favoured of Fortune, and of Her,
A Poet, Prince, Philosopher,
For many a winter, many a spring,
May glorious Oscar rule as King !
And may the Light of Bhârati new
That's glorious borne as here you view

Shine ever and ever, may ever shine,
So long as Sun·and·Moon do shine,
So long as proudly stand the Hills,
So long as rolling ocean reels,
So long as Scandinavia stands,
So long as are true India's Lands.

IDYLL II.

Thanking the People of Norway and Sweden for their hospitable reception of the Congress.

अथैकदा शैलसुता प्रसन्ना
प्रदक्षिणां सा जगतः सुताभ्यां ।
दिदेश कन्यामणियुग्ममत्र
सिद्धिं च बुद्धिं च पणं चकार ॥ १ ॥

स बर्हिवाहो दिशि संप्रतस्थे
गणाधिपो मूषकवाहनश्च ।
प्रदक्षिणीकृत्य शिवं शिवां च
स आप्तवाँस्ते शशिसुंदरास्ये ॥ २ ॥

प्राप्ते पुनः स्कन्द उमानुतापं
सौहार्द्धृद्धा भृशमीयुषी हा ।
सा लज्जमाना पुरुषानभिज्ञ–
मिलाभिधं खंडमियं प्रपेदे ॥ ३ ॥

विरतिमुपगतो ऽयं देवसेनाधिनाथः
प्रतिभुवममराणामीषिवान्स्वर्गमत्र ।
प्रकृतिमनुपमां तां सुस्मितां वीक्ष्य लक्ष्मीं
सुहृदयजनतां गां वासमंगीचिकार ॥ ४ ॥

स्वर्गोत्तरापथोपास्व्यः स्कन्दावर्त्तसुहृत्तरः
प्राप्तस्वतंत्रयैषो ऽयं भारत्यापि समीप्सितः ॥ ५ ॥

जना जगति मोदन्तामातिथ्योल्लासमानसाः
स्कन्दिनो ऽद्वन्द्वनः प्राचीविद्याध्ययनलालसाः ॥ ६ ॥

ENGLISH TRANSLATION.

1. Once upon a time Pârvatî (*lit.* the daughter of

the Mountain), well pleased, directed her two sons to perform a voyage round the world; and offered as prize two beautiful damsels, viz. Siddhi (accomplishment) and Buddhi (intelligence).

2. He (*i. e.* the God of War) riding his peacock set out on his journey. (And) here Ganes'a (the God of Wisdom), riding his mouse, obtained the two sweet damsels with their faces as beautiful as the moon, having gone round (his parents) S'iva and S'ivâ (*i. e* Pârvatî).

3. Now when Skanda (the God of War) returned, the affectionate Umâ (Pârvatî) became very sorry. (And she) being abashed removed herself to the Continent known as Ilâvartta, unknown to men.

4. The General of the Army of the Gods was greatly dejected. He desired a land that would rival the Svarga (or Paradise) of the Gods. Here, having seen Nature incomparable, and Beauty sweet smiling, and a Land full of the people of good heart, he fixed his residence.

5. That is that Skandâvartta, or the Continent of Skanda, known as Svarga (Sverige, Sweden), and Uttarâpatha (or the North, Norge, Norway), very friendly. That has been found by Freedom (also as her home). Even Bhâratî (the Goddess of Learning of Bharata, India) likes to repair to it.

6. May the Scandinavian People, free from evils, rejoice in this world, with their hearts delighting in hospitality, and with their minds bent on learning the lores of the East !

METRICAL TRANSLATION.

The Goddess mountain-born did once
A voyage round the World her sons,
The fiery God of War Skanda,
Ganes'a of Wisdom God, command ;

She offered prize for marriage meet
Accomplishment, Intelligence sweet,
Siddhi and Buddhi beauties rare,
To him that home doth first repair.

Mounting his peacock Skanda flies,
To get the start, to win the prize.
Ganes'a cunning still, he schemes,
His parents Heaven and Earth both deems.

He mounts his mouse, he goes them round.
The much coveted prize he found.
When Skanda from his voyage is back,
No prize ! fond Mother is taken aback.

In sorrow Pàrvatì hides her face,
Ashamed, she suddenly leaves the place,
To Ila's continent she flies,
Where of the harder sex none hies.

The God of War, full of disgust,
His heavenly home he left, in quest
Of lands that would be Paradise
To him, and more than that likewise.

And here unrivalled Nature found
He, Beauty smiling sweet around,
And Peoples of good heart possesst,
He made it home, his heaven, his rest.

His North Way Norge was yclept,
His Svarga, Sverge, true and apt.
From Skanda, Scandinavian named.
Throughout the world those countries famed.

May Peace, Prosperity, ever bless
The Scandians ! May they ever address
To studies of the Orient Light,
To whom guests foreign are delight !

IDYLL III.

Descriptive of the reception accorded to the Congress.

कुसुममुपहृतं मे सर्वदाहं वहिष्ये
सहृदयमरविंदाख्या शशांकास्यया तत् ।
सरलललितभावं कोमलत्वं रसाढ्यं
प्रतिमितमिदमस्मिन् पुष्प एतत्प्रसन्नं ॥ १ ॥

कदापि नहि विस्मृतेः प्रथमथेप्त्यति स्वागतं
महोदधितरंगिणी प्रणयरंगिणी प्रोज्ज्वला ।
ध्वजैर्नु करपल्लवैरधरनेत्रमुग्धांबुजैः
स्मितै रसिकरश्मिभिर्वलसितैस्सुहर्षान्वितैः ॥ २ ॥

प्रदीपमधुराक्षरैः किसलयादिकेस्तोरणैः
प्रसूनचयवर्षणैरनलतारकोद्वर्षणैः ।
स्वभावललिताप्सरोरसिककिन्नरैर्गायनै:
अलौकिकमनुनर्त्तनैर्दृष्टमनोहरैर्लास्यकैः ॥ ३ ॥

सुधासवमहोत्सवैरथ रसाकरैर्भोजनैः
सरिन्नगसरोवरप्रथममहर्घ्यसंदर्शनैः
निरंतरमहोदिनेदिनइहाभिसंमोदिताः

सुराः किमु गृहागता अतिथयो नु भावीरताः ॥ ४ ॥
अदृष्टपूर्वं वृत्तेषु काव्येष्वश्रुतपूर्वकं
स्कन्दिनामिदमातिथ्यमानन्दिनां नु नन्दतात् ॥ ५ ॥

ENGLISH TRANSLATION

1. The flower that has been presented to me by
the Lady with her eyes like the Lotus and the face
like the Moon, I shall ever bear with my heart. (For)
there is imaged, smiling, in this flower, her simplicity
and sweetness, and her tenderness full of sentiment.

2. Never, never will that welcome be forgotten
like the shining river of regard, surging like the great
Sea. What with bannerests, the hands (like tender leaves)
the limbs and eyes like the sweet lotus, with smiles of
sweet rays, and with amusements mixed with intense
delight !

3. With sweet words (of welcome) inscribed in illuminations, with evergreens and festoons of leaves, with
the showering of flowers, with the breaking forth of
clusters of Stars of Fire (in fireworks), with music
as of the divine choristers and of the naturally sweet
fairies, and with opera dances unusual, delightful to the
eye and to the mind,

4. With the serving of the mead of Gods and of
the festivals flowing with wines and viands of all
deliciousnesss, with the showing to us the Lights of the
Rivers (waterfalls), Mountains, Lakes and best of
places, O the Orientalists have been entertained here
from day to day without stop and cessation as if they
were the Gods that had repaired to their houses as
guests.

5. What was not seen in life, what was never heard in the songs of Poets, was this hospitality of the Scandinavians.—May it resound (throughout the world)!

IDYLL IV.

Descriptive of some touches of the Trolhatta Falls last visited by the Congress.

नृत्यति गायति कूजति मधुरं सुंदरतरं हसति फेनैः

रमते कमते किरणं रमणं तरणेस्तरंगिणी रमणी ॥ १ ॥

हरिरपि निशि निशि दिक्षि दिशि पिपासति रसं नु चुंबति सुवदनं

अमृतकरैरालिंगति हृदयं मणयी स्फुटं विशति सरळं ॥ २ ॥

समुच्छलति कम्पते मधुरनीलदुग्धस्मितां

शशांककरवेष्टितां निशि दिनेशभाभार्णितां

दिने क्वचिदियं पुनर्नवनवां मनोहारिणीं

बिभर्ति सरिद्दूतां श्रियमहो नु वेणिच्छलात् ॥ ३ ॥

1 This beautiful River dances, sings, coos sweetly and smiles beautifully with her (white) foam. She plays about, and she woos the sweet ray of the Sun.

2. Night after night, and from place to place, even the moon–god desires to drink her nectar, and kisses her beautiful face. He embraces her with his ambrosial rays. And he, full of love, enters her open plain heart.

3. O, she bounds forth, she shakes her sweet greenish (waters smiling) milk-white (with the foam), entwined in the rays of the moon at night, and burnished with the light of the sun sometimes. She bears her ever-renewing wonderful beauty charming to the mind in the form of her tresses as it were. How lovely !

APPENDICES.

APPENDIX A.

CORRESPONDENCE *anent* THE DEPUTATION AND WORK OF
MR. H. H. DHRUVA AT THE CONGRESS.

(1.)

*(Letter from the Honorary General Secretary Count
Landberg to H. H. the Gaikvad of Baroda.)*

HIGHNESS,

The International Congress of Orientalists will
meet at Stockholm the 2nd September 1889. His
Majesty the King of Sweden and Norway, the August
Patron of the Congress, has commissioned me to invite
Your Highness, as a liberal Patron of Sanskrit litera-
ture to be present at that meeting.

His Majesty, my gracious King, should be very
glad to make the acquaintance of Your Highness to
get the opportunity to thank Your Highness for the
kindness with which Your Highness received T. R.
H. the Princes Oscar and Carl during their last journey
in India.

The Congress should also be highly honored, if
Your Highness would graciously accept to be "Honorary Member" of the Congress, with H. M. the Emperor of Germany. H. M. the Sultan, H. R. H. the
Arhduke Rainer, H. H. the Khediv of Egypt whose
patronage has highly promoted the Oriental studies.

The Congress should be very indebted to Your
Highness if Your Highness would allow any Indian

Scholars to attend to that meeting, the approach between the Indian and European Scholars being very necessary for the advancement of the science, would thereby be greatly facilitated and the August Patron of the Congress should be very satisfied to see in His Capital such illustrious guests.

I have &ca.

(Sd.) COUNT CARLO LANDBERG Dr. Ph.

Secretary General of the VIII. International Congress of Orientalists.

Stuttgart, Germany, the 9th Septr. 1888.

(2.)

Reply to (1) of H. E. the Divan of Baroda to Count Landberg and credentials of Mr. H. H. Dhruva.

HUZUR CUTCHERRY,

Baroda 24th December 1888.

No. 3805.

To,

COUNT CARLO LANDBERG Dr. Ph.

Secretary General of the VIII. International Congress of Orientalists.

Stuttgart,

Germany.

SIR,

His Highness feels thankful for your letter of the 9th September on behalf of His Majesty the King of Sweden and Norway, inviting His Highness to the International Congress of Orientalists. It would have given His Highness great pleasure to have been present on the occasion but as His Highness has recently returned from a long tour to Europe, he regrets his inability. His Highness feels honoured in the offer made him to be Honorary Member of the Congress and accepts it with pleasure. A native gentleman, probably Mr. H. H. Dhruva, B. A. LL. B. from this side will be sent in due course to attend the meeting of the Congress.

I am &c.

(Signed) LAXMAN J.

Prime Minister

Baroda State.

(3.)

Order of nomination of Mr. H. H. Dhruva as Delegate of His Highness to proceed to Europe to attend the Congress.

શ્રી

જ. નંબર ૭૦૭

યાદી મેહેરબાન રાવ બહાદુર હરીલાલ હર્ષદરાય ધ્રુવ બી. એ. એલ. એલ. બી. અમરેલી પ્રાંતના જડજ સાહેબ તરફ હજુર ઇઅેજી આરીસના મેનેજર તરફથી લખવાની કે

યુરોપખંડમાં આ દેશની ભાષા જાણનારાઓની સભા આવતા સપ્ટેમ્બર સને ૧૮૮૫માં ભરાવાની છે. તેમાં આ સરકાર તરફથી આપને મોકલવાનું ઠરેલું છે ને આપના જાણવામાં છેજ. હવે તે સંબંધે આપના જવા આવવા વીગેરેના ખર્ચ સારુ આપને સરકારથી રૂ ૩૦૦૦) ત્રણ હજાર કલદાર તથા આપના માગ્યા પ્રમાણે આપના છ મહિનાના પગારની રકમ રૂ ૨૪૦૦ ચોવીશસો કલદાર એડવાન્સ આપવા વીગેરે બાબતમાં મેહેરબાન નામદાર દીવાન બહાદુર દીવાન સાહેબે તા૦ ૨૭ની ઇશ્વારીનો મેમો કર્યો

22

તેની એક નકલ આપની માહીતી સારુ આ સમાગમે મોકલી છે તે ઉપરથી આપના જણુવામાં આવશે. આપે આ કામ માટે જુન મહીનાથી જવાની જરૂર બતાવી છે તો તે મહીનાની કોઇ તારીખથી જવાનો ઇરાદો રાખો છો તથા ઉપર પ્રમાણે આપને રૂ ૫૪૦૦) આપવા હવા છે તે આપને કેવી રીતે (એટલે તે રકમ શૈશરી કાંઇ રકમ મુંબઇ એક ઉપરના ચેકથી તથા આ-કીની રોકડ) લેવાની ઇચ્છા છે તે ખુલાસેવાર લખી જણાવશો. એટલે તે પ્રમાણે એ રકમ આપને આપવા વિષે હજુર તીજોરી તરફ હુકમ મોકલાવી આપવાની તજવીજ કરવામાં આવશે.

એ સભા ભરાવાની તેના સેક્રેટરી તરફથી આવેલાં કાગળની નકલ તથા તેના જવાખમાં આપને આ સરકાર તરફે મોકલવાનું ઠરેલું છે વીગેરે મતલબના તેમને આંહીથી ગયલા પત્રની નકલ એ રીને એ નકલો આપને જણુવા સારુ આ સાથે મોકલી છે તથા આપના નામનો મુંબઇ મેશર્સ થૉ-મસ કુક અને સનનો તા૦ ૬ ફેબ્રુવારી સને ૧૮૮૯નો કાગળ આ સાથે પા-છો મોકલ્યો છે તે પહોંચ્યાનો ઉત્તર મેહેરબાનીથી લખશો.

તારીખ ૯ માર્ચ સને ૧૮૮૯ મુકામ વડોદરા.

Sd./ S. PEISHWAI

મેનેજર.

(4.)

Mr. H. H. Dhruva's Letter to Count Landberg propos-
ing to go to Europe and naming Subjects
of his Papers.

AMRELI (Kattyawar)

India *8th June 1889.*

To,

COUNT C. LANDBERG,

Secretary, VIII. International

Congress of Orientalists

10 Goethe Strasse, Stuttgart.

Wurtemberg Germany.

SIR,

I have the honor to enclose herein copy of order
of my appointment with its translation by H. E. the

Divansaheb to attend the VIII. International Congress of Orientalists assembling at Stockholm-Christiania next September as a Delegate from H. H. Srimant Maharaja Sir Sayajirao Gaikwar G. C. S. I. &c. of Baroda.

Under the order, I may be permitted to add that I am going to be present at the coming Congress. You will, therefore, do me the favor of sending me a card of Membership to the address of Dr. Buhler, 27 Cottage Gasse Wahring Wien, Austria, where I will be about the close of July as I leave India on the 5th of July by the Austro Hungarian LLoyd Co. Steamship, Maria Terisa. I will pay the money for the card either to Dr. Peterson at Bombay or to Dr. Buhler at Vienna.

I propose to read two papers before the Congress·

(1) The Neo-Vernaculars of Western India with special reference to the Old and Mediœval Gujerati Language and Literature.

(2) Light shed on the History of Gujerat by tho antiquities and archœological finds in Baroda State.

I have the honor to be
Sir,
Your most obdt. servant
(Sd.) H. H. DHRUVA
District Judge, Amreli,
Delegate to the VIII. International
Congress of Orientalists of H. H.
Srimant Maharaja Sir Sayajirao
Gaikwar G. C. S. I. of Baroda
State, India.

(5.)

The Morning Post of 2nd September 1889 on the work of Mr. H. H. Dhruva and Mr. J. J. Modi at the coming Congress.

The eighth International Congress of Orientalists which opens to-day at Stockholm, under the presidency of his Majesty King Oscar of Sweden and Norway, is likely to prove a more than ordinarily interesting meeting. Not only is the list of delegates unusually brilliant and comprehensive, including the very pick of European scholarship, as well as representatives of several of the ancient communities of the East, but some of the subjects to be discussed in the course of the meeting are such as will have considerable attractions for thousands who lay no claim whatever to rank among professed Orientalists. The great States of Europe, in all of which Oriental studies are now fostered by their respective Governments, send accredited delegates, as do the leading universities of the Continent. Among the distinguished men present at Stockholm to-day are Professor DILLMANN, the Ethiopic scholar, who presided when the Congress was held at Berlin; SCHRADER, first of all authorities on Assyrian cuneiform; and FRIEDRICH DELITZSCH, as great a Hebraist as his father. Holland sends the famous Arabist DE. GOEJE from Leyden; Italy the well-known IGNAZIO GUIDI; France DARMESTETER and SCHAFER, as well as two Academicians; while MAX MULLER and Professor SAYCE, LUBBOCK BENSLEY, Lord Almoner's Professor of Arabic at Cambridge and Dr. CHARLES H. H. WRIGHT represent Oriental scholarship in this country. Delegates from Brahman, Buddhist, Moslem and Jewi-h communities meet on common ground at the Congress, along with those entitled to speak in the name of the Propaganda Fide of the Catholic Church and the Protestant British and Foreign Bible Society. Several ladies noted for their attainments as Orientalists are also present. Among them are our countrywoman, MISS AMELIA B. EDWARDS, and the more celebrated Madame DIEULAFOY, one of the dozen Frenchwomen who have obtained the " Legion of Honour " from the Republican Government—who so courageously helped her husband in the seven years' excavations he carried on at SUSA in the land of the ancient Babylonians, and who appears at the Congress in the male costume which, as the result of experience, she prefers to the more ornamental attire of her own sex. But the personal interest of the meeting will centre in the two delegates from Hindostan, H. H. DHRUVA representing the GAEKWAR of Baroda, and JIVANJI JAMSHEDJI MODI, the High Priest of the Fire Temple of Colaba, who represents the ancient community of Eastern Fire-worshippers.

The papers these two gentlemen are to read to the Congress are those which will attract the most general attention on the part of laymen and outsiders at all events, who can hardly be expected to take an absorbing interest in the origin of pronominal particles in Sanscrit, the existence of a true *vau conversine* in Assyrian, or cognate topics of a like practical value, which so often form the theme of discussion at Orientalist gatherings. The High Priest of the Colaba Fire Temple will deliver two. addresses—one on the "Homa," so often referred to in the Avesta, or Bible of the Parsees, and the other on the "Funeral Ceremonies" of the Guebres, or Fire-worshippers. The latter is likely to be widely read and discussed, for the topic is one on which the most diverse opinions are held, and which hitherto seems totally incomprehensive to those who do not belong to this ancient and most mysterious sect. The Fire-worshippers are the remnants of the oldest religious body the world has any knowledge of, their cult is a survival, in almost primitive form in some respects, of the once universal sun worship, to which early mankind was addicted, and an explanation of their mode of disposing of the dead, together with an exposition of the ideas underlying the strange ceremonies that are customary among them at death, and interment, can hardly fail to throw much light on archaic beliefs and customs, especially with reference to the hopes of hereafter entertained by our Old World progenitors. As most people know, the Fire-worshippers do not bury their dead. They place the bodies of those who die on elevated stages, exposed to the air and the attacks of predacious birds, kites, ravens, and carrion crows until the flesh has all disappeared which happens soon enough in most cases, when the bones are carefully collected and interred in the strange and eerie-looking cemeteries owned by the sect. The practice though very ancient, is rather abhorrent to our notions.

And those who have witnessed the funeral ceremonies of the Guebres, who have seen the birds of prey following the burial processions, who have watched the kites and crows circling round and round as the corpse is borne along and laid upon the stage, ready and eager to pounce upon it and tear the flesh from the bones, are not likely to say much in favour of this mode of disposing of the dead. But then, in the question of burial, custom is everything, and use makes strange and painful practices tolerable. The custom of the Parsees, however, is so utterly opposed to the natural feelings or, as some say, the natural weakness of humanity, that there must be some deep reason for a practice that seems so needlessly brutal. The Fire-worshippers reverse the practice of the ancient Egyptians, who thought so much of the body that they did their utmost to preserve it from decay for all time. The Parsee thinks so little of it that his one object appears to be to secure the total destruction of his "soul's earthly shrine" with the utmost rapidity. And it will certainly be interesting—if only by reason of the old-time universality of fire-worship—to learn from so authoritative a source as the High Priest of the Colaba Fire Temple, the religious and metaphysical beliefs that underlie the strange and, to most men, repugnant, funeral ceremonies of this sect. His remarks on the "Homa" or "Soma" the sacred beverage of the "Avesta," will appeal to but a limited public in comparison with the other topic.

The subject on which the delegate of the GAEKWAR

of Baroda will address the conference is certain to
provoke no little discussion in the learned world, for
it will appeal to a far wider circle than that engaged
in Oriental study and research. The whole scientific
world will be interested in MR. H. H. DHRUVA's paper,
which will deal with nothing more or less than the
"Lost Books of Euclid," for, it is alleged by this
gentleman that a Sanscrit copy of the missing books
has actually been discovered at Jeypore, in Rajpootana.
The discovery of the books, if confirmed, would be as
remarkable a fact as their preservation for so long
a period, and in a foreign garb, too, a Sanscrit translation. The matter is certain to create some sensation,
and though the budding youth of the kingdom entering
mathematical studies would probably learn with more
satisfaction that the existing books of the Greek
philosopher were lost than that the missing ones had
been found, the discovery will prove a circumstance of
the greatest interest and gratification. The two papers
to be read by the High Priest of the Fire-worshippers
and the delegate of the GAEKWAR of Baroda would
be sufficient to invest the present Congress of Orientalists at Stockholm with more than usual interest even
if the list of scholars attending it did not mark it out
as an exceptionally brilliant gathering. Apart from
these, however the other papers to be read and discussed
can hardly fail to be of value, especially to those desirous of understanding Eastern peoples, customs, and
modes of thought. For Englishmen, naturally, a gathering of this kind has an especial importance. Engaged

in the administration of vast Eastern possessions, peopled by a diversity of Eastern peoples whose customs, laws and practices are the outcome of the ancient religious beliefs of the early races of man, all that throws light upon these is of interest and value, for it helps to a clearer understanding of them, and thus facilitates intercourse. Looking at the Congress from an objective point of view, we may say that the field in which our great Orientalists labour is one of the most attractive to which men of culture can devote themselves; and though now and then there may be a little needless threshing of straw, the results, in the main, are to be welcomed as adding to the sum of human knowledge, and are calculated, moreover, to be of help in solving the difficult problems arising out of the relations, in these days, between the West and the East, and the contact of their respective civilisations.

(6.)

Dr. Buhler's report to Dewan Bahadur Manibhai Jasbhai about Mr. H. H. Dhruva's work at the Congress.

September 29–89.
27 Cottage Gasse.
Wahring.

My dear Sir,

The Congress is over and I must write to you a word about your representative Mr. Dhruva. I am very well glad to tell you that he has done exceedingly well and

23

has earned the approval of every body with whom he has come into contact. He has read some very interesting papers, has written and recited two nice small Sanscrit poems; and the manner in which he has done this and has behaved generally was perfectly gentlemanly and in good taste. The Aryan Section has also shown its appreciation of his merits by voting him its thanks and by requesting that a letter of thanks be addressed to H. H. the Gaekwar for the generous interest he has taken in the Congress. The King of Sweden seems to have been much struck with Mr. Dhruva. He spoke to him very nicely in the public sitting. In answer to his address, he frequently took notice of him at the various festivities and he has decorated him with the Swedish medal for arts and sciences. The last honor is a great one, not frequently given and given to the most distinguished scholars.

I shall write officially to H. E. the Dewan by next mail. But I wished first to let you know, as you have taken so kind an interest in the matter.

Believe me

Yours very sincerely

Signed, G. BUHLER.

To

Dewan Bahadur

MANIBHAI JASBHAI.

(7.)

Dewan Bahadur Manibhai's note to Mr. H. H. Dhruva
enclosing No. 6.

Baroda, 14th November 1889.

My dear Sir,

I have pleasure in enclosing for your information
copy of a letter I received from Dr. Buhler in connection
with your deputation to the Oriental Congress in Europe.

Yours very sincerely
MANIBHAI JASBHAI.

To

Rao Bahadur
HARILAL H. DHRUVA
B. A. LL. B.
&c. &c. &c.
Baroda

——

(8.)

Copy of the Swedish Diploma (Certificate) of
Literis et Artibus
conferred on Mr. H. H. Dhruva by H. M. King Oscar
of Sweden and Norway.

——

Royal  Seal.

Att. H. M. Koniingen af Sverige och Norge i
nader behagat tilldela

H. H. Dhruva

delegerad från Gaikwareu af Baroda
Medaljeu **"Litteris et Artibus"**
att i hogblatt band å brostet baras, far jag på nådigste
befallving harmed meddela.
Stockholms Slott den 6 September 1889.

Sd/. NILS VON ROSEN
Forste Hof Marskalk.

(9.)

Dr. G. Buhler on the researches of Mr. H. H. Dhruva
in regard to the Gujerati Language at the VIII.
and IX. International Congresses of Orientalists
(1889 and 1892): Extract from his letter
dated 8th March 1893.

......" I have also just to-day corrected your paper
on the Gujerati Language of the 14th and 15th centuries, for which as well as for the other the thanks
of the IX. Congress of London were voted. Your
paper on the Language is very interesting and, I am
sure, nobody will deny that you have done a great
deal for the Language and antiquities of your native
country. Most of the forms you mention are to be
read in every *Tabo* or *Avachurn* of the Jain Yatis,
and in their Ràs, Sajjhâi and other Prakrit compositions.

"I am glad to see you have altered your view
about *Chand Bardai*. The Ràsâu, which goes by his
name is, indeed, a late forgery, as Kaviràj Muràrdhù

and Shyâmaldas have asserted long ago. My pupil Mr. Morison, is at present at work on a Sanskrit Kâvya, called Prithivîrâja-vijaya, written by a Kashmirian poet in the service of *Prithiviraja* (name lost) and commented on by Jonarâja between S'aka Samvat 1370 - 1380, which I found in Kashmir 18 years ago, and which has been lying in the Deckan College unused until now. This poem gives us a very long pedigree and full account of the Châhouvânas including the early part of P.'s career. This pedigree and account *fully agrees* with the inscriptions, but *contradicts* the Râsâu on every single point. It is now perfectly plain that the Râsâu is worth nothing. Mr. Morison's first article appears in No. II. of Vol. VII. of our Journal." (The Vienna Oriental Journal 1893.)

APPENDIX B.

Message of Mr. H. H. Dhruva, Delegate of H. H. the Gaikwad of Baroda to H. M. King Oscar II. August Patron of VIII. International Congress of Orientalists.

Stockholm, den 2nd September 1889.

YOUR MAJESTY,

His Highness the Maharaja Gaikwad of Baroda was not a little gratified to be invited to be present at this grand assemblage convened under Your Majesty's august Patronage. His Highness sends his hearty greetings to Your Majesty and the assemblage of Orientalists and his cordial hearty thanks for the interest Your Majesty and the Congress take in subjects which His Highness is also most deeply interested in. May it please Your Majesty to accept the present of the volume of Dabhoi Antiquities which His Highness has been pleased to send with me for Your Majesty as also some coins, facsimiles of As'oka edicts and some Gujerati Volumes which I humbly offer on my behalf. I again thank Your Majesty and the International Congress of Orientalists for the deep interest you take in our ancient Literature and in the Subjects that we are deeply concerned and interested in, on behalf of our State of Baroda and my countrymen, I mean the Hindoos, nay, the Natives of India. I will convey to His Highness when I go to Baroda the kindly and hospitable reception accorded to me and His Highness will ever appreciate the friendship of Your Majesty contracted under such happy auspices.

APPENDIX C.

3-9-89.

Dr. Burgess contended that there were in King Jayasinha's Library Mathematical works in Latin &c. and probably the Sanscrit work was a mere translation of a European recention. There were all the 15 Books published in Europe in the 17th century. And so there was nothing lost and nothing new here.

Dr. Bühler held that the Hindu adopted a Greek version and foisted it on the world as Hindu. But it is interesting to note that such a view existed and such a procedure was found.

Mr. Dhruva replied : " the question is left open. The materials brought to notice to-day were not within my knowledge and then as I got the work a little before starting, the paper was written in steamer If this work had a Greek origin and if it had a proper original before it there would surely have crept in terms from it as we know in the case of astronomy. But there is only one term *kendra* which the author might have borrowed from astronomical writers and not from Greek or any European original direct. But more light is needed and we shall have it by and by.

APPENDIX D.

(4.)

Col. Prideaux's reply to Mr. H. H. Dhruva's letter dated 10th September 1890 enquiring about originals of Rekha Ganita at Jeypur.

31st May 1890.

MY DEAR SIR,

In reply to your letter of the 27th inst., I beg to state that I find on enquiry that there is a Ms. of the "Rekhâ Ganita" in the Palace Library, but I understand it has at present been lent to Dr. Handley and is in charge of his Assistant at the Museum.

The Office in charge of the Palace Library is unable to give any information about the original Greek, Latin or Arabic Works from which the 'Rekhâ Ganita' is said to have been compiled by Maharaja Savai-Jey Singh. Nor does there appear to be any Catalogue of the Library. About 8 years ago I accompanied Prof. Peterson of Bombay to the Library and an application to that gentleman might throw some light upon the works contained in it.

Dr. Hendley is the best person to apply to on these subjects, but at present he is on leave at Simla where my address is " The New Club," but until his return to Jeypur in about six weeks, I do not suppose he will be able to render you much help. I would recommend your writing to him later on. I may add that I feel some doubts as to whether the Maharajah will be willing to lend books or Mss. from his private Library. •

Believe me

Yours very truly

N. S. PRIDEAUX.

(5.)

Reply of Dr. Hendley's letter to Mr. Dhruva's letter of 10th September, 1890 enquiring about originals of Rekha Ganita at Jeypur.

THE NEW CLUB.

SIMLA, *June 8th 1890.*

Dear Sir,

I shall not be in Jeypur I think until July 17th, when I shall be able surely (*sic.*) to reply to your letter at full length. There is a private copy of the work you mention at Jeypore. It was lent to me and I have had extracts made from it. I will put you in communication with the owner on my return.

I could not find any Latin versions of Euclid in the Palace Library. There are some mathematical works but none bearing on your research.

Yours sincerely

T. H. HENDLEY.

(6.)

Dr. Hendley's notes about the originals of Rekha Ganita at Jeypur with annextures.

JEYPUR, *October 2nd 1890.*

DEAR SIR,

With reference to your letters to Col. Prideaux and myself I have now the pleasure to send you a memorandum on the books of Euclid by Pandit Braj Balabh of the Jeypur Museum from which it appears that the book was translated from the Arabic.

Yours truly

T. H. HENDLEY.

There are no Greek, Latin, Arabic or English Versions of Euclid in the Palace Library.

Translation of Hindi Notes by Rameshwar Jotishi of Jeypore.

THE OWNER OF THIS BOOK.*

Euclid who composed the book was the son of Nocrades and lived in Alexandria in the time of Ptolemy Lagons. This man passed for one of the best Scholars of the time and the book was compiled during his reign. The Chapters were in detached portions and Euclid collected them all together and corrected

---

* Translation of the Sanskrit S'loks as in the beginning of the Samrât Siddhânta has not been given here as they are almost the same as those in Rekhà Ganita translated in the paper.

H. H. D. 1893.

the propositions, adding several new modes of proving the propositions and exercises and the book was called after his name. Euclid was translated into several languages, Greek, Latin, Arabic and dates before 280 B. C.

In 1840 A. D. it comes to 2120 years. Then during the reign of Jeysingh the Maharaja of Jeypore, Jaggannath Pandit translated it from Arabic text into Sanscrit and since then it was translated into Hindee by Champa Ram, Guzeratee Brahman of Sehore under instructions from Col. L. Wilkins for the Sehore School. It was translated into Hindee in the year 1840 A. D.

(7.)

Dr. Buhler's letter on earlier notes of Rekha Ganita.

WIEN, AM *June 9th 1891.*

Oriental Institute
University.

MY DEAR MR. DHRUVA.

In looking through the old vols. of the Journ. Beng. As. Soc. I came across a paper in Vol. VI., in which Mr. L. Wilkinson describes the Sanskrit Euclid, written for Jesingh of Jeypur. I think the work is the same as that which you have obtained and wish to publish. I transcribe the first verses* in order to

---

* These verses have not been given below as they are the same as those in the paper.   H. H. D. 1893.

enable you to judge of this matter for yourself. You had better read Mr. W.'s article before you publish your edition of your Ms. The Sanskrit book is, of course, nothing but a translation of a European work. Dr. Burgess has also found the particular editions according to which it has been made.

I write this in great haste in order possibly to prevent that you overlook Mr. W.'s article. About other matters I shall write soon.

With best regards

Yours Sincerely

G. BUHLER.

(1.)

Extracts from Dr. G. Burgess's letter about the early reprints of translations &ca. of Euclid in Europe.

22 Seton Place, Edinburgh
21st Oct. 1889.

MY DEAR SIR,

I have just received yours of 18th and am happy to give you such information as I can lay my hands on at once. A mere list of the translations into different European languages would fill several sheets and would be of little use to you : I shall give you only therefore the more important ones in Latin, English and Greek. ... ...
... ...
You will see from the above that though before Zambertus the European versions were translated

from Arabic Translations, and based on Adelard's ms, yet about 1505 the Greek Mss began to come to light, and these Mss contained 15 books and 485 props, while Adelard's wanted 18 propositions of these and had 30 others not in the Greek. Rhodius (Witteberg 1609) &c., Richard (Antwerp 1645) published Latin Editions of 13 books, but the best known were Commandini's (15 books) and Barrow's (also 15) ; and most probably your Jeypur one is from one of these or from Gregory's. The 14th and 15th books are generally ascribed to Hypsicles, and were omitted by Rhodius, Richard and others ; and the Berlin ed. 1826 gives only these 13 books, but based on three Mss at Munich and the works of preceding editors based on about 32 others. Our Greek Mss are therefore by no means rare and have been fully utilized, so that we are not dependent at all on the Arabic versions now, which Zambertus showed were very inaccurate. More information I think you would find in the Penny Cyclopœdia—which I cannot now refer to as I sold it before leaving Bombay, under "Euclid", "Burnard Dr. E." "William Jas." "Gregory, David," &c. which were written partly by De Morgan and are very accurate.

As to the European mathematical books at Jaypur, I would suggest your applying direct to some one there : Dr. Hendley could perhaps help you, by suggesting some pandit or other to communicate with. I remember seeing several Latin books on Mathematical subjects, among them Hausteed's Histo-

ria Coclistis (but whether the edition of 1712 or
that of 1725–I cannot say). It would be most interesting to get as complete a list as possible with
the dates of publication and print it with your paper.
Gregory's Oxford edition is a very big folio, Barrow's
is a small 8 vo.

I hope these hurriedly written notes may be of
use to you.

Ever Yours Sincerely

J. BURGESS.

SOME SPECIMENS OF PROVINCIAL AND CLANNISH GUJERATI.

(to refer to pp. 48 &ca.)

(1.)

Songs popularly sung in Malava (Rutlam) by laborers in opium factories, collected on the spot.

રાગ ખુમાચ.

નંદ રાણી પટ તુમ ખોલહો, તેરા બાલ મુકંદકુ દેખત હો–ટેક.

કાઇ ગોકુલજી રે બીંદ્રાખીનજી, કાઇ નંદ ગામ બરસાનાજી–૧

કાઇ નેન ભરેરી કાઇ સેન કરે, કાહી ઠાડીજી માડી અરજ કરે–૨

દખજી મટનીઆં સીરપર લેઇ, કાહી લાજજી મારી વા અરજ કરે–૩

મીરાં કહે સુનરી સખી, કાઇ ગંગાદાસ દરસનકુ આએ–૪

રાગ બીહાગ.

સામ મેરા નેનંમે ખસરો, લોગ કહે મજરોરે––ટેક

બીદી બાલ નેન ખીચ કજલા, સીનગાર બન્ષો અજરો–૧

ગોરી ગોરી બૈહીને હરી હરી ચુરીઆં, પોચનકો ગજરોરે–૨

મીરાં કહે પ્રભુ ગીરધર નાગર, સામ સુંદર અજરોરે–૩

કાફી.

બઇ મીરાં રામ દીવાની, મેરા દરદ ન જાનત કોય––ટેક.

ઘાયલજી બાત ઘાયલ જને, સો કાઇ ઘાયલ હોય. બઇ૦ ૧

સુલી જો ઉપર સેજ હમારી, પોઢણુ કેસી ઘુધ હોય. બઇ૦ ૨

જડી ખુટીસે ભલા કારજ નાહીં, ખેદ લીઆ સખ જોય. બઇ૦ ૩

મીરાં કહે પ્રભુ ગીરધર નાગર, ખેદ સાંમરીઆોજી હોય. બઇ૦ ૪

મારૂ પરજ.

સામરાજી ઓલો કયું નહીં માસુ (૨) ટેક.

જો તું અમસે રૂસ રહોલા, તો હમ રૂસા તો મના નહીં થાસુ. સામ૦ ૧

જે તુમ હમસે એક કહોલા, એકકે લાખ સુનાવુંગી થાસુ.   સામ૦ ૨
મીરાં કહે પ્રભુ ગીરધર નાગર, કપટકે ગાંઠ ખોલો કઢું નહીં માસુ. સામ૦ ૩

───────

રાધિકા ગજરા પ્યારીજીકા ગજરા, હે તારા રાધે રાણીજીકા અજરા—ટેક.
મેં જલ જમુના જાતી ભરનકુ, ભર આઈ ગગરા બસર આઈ ગજરા.
                                          હે ડારો૦ ૧
તુમ મત જાણો બણ્યો હે ફુલકો, રતન જડત હો મોતીઆં હે દો ગજરા.
                                          હે ડારો૦ ૨
મીરાં કહે પ્રભુ ગીરધર નાગર, સાંમસુંદર ઘડાવે મીરે અજરા. હે ડારો૦ ૩

───────

રાગ કાલીંગડાનો કેરવો.

સાગ્ન પરીક્ષિત જીન સુનાઓ હો સુખદેવ ભાગવત આઓ—ટેક
કલજુગ કે પરતાપ માહા બબ રાજ્ય કે મન ભાઓ
ભરત કલેવર સરપ હાથમે ડસીકે ફંડ પેરાઓ.   હે સુખદેવ૦ ૧
ડસી પુત્રકા સાપ બચ્ચા જદી તક્ષક નાગ ડસાઓ
સુનકર સ્રાપ મગન ભઓ રાજા સબસે ફંદ છોડાઓ. હે સુખદેવ૦ ૨
ખાન પાન સભ ત્યાગ કરીઓ જમુનાહઠ ધ્યાન લગાઓ.
વાં આઓ સરી સુખદેવ સ્વામી આઘને જ્ઞાને સુનાઓ. હે સુખદેવ૦ ૩
ક્રસ્ન ચરીત્ર અમ્રત પાખેકે વઈકુંઠ ધ્યામ પઠાઓ
નરસીંહનો સ્વામી અંતરજ્ઞસી રમઝમ ઘટ છાઓ.   હે સુખદેવ૦ ૪

───────

કાલીંગડો.

રંગીલી જુમખાવાલી (૨) ખાજુબંધ એરખાવાલીએ
અંજખીન અંખીઆં કાલી (૨) દેસી તુ ઓત રૂપાળીએ—ટેક.
તારી મટકીમે કંઇએ રાધે સાંભલ મારી બાત (૨)
દાની લીઆ ખીન જવા નહીં દુગા (૨) નંદભાવાક્ષી આણુ-રંગીલીજુમ. ૧
માહારી મટકીમે હે જોઇએ થારે શા પડી છે પુછ
દાન લેવાનો મુખડો જેવું (૨) મોઢે નથી છે મુછ, ચલો જ નંદના છૈયા
અમે ગોકુલમે રહા રે. રહાનો ભેદ નહીં જાણું પુગ ખીના પાલવ તાણોરે. ૨
હું છુરે બાખા નંદનો છેલો કાંનજી માહારૂ નામ

દાન લીઆખીન જવા નહીં દુગા તારા ગળાખી આંખુ-રંગીલી. ૩.
હું છુરે ભ્રખભાણુ દુલારી રાધકા મારા નાંમ
દાન લેવાનો સાખલો હોય તો આવજે ગોકુલ ગાંમ
ચલો જ નંદના છૈયા અમે ગોકુલમે રહા રે. રહાનો ભેદ નહી જાણું
પુછા વીના પાલવ તાણ્યો રે. ૪
ખાયા નંદનો મીઠ઼ડ઼ો ગાવે સો માહારે મન ભાવે
નરસીંહનો સ્વામી અંતરજામી દુખમે સાક઼ર પાવે-રંગીલી. ૫

રાગ ભેરવી.

ભોરે બાજી હરખી મોરલીઆં, કેસે ધરે જીઆ ધીર—ટેક.
ગોકુલ બાજી બીંદ્રાબન બાજરે, ઇ઼ જમનાંજીકે તીર. મોરી આલી. (૨) ભો૦–૧
સુનત સવણુ મોરી સુધબુધ વીસરીરે, સુધ ના રેત શરીર. મોરી આલી
(૨) ભો૦–૨
નાગર હરીઆં કહે કર નેરીરે, આખર જાત આહીર. મોરી આલી (૨) ભો૦–૩

ભેરવ.

જ દીન ઉઘામો પન ખીસારે, તા પન ખીસાર પાવ ઘડી—ટેક
ભજબાને ભજુ તજુ નહી વીનકુ, આહી ઠેવ માહારે પરાપરી (૨)
આ મેરા મેં ઉનકો ભીલ, ભરત હેત યા દેહ ધરી (૨) ૧
સેના સજના ઓર રહી દાસા, સીવરી ક્લીએ ફુલ હીણી
લાકઇ જુટા ઓર આરાગા, રસીયત કા અયો માન ઘટી (૨) ૨
ધ્રુપતા કા ચીર હરી દુસાસન, ભગત જન વાચ઼ે સાહ કરી
ખેચત ચીર બોહત લગઇડીએ, ફેરવ લાજમેં ધુર પડી ૩
મેરોહી ધ્યાન નામનીજ સુમરન, અષ્ટ સીદ્ધ નવ નીધ સહી
કહે રોહીદાસ વાધ ઉર કાખ઼ો, જે સમરે સીતા રામ હરી ૪

રાગ સોરઠ.

(ગીરનારીખ઼ દરભારી. બપોરી મધ્યસતે.)
ઘણા દીન ખીતારા ખીહારીજી, આલુ થારી આવે—ટેક.
નીસદીન નેણુ નીહાસ્ત મારગ, ધર અંગણ઼ુને સુહાવે; પ્યારા (૨) ૯૦–૧

ચડકે અટારી ને ચોદીસ જોવાં, કહુંએ નજર નહી આવે. પ્યારા (૨) ૫૦-૨
ઓ દીન કથ હોસી બગતાવર, જુગ બલ કંઠ લગાવે. પ્યારા (૨) ૫૦-૩

સોરઠની કાફી.

રાહે થારી સુંદડીમે ખળ્બો છંદ. (૨)—ટેક
જેસી રંગી જેસી આખ હુકે તારે (૨) છીટક રહ્યા છે પુનમચંદ (૨)-૧
જેસી રંગી જેસી હીર હુઓ કનીઆં (૨) સોઅે રહી છે ગોરે અંગ (૨)-૨
તીન લોકકે ઠાકુર ક્હીએ (૨) કર રાખો છે બાજુ બંધ (૨)-૩
સુરદાસ પ્રભુ કાલી કામળીઆં (૨) ચઢતે સકત દુજે રંગ (૨)-૪

સોરઠ મલ્હારી.

સખી ઇંદર બરસત સેસધાર, ખીર ખાંડી આર્ખ ખાહાર (૨) ટેક
જરમર જરમર મેઘલા બરસે (૨) હાં જીણ્યું જીણ્યું પડત કુવાર
રાજ ખીરખાશી૦-૧

દાદર મોર પપૈયા બોલે, કોચલ કર રહી ગાજ. રાજ ખીરખાશી૦-૨
ચંદ્રસખી ખન બાલકૃષન છએ, ઇંદર કર રહ્યા ગાજ. રાજ ખીરખાશી૦-૩

ખુમાચ સ્વારી.

જ્યારે લાગા છે સબદકા બાણ, ઘાયલ કું જીવે (૨)-ટેક
સબદ મારાં મર ગઓં, સબદા છોડ્યા રાજ;
જ્યાં એ સબદ પેછાનીઆં, જ્યાં રાસરગા કાજ. ઘાયલ-૧
સબદ સબદ સબ કોઈ કહે, સબદાં હેરે અલેક;
જિભ્યાપર આવે નહીં, નીરખ પરખ કર હેખ. ઘાયલ-૨
ચોપડ રાલી ચોવડે, સારો ઝીયો સરીર;
સતગરૂ દાવ બતાવીઆ, ખેલે દાસ કબીર. ઘાયલ-૩

રાગ કલ્યાણ.

કાનરકારે હો મનવારે લાલા, તુમસે લાગો રંગ, અેજી લાલ તુમ—ટેક.
કરખી ચુરીઆં કરક કરક ગઈ, અંગલી મુરક ગઈ ગગરી ઠુરક ગઈ;
તખ હુન છાંડો સંગ, અેજી લાલા તજુઅન છાંડો સંગ.   ૧

અમારી ભુવનમે લુપચુપ આવે, સેનમે હમકુ ઝુલવાવે;
નીરખત હોત આનંદ,એજી લાલા.   ૨
ખીજઈ ખીનતા સબ મીલ આઈ, સુરદાસ તુમરે બલીહારી;
મુજ બલ ભેટત અંગ, એજી લાલા.   ૩

_____

રાગ કલ્યાણ.

સામરી સુરત બનસીવારા ગીરધારી, મેરા મન હરલીયાં જઅ. એજી—ટેક
બીંદ્રાબીનકે કુંજગલનમે, ક્રાંન રાસ કીઓ એક છનમે;
સેન લગાતો જઅ એજી મુસે સેન લગાતો જઅ   ૧
જુમનાજી તીરાં તીરાં ધેન ચરાવે, બંનસીમે કછુ અચરત ગાવે,
મોહ લીની ખીજનાર, એજી   ૨
ખનજી ખીનતા સબ મીલ આઘ, સુરદાસ તુમરી બલીહારી;
બહીઆં મુરકતો જઅ, એજી મેરી બહીઆં મુરકતો જઅ. એજી ૩

_____

(2.)
Specimens of Charani and Kathi popular verses sung
in Kattyawad.

_____

લાખણુશીના તથા માણુકદે.

લાખણુશી લેને લાડ, આજુની એકજ ઘડી;
પરોડીયાના પરીયાણુ, સવારે સરગ પધારસું.
જતી હોતો જ, મારો રહો દણીઆત છે;
હેઠ દેને સારીસું અખાઉસે. ઉઘુનો ઘણી.
અઝુજને અલણુ, કોઈ સાને સમજેઅ નહી;
ફેરા ફરીને બાંધ, લાખણુશી લોહીયાળો થઅો.
અમે ચડીયા સકાર, મારેલ વનમાં મરઘલો;
તેનાને ઉડ્યા તરશકટ, લોહીયાળાં અમારાં લુગડાં.
દાદા મ કરે દાખડો, વીરા મસડાવે વાર;
જે નર ન મુવો ઘરને આગણે, એ નહીં મરે ટોડા બાર.
કેઠવી હોજે લીંબડી, સીતલ હોજે છાય;

અક્ષર હોજે અમોલખું, બોધ પોતાની બાપ.
સોના જેડી સેબળે, રૂપા જેડો જુ;
તુજને પુછું ગોવાળીઆ, કન્અે ઘરે આઠું મુઠ.
સોના જેડી સેબળે, રૂપા જેડો જુ;
જે ઘરવાળો લાખણશિ માલતે, એ ઘર માઠું મુઠ.
નવ નવ કંટારોડ નાખીઉ, અમારી સઘ સાજ ન રઈ;
માગ દેજે માનવીઆ, મારે જવું માણહને મોલ.
સરગ પધારો ભલે કરી, મ જાનજે મરી;
રેજે આપણા શેરમાં, ઉંડા મુલ કરી.
કંથજા કાયર મ થા, ઘર વીંઢું ઘણે;
કાઠ કટારા કર દુખડાં, જાણે ગડેરલને થકે.
દાદા કેરા દાખડા, વીરા ચઅવી વારૂ;
જે નર ન મુવો ધરને આગણે, એને મારકે ટોઠ બારૂ.
રાત થોડી ને રણ ઘણું, વાસે ચડું કેકાણું;
અંધવ હોજે અમોલખું, તોય પોતાની બાંધ.
વેદ્ય આમ કર વૈદ્યપણું, મ જાલ મોરી બાય;
વાલા લાખણશિની કટારી, આખડી વાંજર આંધ

સામળી ઢેઢના દુહા

નાણા નાખો અગલા, માલ વોરીઆ સમાલ
જેને દુજણે દાણી ગણ છુટીએ, ઝણીઉ મેલ કેવાય
સાંભળે સાંગડવા ઢેલ, સામઝ માણસનો ગુણ ગાયે
એને કાઠનો તારા શેરમાંથી જએ
કાબેરી ને બાબેરી, બમી ભાગડીએ વણાય
અજર મેઅેમાં અેછીએ, કાળી ક્રબળ કેવાઅે
ઝાળાં બચઘાં કોયલના, કાળા ગરનો કાગ
કાળે તારી ઘેરલનો છોટલો, છઠો કાળો વાછગી નાચ
આતરમાંથી ઉમટ્યો, દક્ષણમાં નચ
જેને પડછાયે પાણી હાલે, કાળો મેઅે કેવાય
ઘોળાં દેખીને ન ઘોડીએ, ઘોળાં મોળને ઢાઢ

કોકે ગેરાં ને ગળસટાં, ભાયસ જણ્યા બીતે વાત

પરચુરણ

નજર કરીને નાખ, અબાસ પંડ ઉપર પાલવ નહી
અસતના અમે, દુબળશી આગળ દાખીએ
નીકળને હવે નાગ, કોકેરા કુઢબાંરૂં ખાઘેરા
લાગસે મોરલીછના માર, તે દીના કુટુટે નાગની
સામળી સોરમ ઘણી, કાનળ થાંડેરૂ આજ
આપણે શેઢા નાપાડો, વાડીઆં, ભવનું મેણું ભાંગ
તુ કુવામાં અલો કેવડો, હું વાડી માયલી નાગર વેલ
તે કેડી ઝાલો મારૂ શેઢલો, મેં કેડી કણ જે મેલ
એં બાંધી તરવાર, જાણે દલીજ તારા ડગઇજે
ચઈબ્જિ રીશાને વાર, પીઆળમાં કેરવ કમે.
આકડાને થડ અરશો, જાણેલો માંગોળી
ખીતીઆખે જખ ખાવલો કરૂ, મારૂ વેજડો કોળી
બાના સું નેહ, કાછાં સું કરીએ નહીં
સરક દે સેણ, સરવાને સાઢે નહીં.
ઘોડાં ધી પાતે, કામણુ કરગરીએ નહીં
સમઝી હૈ ચઢે, પ્યારાં પોતાના કરે
ભલસારી લાજરો, જેના હોય લાંબા પાન
ઘોડે પાછું આવીઉ, ખુઢાં ખ્યાં જુવાન

ઘટ જુનાની પોળ, કેદામે કુંડ દેખીશ નહીં
રતન પડરો રેાળ, ત્યારે મુ સંભારીશ મંડળીક
નહીં વાગે નીશાણુ, નખી હુ ફળશે નહી
ઉમટશે અશરાણુ, સારે મુ સંભારીશ મંડળીક
જખો બાંગો ખેલ પડી, ઘેરા ઢઢ ગીરનાર
દુહો હમીર એ મારીઆ, સોરઠના શણગાર
કવણ ખટઝવે કમાડ, મછી છે રાણુકદેવની
જનખુશે જે રાહ ખેંગાર, ભટક ખાનજ તોડરે

મારા મહેલુ હેક, કેણે તંબુ તાણીયા
શધવો મોટો શેઠ, ખીજ વરતાવ વાણીખા
સ્વામી ઉઠો સૈન લઈ, ખડગ ધરો ખેંગાર
આ છત્રપતીએ છાપ્રો, ધઢ જુના ગીરનાર
તરવરીઆ તોખાર, હઉન ફાટુ હંસલા
મરતા રાહ ખેંગાર, રંડાપો રાણકદેવને
કૂટ કૂટ ધોબજરા ગીરનપ, ખરેડી ખાગો નવ થઓ
મરતા રાહ ખેંગાર, રંડાપો રાણકદેવને
ગરવો લાલ ગલાલ, ખરેડી ખાગો થઓ
એટલે રેતે ઓધાર, તારા ચોસલ કોણ ચડાવશે
રેરે મારા ઓધાર, તારાં ચોસલ કોણ ચડાવશે
ગયા ચડાવણહાર, રંડાપો રાણકદેવને
બલુ પાઠણુ દેશ, જીસે પટોળા નીપજે
સરવો સોરઠ દેશ, લાખેણી મલે લોખડી

___

વાકીઆના જેઠ સુરવાળના.

રાવજીને મલક ચુથાંણો, કોપ થો કાળો
મેડીઉ મેલાવશે, જેનો વેરી જેહુરવાળો
ગઢ ઘેરા આખડીઆ તણો, આડી ને ચોંઝીયાળા
એમાંથી ઉઠીને આલગ ગઓ, વાંકા જેહુરવાળ
ઘોડાને ઘુધી બાંધીએ, ગાજને દઓ ગાળ
પરજુમાંથી પાલ, જટપટ લેવાળો જેહુર
ખીજને કાળી બાપડા, કેણે વેર ન થાપ્ર
જમીસાટ જરૂર, જગાઉવાળા જેહવા
જગત બધી જોઈ, સારી સીમ સાઝીઆ વઠરની
ગાજડે દઠને લીધા ગરાસ, વડો વાંઝીઆના ઘણી
સજણ તમને વારતા, ખજરે બેસવા મ જાવ
ફુળીઆમાં વાવીએ એલચી, અમે ફોલીએ તે તમે આવ
જેની જોતા વાટ, સવારે સામા મળાં
ઉઘડા હૈયાના હાટ, કામ મળે નઈ કુંચીઉ તણુ

હૈઆની કરૂં હાટડી, મનની કરૂં બન્નર
તનનાં કરૂં ત્રાજવાં, વાલાં સું કરીએ વેપાર
ઓશીઆળા અમે, ટોડાજલ ટળાં નઈ
તરછોડાં તમે, મેણ્ના જલરાં માગડાં
સૌ સૌને આસરે, સૌ સુવાને જઅ
ખોરડ ખાવા ધાય, નળીએરવાળોના ગજ

ખુટક.

કયાં કોકણ ને કાચ, બેણીની બીઝપ નહીં
ઘડી કને ઘરવાશ, એગમશી દાઝુ પડે
તમે વણુકર ને અમે ધણાર: નાતે નેડો નહીં,
ગણુરો ઉગે માર, જતનો પુછું જોગડા

આવારાળા રાણી ગવાળાના દુહા.

વાધણીઆ સાઠુવેર, કોઇ રાજ ન પામેલ રહે
દેવાવાળાને દેહ, બાળી દીધો ભાવલા
ભાવો ને ઉગલા એ, જે ભાર થતા તે પાછાં ફરે
તો તો મલકમા મે, કોઇ વાધાસાઇ વરસત નહીં
ભાર વરસનો ભાવલો, આખાં ગળે ગામ
રાણી ગપે ડોઢો થઆ, નવખંડમાં રાખું નામ
ભાખુને તારીખ કરી, કોઇએ ન ઝાલે કાન
મળો રાણી ગનો ભાવલો, ડોળી એસારી ઠામ
ટોપી ને તરવાર, નર બીજને નમે નહીં
સાહેઝ મહીના ચાર, ભાન રાખો તે ભાવલા

પરચુરણ.

હાથ છે એમ પગ હત, તો તો દરીઆ માઝગ દેત
લંકાનો ગઢ લેત, રાવણ વાળો રાણીગા
કાળીયાણી કડે પાતળી, હળવી લીએ હેલ
બગસરાની બન્નરમાં, ઠળકતી ચાલે ઢેલ

દળામણ જેઠવાના.

ચુંટી હરન કે અગમે અહંએ.
પળ બહુને હરી હેસ્લા, વહેશી હેન્દ્રે
હેલા હરબીએ, બંદ્ર ને ગચ્છ ક્લશ
હેરાકું આહેર, બંત ક્રહ્દ નહી હેનહ્દ
હળમણું દ્ર ને હરારકે ક્રહતો નહ્દ.
ઉન્દ્રરા ને બત્તે, ચન ચલ ચોખ્ખું, ચન્દ્રા
બારલ બ જ્યતી બ્યા, હેઈ ચાંચલ ચેન્ચલુસ
ક્રમ છે કચન કે, ચેનરકે અબ્ર ઉરિલા
ચઠ ચન ચરિએ, એઇસે આમ્બીઆ નહી
ચડચકું ચનતા, ચોની ચેનચકું ચિખ્ખે.
ચાના ચરી ચેનચકું ચચે, પચાપચે ચચાલર
જૂના ચેઈચેરા ઇચ ચેહ્લ, નચા આચ્છી ચાસ
ચાઈ ચેઈઠી ને ચરરેા, ઇેર્ફ ભચર બાચું હાથ
ચાઈ આચખ્ચું ચનચરે, બાણી જેઠવાની જન
ચાઇ ચને ચાની ચડી નદીએ ચરનાં નીર
ચેક ચચનને ચારચે, સુચાચું અચારાં ચરીર.
ચાયચીઇ ચ ચાઇ, ચાયચીએ ચન ચેઈચે નહી
ચચાળુ આચેાચી ચાઇ, ચરખી ચુઇ હળામચુને
ચાજુચ ચ ચાઇ, ચાજુના ચાઇરનચ નહીં;
ચચાઇ આચેાચી ચાઇ, ચેઈરા ચારે હળામચુ જેઠવે.
ચાણીઆ તું ચચાણીએ, ચેઈર્ફ ચીચારી ચેાચ,
હળામચુ નારા ચાઇ્રાં, ચાદને ચચટ ચેાચ.
ચાણીચ નારે ચાઇકે, અચે હેઈ હેઈ ચચ્તુ ચીચરા;
ચેક હેઈચાનેા ચાર, ખીચે હળામચુ જેઠવેા.
હળામચુની હચચાલ, ચારા દલચાં દીચલ રહી;
ચુંચીઇર્ફ રઇ ચચાઇ, ચઠેલચાં જેઠવાના.

કુંવર કોઠાળીના દુહા.

રાણો ચીચાબ્ધા ને કુંવરની દોસ્તી થઇ સાથે

ડુંગરે રહેતાં હતાં પછે રાણો ચાચઈ આવ્યો ને કુંવર રઘસાણો.
ઉડી આવ્યો કાગ, કોઈ વનરા વીધીને
સાણે અમણા સેણ, કે ઉડીને આધા ગયાં.
ગર લાગી ને ગુઢાગળા, પેટે વધ્યો પીઉ
કાગડા કુંવરને ભખુજે, રાણો ચાચઈએ રીઆ.
વેણુ લવે ઉતાવળી, નર વાંખળ કે તીર
ચાલો લગાડો શીપરે, રખે સાજણુ ઘોઈ ગયાં હોય શીર
તડ તડના બે તીર, કોઈ પાપણુના વુઠે નહીં
સોસરવા અંગ સરીર, સાથે ધાસા જણુના.
બાળે ખીજની ચાલ, ડાફકતી ઉગલાં ભરે
હસના તે જેડી ચાલ, બોય કોટાળી કુંવરને
બાળે ખીજના વાળ, કોઈ એક થાય ઉચેરા
કડલગણુ કાબ નાગ, કોટાળી કુંવરને
કુંવર કાળી નાગણી, સકેલી નખમાં સમાય
તેનું કરકું ડગ ન ભરે, કોટાળી કુંવર કેવાય
રાણા કે રાત, બીશીને બથ ભરીએ નહી
ઉર અમારાં, કુંવર કે ક્યડાઇ ત્યાં
કુંવર ઉચળે તેા ભલ ઉચળે, તુકાં ઉચળ ડુંગર સેણુ.
કાલે કુંવરને મનાવશું, તું પડોરે પાણુ
રાણો તે રાતે ફુલડે, ખાખરની છલીઆ
સાજણુ ઘેરા સામદા, જણે કોક આણા તવળીષ
બાળે ખીજના ઉર, હાલે ત્યાં હસ્ખસે
કે અણુઆિારાં ઉર, કોટાળી કુંવરે

સોનસડીયાણીના દુહા.

સોનને સમજવો સાનમાં એના પીતાને કે
કરતું કુંવરીનું વેશવાળ, મેમાન ભજના છે,
મેમાન ભજના છે તે જડોરા જમ
અને ઘરે ચોરાશી ગામ.
પછે કેસ પીઆ હે બાંદી, એટલા થોક લખીને બાઈ બાજુને હ

સ્રીાનને સમજવી સાનમાં એના પીતાને કે
સાને વેલને સાખદી કરી ને ભુભલીએ જવું કેં
જતના રજપુત જેડવા, હ્ાબાડગર કેં
આબાડગર કેં તે જેડવા, સુખદુખ તે મારા શરીરને વેડચા
પછે ફેસ પીયા દ બાદડી આગળ ગાપને ફ્રાજલ પરી
સ્રીાને વેલને સાખદી
સ્રીાનુ સગા લઈ માદળીયુ મઢાવીએ તે જમો કામી જેડવા
જમો કામી જેડવા તે જેડે જડી અને સોન રથ જેડી મારગે ચડી
પછે ફેસ પીયા દ બાદડી હલામણુ મળે તો મોતીએ વધાવીએ
સ્રીાનના સગા લઈ માદળીયુ મઢાવીઆ
સ્રીાન સોનાનુ ટીડડું હલામણુ કળાએલ મોર
હ્ાલરીઆ ગયા દેશવટે તે દુના પડા વનજેગ
ને દુના પડા વનજેગ તે વડીસાને સાખ ભરી સરકારમા દીધા
પછે ફેસ પીયા દ બાદડી સોન વીખડી હલામણુની જેડ
સ્રીાન સોંનાનું ટીડડું હલામણુ કળાએલ મોર

પુતળી સલાટની દુહા.
ખરચી ભરડાની, હીફરડી હ્યામાં
તનમાં તે તરડી, પાસ લીઉ ખટકાવે પુતળી
હાથનેા વળાવું દીવડેા, આગળીઉની વણ્ાવું ચાદ
પંડના પડાવું પાટીઆં, સેવું પણે પુતળી સલાટ
તળાવનાં તરશાં, ભાંભળ નીર ભાવે નહી
મીઠાં જળ મણે, પાલરપાઆં પુતળી
ફંસારા ઘડને કળશીઓ, નાલેસનીચે ઘાટ
પરખેતરમાં પુતળી, સાચું નાણું સલાટ

મારૂ ઢોલાના દુહા.
ઢોલેા ધુવે ધોતીઆં, મારૂ એ ધાન ન ખાય
ખોડા ધાને કરલીઆ, ઢોલો ગામ ન જાય
ખોડા થાઉ તો ડંભ ખાઉ, બાંધી મુખે મરૂ

જબ ઢોલાને સાસરે, તો હરીઅલ મગ થરૂ
જૂણી ડંભારણીએ ડંભસૂં, શીશસુ તાતાં તેલ
ખોડો થાને કરલીઆ, નીરીએ નાગર વેલ
દીધ ગઐો દળ ડુંગરે, વચાં ગમ્મા વડે
ફટકાળી સાંજના કરલીઆ, રાખો મને રણ થળે
તાણી ભીડો ગાતરી, વોછી મેક્ષે વાધ
કાઢા ડાખા પગની કાંકરી, તો મારૂ ભેટાઉં આજ.
ફર લાગ આ પરદેશમાં, કેની ન કરીએ આળ
તુજકુ સબકાવીઆં કાખડીઆ, ને મુંજકુ દીધી ગાળ
મે જાણ્યુ રખારી રાયકો, મે જાણ્યુ ચારણ ભાટ
ન જાણ્યું ઢોલાનો કરલીઆ, નીકર પસલીએ પાણીપાત.
ઢોલા આવને ઢોલીએ, મારૂના નીમ જાણ
કડકસે ને કા સાંભળે, ખેંચી ભલી કમાન.
મારૂ ચલી મોલા ઉપરે, ઉઘાડા મેલી કેશ
જાણુ કોઇ છત્રપતી ચાલીઆ, કોઇ મલક નમાવા દેસે.
ઢોલો ને મારૂ ખ વઢીઆ, લવીંગની લાકડીઆં
ઢોલે અ મારૂ ને મારીઆં, ફુલની પાંખડીઆં
કાળે માથે માનવી, ભગરે માથે ઉંટ
નગણ્યાને ગુણ કરા, તાણી બાંધા ફુડ.
કાંટા ન કરે કરલીઆ, ચરે ખીજાં ઊંટ
લાલેડો લાંઘણ કરે, જેણે ચાખેલ ચંદણુ રૂપ
મારૂ મારૂ મેં કરા મારૂ ઘેલડીઆં હોય
પાણી પીતા કરલીઆને, સબકાવી કાપડીઆં
મારૂ મેલે લુગડે, ઉભી ઠામ ફઠામ
કાંતો સાજનો કાળ પડો, કાં ઘોખી ગઐલ ગામ
મારૂ જેસી પતક્ષી, જાણે ખાંડેણ ધાર
જેમે આવી લથડી, ટુકડ ભઆ ત્રણ ચાર
અમદણુ ચંદણુની મારૂ ઘડી, તે નારે જપડા ચાર
તેના ઘડો એક ચંદલો લખ ચોટાડો લેઢાઇ
હાથે ચુડી હેમની, હેમ સરીખા હાથ

મોરા ઘડા મારતો જેદી નવરો દનો નાથ
પગને પાની પતલી, છુટાં નાગડનું
ઘરની સંપત હોય નો, ઢોલા લાવ મારૂ ઘરાં
કડાં ખટુકે ખટજ, દોરી તાણે દાશ
ભ્રણુ ઢોલા તારૂ માથરૂં, મારૂ હું દો ઘરવાશ
ખાવું ઓભાયમાં, ભુખ વણુ ભાવે નહી
દુહો દેહમાં ઉલટ વણુ આવે નહી

_____

ઓઢો જામને હોથલ પદમણીના.

મારીશ તુને મોર, કોઈ શીંગણુના બાણુ સાધીને
સત ના તું ચોર, મારા ઓઢાને ઉદાશી ક્યૉ
મોર કે હું ડુંગરનો રાજીઓ, પાપે પેટ ભરૂં
મારી રતે ન ઓલું, તો ડુકે ફાટી મરૂં
ધરા વીના ધાન ન નીપજે, કળ વીના માઢુ નાથ
ઓઢાને ઘરે ઝખરો, જેને માથે હોથલ પદમણી હોય
જોઇ વોરીએ જાત, જતે જોઓ નઇ
પડે પટોળે ભાત, ફાટે પણ ફીટે નહી.
રતન ને રાણુ, ખીજાં કાચાં ને કરમદાં
કાકે જુવાનને જાણુ, રાતે સાઢળે રતની
ન.ખાં દીસે જડ, ગોઢાળીં ગુંદરણુના
જાજ ભણુજે જુવાર, રેટા વાળી રતનને
ન.ખાં દીસે જડ, કોઈ જુંડાળાં જર તણા
જાજ જાણુજે જુવાર, સોટલવાળા સઈદને
કોઇ રાખા ઇતીની રાખ, દાઝે તોય ડાકણુ થઇ
નઇ સુવાવડનો સોભાગ, બાભરીયા બાળ કુંવારી
પાનાળા પેરીને, પેલ કાંઠે ચાલેલ નહી
વર તુરી વરમાળ, કઉં કર જળાના ધણી
હયામાં હતી હામ, જાણે હાલરડાં હીંચોળશું
નહી સુવાવડનો સોભાગ, બાભરીયા બાળ કુંવારી.
ખંડાણોમે જાણે વરા પેલીને વરસસે.

વરશે દેશ વીદીશ, ઉજળી ને જીનાળોરા
મે મે કરતાં મે, અમારી જીભડીઉ જાય થઉ
તોય ન વરશે મે, ઉજળીને ઉનાળોરા
વાદળે ને ઘટાઉ કાઠીઉ, ડુંગરડાં ડમર
પેલું ભાણુ પરમાણુ, વાણુ સૂચે ડુવાધડા
નજર કરો તો નંગ, નકર નેણાને વારો
ઉપર વાડાના સજણું, કાંડાસે થૈથે મારો
હરેરમાં હુઆ, કોઇ ઝુરો કોટ ભાળીને
નઇ મારે નખાખ, ઉગારે ઉનાનો ધણી
કોઇ હરેરમાં હુઈઆં, મરવા નઇ દેવે
કાલે કાળા વરસસે, ઉગારના વાળો એહ
વણુ સગે વણુ સાગવે, વણુ નાતરીએ નેગ
સંધાય વના જીવીએ, તું વના મરીએ મે
સાજણુ તમને વારતાં, નદીએ નાવા મજ્જવ
ફળીઆમા ગાળે વાવડી, અમે શીચીએ ને તમે નાવ

ખુટક દુહા.

નકરીએ નંગ, કોઇ સખીઆ જીવ સંતાપવા
દાઝે પોતાની દેહ, આઢે પોર ઉદાશી ડરે
વાલા આડી વાડ, કાંટાળી કરીએ નહીં
જખરક લાગે ઝામ, ભાઝારડીઆ વઝની
નાના સુ નેહ, કાલાં સું કરીએ નહીં
સટકેથી દે શીખ, સરવાળુ સોઢે નહી
જેનોને જાણે જીવ, તેના આતમને ઉચાટ ધણી
નહી નાડુમાં નીર, દનસુ મોતીવા મરે
જેનો ન જાણે જીવ, તેના આતમને ઉચાટ નહી
નવે નાડુમાં નીર, દન ઉઘો ખાવા ચડે
માઆ રાખો ને માનવીઆ, જજ્જ રાખોને હેત
બોલાં ચાલાં માફ કરો, અવગુણ કરા અનેક
અમે માગુ તેલ, તે દી અમુલાં ઉતર દએ

હજી ચટ્ક્ષે મેલ, જેલું નઈ ઓરીચી
તમે માગ્યુ તેલ, તે દી કાચુ અકુપે નહી
પણ દ્રાગને ફુલેલ, આવને વાળે નાખુ વીજરા
ખીજની ઓથીએ, કોઈ હૃપાવી સે રાસું નહીં
તારા માથાને મોવાળ, મને વાલપ લાગી વીજરા
વઈ જણ્દ આડો વીજણો, જણુલ આડી ભીત
પડહે પડાવા તું કરે, બાળપણુની પ્રીત
કોઈ વાઢ વળી સુજ્ઞ, ભુડે ભોય ભુભલીની
એક્ષીલો અસ્વાર, મીરે ન બાળુ માગડા
તું ખેટા ને હું બાપ, ક્યાં આલખન છ આરશી
માંગડો ને મરતે, સમર તુરો આરસી
તારાં નેત્રાં બાળુ તણ્ઘ, કોઇ આગે ન વસળોઈ
ગરને ગડકાનોઅ, નાઢા ભારીથી ના જડ્ઘા
ના ઝાળ મરાએ નહી, સાવાતને હરમત સોત
ખોડાને વેલું ખોત, સૌને માથે સુરાવ
અમે પરદેશી પાન, કોઇ વાતે વીટોણે આવીઆ
કોણે ન દીધાં માન, ઉડીને અગણાં રીઆં
કોઈ હાકમને વળગેલ વીર, ભવે દુખ ભાગે નહી
ચરખે ચાપો વીર, ઘણેરો ચરખાનો ઘણ્ઘ
અમરેલી એ આવેલ, કોઈ જોડે રમવાને ભાલે
મરડીઉ ખોલે, ચડી નાર એ ચાંપરાજ
કોઇ અમરેલીએ ઓલો, ભડ રમવા ભાલે
ખીળડી સું ખગલે, ચડી નીરખે ચાંપરાજ

૬

(3.)

Specimens of Harauti songs and document writing at
Boondi-Kotah (Rajputana.)

HARAUTI SONGS.

ગરમીકી આસમકો ગીત.

મ્હારા હાલીનકા* હાથમે ગુલાબખ્ત્રી છડી
મારા કેસરિયાબ્રી પાઘમે કછનારબ્રી † ક્ત્રી
મારા નોબ્રીલા શીસે જમે દૌઈ કામણ્યાં ખડી—ટેક.
બાગાં જબ્બે સાહિબા ઢોલા લીમુ લાબ્બે ચાર
છોત્રીસી નારંગી લાબ્બે હીવડલાકો ‡ હાર—મ્હારા૦
મે § ખરનેજેછિ ઢોલા ઉદયાપુર મત જાઈ
ઉદયાપુરબ્રી કામણી થાંને રાખેગી બલમાઈ×—મ્હારા૦
કુવા તું સરનજીવણો + ઢોલા નિર્મલ થારો નીર
ગુલહંજ() પાણી ભરે કોઈ હૂ હૈ આડે શીર—મ્હારા૦
ગેલે ÷ ગેલે જવતી ઢોલા ગેલે પડ્યો રૂમાલ
નીચી હોર ઉઠાવતી કોઈ ખેલ ગયો કુલમાલ—મ્હારા૦
ક્યા પીલાકો પેહેરવો ઢોલા ધૂપ પડે રંગ જાઈ
ક્યા લડકાબ્રી દોસતી કોઈ બીડ પડે ઉડ જાઈ—મ્હારા૦
કુવા મેર + કુલામડી × ઢોલા બાગાં મેર બબૂલ ✛
ગોરીજી ઉભી પાતલી જીકે હાથ ગુલાબી ફૂલ—મ્હારા
દેહે લપટકે ક્યા કરો ઢોલા લાવણ્ડ્યુસું કુલ જાઈ
કા ॥ સાહેવા૦ મારી સજ્જસું ઉડ જાઈ—મ્હારા .હુલીડાકે
હાથમે ગુલાબખ્ત્રી છડી, મારા પાતલિયાને વિસરન એક ઘડી.

THE SETTING MONSOONS.

કાલીજી આદલિયાંબ્રી રેખ ખીજલી સોહાઈ% લાગેૂ

---

* આશીજ. † દાડમ. ‡ the heart. § રોકું છું. ×બિરમાવી. +અમર-
પાણી. () a beautiful woman. ÷ a road. + a side. × creep-
er. ✛ a Babul tree. ॥ ઓદામન (કાયું મન). ₀a Lover.
% sweet. ૂ beautiful.

મારા એહેલ હેઠ, કેણે તંબુ તાણીયા
શધવો મોટો રોઠ, ખીજ વરતાવ વાણીયા
સ્વામી ઉઠો સૈન લઈ, ખડગ ધરો ખેંગાર
આ છત્રપતીએ છાંઘઓ, ઘઠ જૂનો ગીરનાર
તરવરીઆ તોખાર, હઉન ફાટુ હંસલા
મરતા રાહ ખેંગાર, રંડાપો રાણકદેવને
ફ્રટ ફ્રટ ઘોળ્જરા ગીરનપ, ખરેડી ખાગો નવ થ્યો
મરતા રાહ ખેંગાર, રંડાપો રાણકદેવને
ગરવો લાલ ગલાલ, ખરેડી ખાગો થ્યો
ઝેટલે રેતે ઓઆધાર, તારા ચોસલ કોણ ચડાવશે
રેરે મારા ઓઆધાર, તારાં ચોસલ કોણ ચડાવશે
ગ્યા ચડાવણુહાર, રંડાપો રાણુકદેવને
ખળુ પાઠણ દેશ, જીસે પરોળા નીપજે
સરવો સોરઠ દેશ, લાખેણી મળે લોઆડી

વાઘીઆના જેઠ સુરવાળના.

રાવજીને મલક સુથાંબો, કોપ થો કાળો
મેદીઉ મેલાવશે, જેનો વેરી નેહુરવાળો
ગઢ ઘેરા આકડીઆ તણો, આડી ને ચોંઝીયાળા
ઝેમાંથી ઉઠીને આળગ ગ્યો, વાંકા નેહુરવાળ
ઘોડાને ધુધી બાંધીઝે, ગાજને દઝે ગાળ
પરજુમાંથી પાળ, જટપટ લેવાળે નેહુર
ખીજને કાળી બાપડા, કેણે વેર ન થાઅ
જમીસાટ જરૂર, જગાડવાળા જેઠવા
જગત બધી જોઈ, સારી સીમ સાજીઆ વઢરની
ગાજડે દઈને લીધા ગરાસ, વડો વાંઝીઆના ધણી
સજણુ તમને વારતા, ખનરે ઝેસવા મ જવ
ફ્રળીઆમાં વાવીઝે ઝેલચી, અમે ફ્રોલીઝે તે તમે આવ
જેની જેતા વાટ, સવારે સામા મળાં
ઉઘડ હૈયાના હાટ, કામ મળે નઈ કુંચીઉ તણા

હૈઆની કરૂં હાટડી, મનની કરૂં બજાર
તનનાં કરૂં ત્રાજવાં, વાલાં સું કરીએ વેપાર
આશીઆળા અમે, ટોડાજલ ટળાં નઈ
તરછોડાં તમે, મેણા જળરાં માગડાં
સૌ સૌને આસરે, સૌ સુવાને જાઅ
ખોરડ ખાવા ધાય, નળીઆેરવાળાના ગજ

છુટક.

કયાં કોકણ ને કાચ, બેણીની બેઘપ નહીં
ઘડી કને ઘરવાશ, બેગમશા દાઝુ પડે
તમે વણકર ને અમે ધણાર, નાતે નેડો નહીં,
ગણુરો ઉગે માર, જતનો પુછું જોગડા

બાવાવાળા રાણી ગવાળાના દુહા.

વાધણીઆ સાટુવેર, કોઇ રાજ ન પામેલ રહે
દેવાવાળાને દેહ, બાળી દીધો બાવળા
ખાવો ને ડગલા એ, જે ભાર થતા તે પાછાં ફરે
તો તો મલકમા મે, કોઇ વાધાસાઇ વરસત નહીં
બાર વરસનો બાવળો, આખાં ગળે ગામ
રાણી ગપે ડોઢો થઆ, નવખંડમાં રાખું નામ
બાખુને તારીખ કરી, કોઇએ ન ઝાલે કાન
મળો રાણી ગના બાવળા, ડોળી બેસારી ઠામ
ટોપી ને તરવાર, નર બીજાને નમે નહીં
સાહેબ મહીના ચાર, બાન રાખો તે બાવળા

પરચુરણ.

હાથ છે એમ પગ હત, તો તો દરીઆે માગજ દેત
લંકાનો ગઢ લેત, રાવણ વાળો રાણીગા
કાળીયાળી કડે પાતળી, હજવી લીએ હેલ
બગસરાની બજારમાં, ઢળકતી ચાલે ઢેલ

હુલામણ જેઠવાના.

વહેલી વાસ સે અવગસે આરીઓ
પણ ભજુને મારી ભોમના, સવેશે સોનનો.
કાપો કઆડીએ, નાખો ને રજુ માંઅ
લેવાલો અલોટે, સંવ સહી નહી સોનની
હુલામણ હ ને, કાનળીએ કપાને નહી,
જેંવા તે જનને, વન વન વીખાસો વાંસડા.
નળીઆ નાખની નળ, ડાર્ક આંદાઅ મેરામણુમા
કરમ છે કપાળ કે, નોનરશે અગર ડેરીઆ
ઘ: વન ઘડીઆં, એરણે આબડીઆં નદી
સઃરઃસુ વાનના, સોની મેરામણ નીપજે.
આના મારી મેરામણ વસે, પતાવસે ક્વળાશ.
જુના બેઅતો હગ મેળ્યુ, નવા આગૌ માસ.
કાગૌ ઘોડો ને કાટવા, ડાર્ક ભમર ભાળું હાથ.
આર્ક આપણી અજરે, ભાળી જેઠવાની જાત
આકઃ અને આની વઢી નદીએ ભરતાં નીર
એક વચનને કારણે, સુકાણાં અમારાં શરીર.
દોયણીઉં મ કાઢ, દોયણીએ મન દૌગે નહી
કમાણ આડોથી કાઢ, હરખી લઉ હુલામણુને.
સાજીઉ મ કાઢ, સાજુના સાટવતલ નહી;
કમાઃ આડોથી કાઢ, જેંવો મારે હુલામણુ જેઠવો.
વાણીઆ નું ક્વાણીઆ, જેર્ક વીચારી ઓલ,
હુલામણુ તારા હાટમાં, સાંદને કપઃ ઓલ.
વાણીઆ નારે હાટડે, અમે દો દો વસ્તુ વીસરા;
એક હેઠાનો હાર, ખીને હુલામણ જેઠવો.
હુલામણુની હઠતાળ, મારા દલમાં દીખલ રહી;
કુંચીઉં રઉં કમાડ, જડેલરાં જેઠવાના.

કુંવર કોઠાળીના દુહા.

રાણો શીઠાઠો ને કુંવરની દોસ્તી થઈ સાથે

હુંગરે રેહેતાં હતાં પછે રાણો ચાચર્ઈ આવ્યો ને કુંવર રઘસાણો.
ઉડી આવ્યો કાગ, કોઈ વનરા વીધીને
સાણે અમણા સેણ, કે ઉડીને આધા ગયાં.
ગર લાગી ને ગુડાગળા, પેટે વધ્યો પીડ
કાગડા કુંવરને ભખુજે, રાણો ચાચઈ રીઆ.
વેણુ લવે ઉતાવળી, નર વાંખળ કે તીર
ચાલો લગાડો શીપરે, રખે સાજણ ઘોઈ ગયાં હોય શીર
તડ તડના એ તીર, કોઈ પાખણુના ડુડે નહીં
સોસરવા અંગ સરીર, સાસે ધાસા જણુના.
બાજે ખીજની ચાલ, ડાકતી ડગલાં ભરે
હસના તે જોડી ચાલ, ભોય કોટાળી કુંવરને
બાજે ખીજના વાળ, કોઈ એક થાય ઉચેરા
કડલગણુ કાબ્ધ નાગ, કોટાળી કુંવરને
કુંવર કાળી નાગણી, સકેલી નખમાં સમાય
તેનું કરતું ડગ ન ભરે, કોટાળી કુંવર કેવાય .
રાણા કે રાત, બીશીને બથ ભરીએ નહી
ઉર અમારાં, કુંવર કે ક્યડાઇ ગ્યાં
કુંવર ઉચળે તો ભલ ઉચળે, તુકાં જ્યચળ હુંગર સેણુ.
કાલે કુંવરને મનાવશું, તું પડોરે પાણુ
રાણો તે રાતે કુલડે, ખાખરની ઘલીઆ
સાજણુ ઘેરા સામદા, જાણે કોક આણુ તવળીસા.
બાજે ખીજના ઉર, હાલે ત્યાં હસખસે.
કે અણીઆરાં ઉર, કોટાળી કુંવરે

સોનસડીયાણીના દુહા.

સોનને સમજવો સાનમાં એના પીતાને કે
કરતું કુંવરીનું વેશવાલ, મેમાન ભજના છે,
મેમાન ભજના છે તે જોડેશ જમ
એને ઘરે ચોરાશી ગામ.
પછે કેસ પીયા હે ખાંદડી, એટલા ચોક લખ્ખીને બાઈ બાડુને હૂ

સ્ોનને સમજવી સાનમાં એના પીતાને કે
સાને વેલને સાખદી કરી ને જુભલીએ જવું ઠેઠ
જતના રજપુત જેહવા, હાબાડગર ઠેઠ
આબાડગર ઠેઠ તે જેહવા, સુખદુખ તે મારા શરીરને વેઠવા
પછે કેસ પીયા રે બાદડી આગળ ગાપને ફાજલ પરી
સ્ોને વેલને સાખદી
સ્ોનુ સગા લઈ માદળીયુ મઢાવીએ તે જમ્મો કામી જેહવા
જમ્મો કામી જેહવા તે જોડે જડી અને સ્ોન રથ જોડી મારગે ચડી
પછે કેસ પીયા રે બાદડી હલામણુ મળે તો મોતીએ વધાવીએ
સ્ોનના સગા લઈ માદળીયુ મઢાવીઆ
સ્ોન સ્ોનાનુ ટીડુ હલામણ કળાએલ મોર
હાલરીઆ ગયા દેશવટે તે દુના પડા વનજોગ
ને દુના પડા વનજોગ તે વડીલોને સાખ ભરી સરકારમા દીધા
પછે કેસ પીયા રે બાદડી સ્ોન વીખડી હલામણુની જોડ
સ્ોન સ્ોનાનું ટીડુ હલામણ કળાએલ મોર

પુતળી સલાટની દુહા.

ભરચી ખરડાની, હીક્ષરડી હઆમાં
તનમાં તે તરડી, પાસ લીઉ ખટકાવે પુતળી
હાથનો વળાવું દીવડો, આગળીઉની વણ્ાવું વાદ
પંડના પડાવું પાટીઆં, સેવું પણે પુતળી સલાટ
તળાવનાં તરશાં, બાંભળ નીર ભાવે નહી
મીઠાં જળ મળે, પાલરપાઆં પુતળી
કંસારા ઘડને કળશીઓ, નાળેલનીએ ઘાટ
પરઘેતરમાં પુતળી, સાચું નાણું સલાટ

મારૂ ઢોળાના દુહા.

ઢોલો ધુવે ધોતીઆં, મારૂ એ ધાન ન ખાય
ખોડા થાને કરશીઆ, ઢોલો ગામ ન જાય
ખોડા થાઉ તો ડંબ ખાઉં, બાંધો મુખે મરૂં

જઉં ઢોલાને સાસરે, તો હરીઅલ મગ થરૂ
જૂણી ડુંભારણીએ ડાંભસું, શીસસુ તાતાં તેલ
ખોડો થાને કરલીઆ, નીરીએ નાગર વેલ
દીઇ ગઐા દળ ડુંગરે, વચ્ચાં ગઆ વડે
કૂટકાળી સાંજના કરલીઆ, રાખો મને રૂણ થઉં
તાણ્યૂ બીડો ગાતરી, વોછી મેલો વાઘ
કાઢો ડાખા પગની કાંકરી, તો માર ભેટાડું આજ.
કર લાગ આ પરદેશમાં, કેની ન કરીએ આલ
તુજકૂ સઘકાવીઆં કાબડીઆ, ને મુંજકૂ દીધી ગાળ
મે જાણ્યૂ રખારી રાયકોા, મે જાણ્યૂ ચારણ ભાટ
ન જાણ્યૂ ઢોલાનો કરલીઓ, નીકર પસલીએ પાણીપાત.
ઢોલા આવને ઢોલીએ, મારના નીમ જાણ્યૂ
કડકસે ને કો સાંભળે, ખેંચી ભલી કમાન.
માર ચલી મોલા ઉપરે, ઉઘાડા મેલી કેશ
જાણ્યે કોા છત્રપતી ચાલીઓ, કોઇ મલક નમાવા દેસે.
ઢોલો ને માર ઇ વઢીઆ, લવીંગની લાકડીઆં
ઢોલે અ માર ને મારીઆં, ફુલની પાંખડીઆં
કાળે માથે માનવી, ભગરે માથે ઉંટ
નગણ્યાને ગુણ કરા, તાણ્યૂ બાંધા ડુંક.
કાંટા ન કરે કરલીઆ, ચરે ખીજાં ઊંટ
લાલેડા લાંઘણ કરે, જોણ્યૂ ચાખેલ ચંદણ રૂપ
માર માર મેં કરા માર ઘેલડીઆં હોય
પાણૂ પીતા કરલીઆને, સઘકાવી કાપડીઆં
માર મેલે લુગડે, ઉભી ઠામ ઠામ
કાંતો સાખુનો કાળ પડો, કાં ઘોખી ગઐલ ગામ
માર જેસી પતલી, જાણ્યૂ ખાંડેની ધાર
જેસે આવી લથડી, ટુકડ ભઆ ત્રણ ચાર
અદણ ચંદ્રાની સાર ઘડી, તે નારે જપડા ચાર
તેના ઘડો એક ચંદલો લઇ ચોટાડો લેલાડ
હાથે ચુડી હેમની, હેમ સરીખા હાથ

મોરા ધડા મારતો જેી. નવરા હનો નાથ
પગવે પાની પતલી, છુટાં નાગફ્ણાં
ધરની સંપત હોય નો, ઢોલા લાવ મારૂ ધરાં
કડાં ખટુકે ખટગ, દોરી તાણે દાશ
ક્રણ ઢોલા તારૂ માયરૂં, મારૂ હું દો ધરવાશ
ખાવું ખોભાયમાં, ભુખ વણુ ભાવે નહી
દુહો દેહમાં ઉલટ વણ આવે નહી

આઢો જામને હોથલ પદમણીના.

મારીશ તુને મોર, કોઇ શીંગણુના બાણુ સાધીને
સત ના તું ચોર, મારા ઓઢાને ઉદાશી ક્યૉ
મોર કે હું ડુંગરનો રાજીઆ, પાપે પેટ ભરૂ
મારી રતે ન ઓલું, તો ટુકે ફ્રાટી મરૂં
ધરા વીના ધાન ન નીપજે, કળ વીના માઢુ નોય
ઓઢાને ધરે ઝખરો, જેને માથે હોથલ પદમણી હોય
જોઇ વોરીઍ જાત, જતે જોખો નહ
પડે પટોળે ભાત, ફ્રાટે પણ ફીટે નહી.
રતન ને રાણુ, ખીજાં કાચાં ને કરમદાં
કાકે જુવાનને જાણુ, રાતે સાઉલે રતની
જાંખાં દીસે જડ, ગોટાળીઁ ઝુંદરણુના
જાજ ભણુજે જુવાર, રેટા વાળી રતનને
જાંખાં દીસે જડ, કોઇ જુંડાળાં જર તણુા
જાજ જાણુજે જુવાર, સોઠલવાળા સઢદને
કોઘ રાખા ઇતીની રાખ, દાખે તોખ ડાકણુ થઘ
નહ સુવાવડનો સોભાગ, ખાખરીયા બાળ કુંવારી
પાનાળા પેરીને, પેલ કાંઠે ચાલેલ નહી
વર તુરી વરમાળ, કઉં કર જલાના ધણી
હયામાં હતી હામ, જાણે હાલરડાં હીંચોળશું
નહી સુવાવડનો સોભાગ, ખાખરીયા બાળ કુંવારી.
ખંડાણુામે જાણુ વરા પેલીને વરસસે.

વરશે દેશ વીદીશ, ઉજ્જળી ને ઉનાળોરો
મે મે કરતાં મે, અમારી જીભડીઉ જય થઉ
તોય ન વરશે મે, ઉજળીને ઉનાળોરો
વાદળે ને ઘટાઉ કાઠીઉ, ડુંગરડાં ડમર
પેડું ભાગ્ય પરમાણુ, વાણ સંચો દુવાધડા
નજર કરો તો નંગ, નકર નેણાને વારો
ઉપર વાડાના સજણ્યું, કાંઠાળે થાથે મારો
હરેરમાં હ્વ્યા, કોઇ જુરો કોટ ભાળીને
નઇ મારે નખાબ, ઉગારે ઉનાનો ધણી
કોઈ હરેરમાં હઇઆં, મરવા નઇ દેવે
કાળે કાળા વરસસે, ઉગારના વાળા એહ
વણુ સગે વણુ સાગવે, વણુ નાતરીએ નેગ
સંધાય વના જીવીએ, તું વના મરીએ મે
સાજણુ તમને વારતાં, નદીએ નાવા મજ્જવ
કૂળીઆમા ગાળે વાવડી, અમે શીચીએ ને તમે નાવ

જુટક દુહા.

નકરીએ નંગ, કોઈ સખીઆ જીવ સંતાપવા
દાઝે પોતાની દેહ, આઠે પોર ઉદાશી ફરે
વાલા આડી વાડ, કાટાળી કરીએ નહીં
ઝમરક લાગે ઝામ, બાખારડીઆ વળની
નાના સુ નેહ, કાળાં સું કરીએ નહીં
સટકેથી દે શાખ, સરવાળુ સોઢે નહી
જેનોને જાણે જીવ, તેના આતમને ઉચાટ ધણી
નહી નાડુમાં નીર, દનસુ મોતીવા મરે
જેતો ન જાણું જીવ, તેના આતમને ઉચાટ નહી
નવે નાડુમાં નીર, દન ઉચો ખાવા ચડે
માઆ રાખો ને માનવીઆ, જગ્ગ રાખોને હેત
ખોળાં ચાલાં માફ કરો, અવગુણ કરા અનેક
અમે માગુ તેલ, તે દી અમુળાં ઉતર દઐ

ફ્ેજ ચટકો મેલ, એલું નહ્ એારીચી
તમે માગ્ તેલ, તે દી કાગ્ુ અ઼઼ુપે નહ્ી
પણ શ્રાગને કુલેલ, આવને લાળે નાખ્ુ વીજરા
ખીજની ઓથીએ, ક઼ાઈ ૬પાવી સે રાસું નહીં
તારા માથાને મોવાળ, મને વાલપ લાગી વીજરા
વઈ જણ્દ આડો વીજણ્ો, જણુલ આડી ભીત
પ્૬હે પડાવા તું કરે, બાળપણુની પ્રીત
ક઼ાઈ વાૠ વળી સુજચ્, ભુડે ભોય ભુ઼ખલીની
એ઼ાલો અસ્વાંર, મીટે ન બાળુ માગડા
તું એટો ને ઙું બાપ, શ્રાં આલખન ૬ આરશી
માંગડો ને મરતે, સમર તુરા આરસી
તારાં નેત્રાં બાળુ તણ્ા, ક઼ાઇ આગે ન વસળાઈ
ગ૱ને ગડકાનોમ, નાડા ભારીથી ના જડઆ
ના ઝાજ મરાએ નહી, સાવાતને હરમત સોત
મોડાને વેલું મોત, સૈાને માથે સુરાવ
અમે પરહેશી પાન, ક઼ાઇ વાતે વીટોળે આવીઆ
ક઼ાણ્ે ન દીખ્ાં માન, ઉડીને અ૱ગાં રીઆં
ક઼ાઈ હા઼કમને વળગેલ વીર, ભવે દુખ ભાગે નહી
ચરખે ચાપો વીર, ઘણ્ેરા ચરખાનો ઘણ્ુ
અમરેલી એ આ્માવેલ, ક઼ાઈ જોડે રમવાને ભાલે
ખરેડીઉ મોલે, ચડી નાર એ ચાંપરાજ
ક઼ાઇ અમરેલીએ આવો, ભડ રમવા ભાલે
ખીજડી સું ભગલે, ચડી નીરખે ચાંપરાજ

(3.)

Specimens of Harauti songs and document writing at Boondi-Kotah (Rajputana.)

HARAUTI SONGS.

___

ગરમીકી ઓસમકો ગીત.

મ્હારા હાલીનજકા✹ હાથમે ગુલાબખરી છડી
મારા કેસરિયાંશી પાયમે કછનારશી † કલી
મારા નોશીલા રીસે જમે દોઈ કામણ્યાં ખડી—ટેક.
બાગાં જાજે સાહિબા ઢાલા લીમુ લાજે ચાર
છોટીસી નારંગી લાજે હીવડલાકો ‡ હાર—મ્હારા૦
મે § ખરનેછિ ઢોલા ઉદયાપુર મત જાઈ
ઉદયાપુરશી ક્ષામણ્ી થાંને રાખેગી બલમાઈ✕—મ્હારા૦
કુવા તું સરનજીવણ્ો ÷ ઢોલા નિર્મલ થારો નીર
ગુલહંજ() પાણ્ી ભરે કોઈ હે હે આડે ત્રીર—મ્હારા૦
ગેલે ÷ ગેલે જવતી ઢોલા ગેલે પડયો રૂમાલ
નીચી હોર ઉડાવતી કોઈ ખેલ ગયો કુલમાલ—મ્હારા૦
ક્યા પીલાકો પેહેરવો ઢોલા ધૂપ પડે રંગ જાઈ
ક્યા લડકાખરી દોસતી કોઈ ભીડ પડે ઉડ જાય—મ્હારા૦
કુવા મેર + કુલામડી ✕ ઢોલા બાગાં મેર ખમૂલ✹
ગોરીજી ઉભી પાતલી જી હાથ ગુલાખી ફૂલ—મ્હારા
હેહે લપટકે ક્યા કરો ઢોલા લાવણ્ુસું હુલ જાય
કા ॥ સાહેવા૦ મારી સન્જાસું ઉડ જાય—મ્હારા .હુલીડાકે
હાથમે ગુલાબખરી છડી, મારા પાતલિયાને વિસરન એક ઘડી.

___

THE SETTING MONSOONS.

કાલીજી આદલિયાંશી રેખ ખીજલી સોહાય% લાગે¶

___

✹ આશીજ. † હાડમ. ‡ the heart. § રોકું છું. ✕ ભિરમાવી. +અમર-
પાણ્ી. () a beautiful woman. ÷ a road. + a side. ✕ creep-
er. ✹ a Babul tree. ॥ ઓદામન (ક્ષ્યું મન). ◦ a Lover.
% sweet. ¶ beautiful.

ચાહી માકા ભવંર* સુજન યાંહી શીરી પ્યા લાગેજ જ —કાલીઝીર

આયાંને § ભંવર ઘડાય રખડી¶ સોહાઈ લાગેજ રાજ —કાલીઝ

કાન્હાને % ઝાલ ઘડાઈ જુઠ્ઠાં ∴ સોહાયાં લાગેજ રાજ —કાલીઝ

મુખડાંને ઐસર લ્યાય ઓતીડાં સોહામાં લાગેજ રાજ —કાલીઝ

હીવડાંને ✦ હાંસ ઘડાય દલડી || સોહાઈ લાગેજ રાજ —કાલીઝ

હાથાંને ચુડલોજ લ્યાય ગજરાં સોહાયાં લાગેજ રાજ

કડ્યાં < ને પટોળોજ લ્યાય સાળુડો સોહાયો લાગેજ રાજ

પગલાં ને પાયલ ╱ લ્યાય ખીંછિયા × સોહાયા લાગે

સીરપર સાળુ લ્યાય કોર સોહાઈ લાગે —યાંહી માકા ભવંર સુજન

આંગળ્યાં ને ખીંછિયાં લ્યાય અણવટ સોહાય લાગેજ

દૃ દૃ ઢાલાંખી ઓટ આરૂણિ છપાયાં રાખોજ +

ચોરી થાંકા બણ્ણુજ સરૂપ હીવડે લગાયાં રાખોજ

શિયાળો.

THE WINTER.

ચાંદા થારી ચાંદણી, ખ્યારી સુતી પલંગ બિછાઈ

જમ જમું જમ દી જમું, કોઈ મારૂણિ ભરતાર

ઝુલડો જુલમ પડે મહારાજ, મેં તો જલું તુમારી સાથ

મારી જોડીલા સરદાર, તુમ આવો મારે પાસ—

**ગજ ખીરીકો |||ચૂંતરો કેસર %% માચ્યો ખીચ

ચોરી માંડ્યો રસસ્યો, આ રંગ ઢોલ્યા કે ખીચ—જડો.

કારી તેં કેરી ભલી, ખાખાં ભલાં અનાર

ચોરી તો માણી ભલી, ખેંચ્યાં ભલાં કવાંણુ†—જડો.

કાચી કેરી કચકચી, કોઈ ખાય છિ‡ હો ચાર

મીઠી લાગે આંબલ્યું, કોઈ અંતપરાઈ નાર—જડો.

---

*a lover. § માથાની રાખડી. ¶ રાખડી. % ears ∴ પી-
પળપતાં (પાંદડીઓ) + હૈયું-છાતી. || હાર. < કટિ. ╱ (વાંકુ ઘરેણું પગનુ
પાયલ) × ઘુઘરા. + concealing under a shield, keep her
screened from rain. ✦ Winter. ** જન્મ ભૂમિ. ||| ઓતરો %% મચ્યો,
† a bow. ‡ had eaten.

તેલ બળે ભાતી. બળે, નાંવ દિયાકો% હોય

એરા જળે જરસ્કા. નાવ પિયાકો હોય—જડૉ૦

જીવવાસું મરવો ભલો, કયું માંઘ્યો ઘરબાર

માર મરૉડૉ સોઈ રહ્યો, કુણ કર ગુમાન—જડૉ૦

કથા પીળાકો પેરવો (ખુદ પડ્યા રંગ જાય) for the other

ધૂપ પડ્યા રંગ જાય

કયા લડકૉક્ષી હોસ્તી ભીડ પડે નટ જાય—જડૉ૦

માર્યા રોજ ગેરી.

મારૂજી આજ કુંગરડાંશી પડ્યો, જડે માર્યા હરણા રોજ

રતન શિખાળો રાજન આઘ્યો.

મારૂજી આજ માળાં મેં શી પડ્યો જડે માર્યા હાળી લોગ—॥

ગોરીરા મારૂ રતન શિયાળા,

મારૂજી આજ બાગાં મેં શી પડ્યો જડે માર્યા દાઉમ દાબ—ગોરી૦

મારૂજી આજ હતામાં શીર્ર પડ્યો જડે માર્યાં મરડ પટેલ√—ગોરી૦

મારૂજી આજ ધૂણ્યાં ને શી પડ્યો જડે માર્યાં રેડવાંજી લોગ—ગેરી૦

ઘાક્ષી તોડ વઘ કર્યો લે મુસળઝી મો સૉઇ—ગોરી

મારૂજી આજ બનજરાંશી પડ્યો જડે માર્યા બાણ્મ લોગ—ગોરી૦

મારૂ સ્ક્ષળે સ્ક્ષળે આપક્ષી ઉનાળે મારા બાપક્ષી.

ચોમાસે માંક્ષ નાનેરે** ખ઼નાવ*—ગોરી૦

મારૂ સ્ક્ષળે સ્ક્ષળે ઓઢણ્યાં ઉનાળે માંને પામર્યાં

ચોમાસે માંને ધનક્ષ રંગાવ—ગોરી૦

મારૂજી સ્ક્ષળે સ્ક્ષળે આવરા‡ ઉનાળે માંસે ડાગળાઇ

ચોમાસે માંને ચોબારા કરાઘો—ગોરી૦

મારૂ સ્ક્ષળે સ્ક્ષળે ખીચડી ઉનાળે માંને લાપશી.

ચોમાસે માંને લાડુડા જમાવો—ગોરી૦

મારૂજી આજ મ્હેલામાં શી પડ્યો જડે માર્યા હાડા રાવજી ભેય—ગો૦

%a lamp. ||cultivators. ¶ places of general resort. √ નાત

પટેલ. ** મોસાળ. * send. † એક જાતની ઓઢણી. ‡ ઓરડા. § અમ્મારી.

THE SUMMER.

નીમડલીકા લાંબા તીખા પાન નીમડલી રતનાળી ઝાલો રે

ગયાજી માકારાજ

કુણુને તોડ્યા ઈંકા પાન કુણુને સતાયો હર્યાે રૂખડો

બાઇજીને તોડ્યા ઈંકા પાન દેવરિયા ચરતાળા* ને સતાયો હર્યાે રૂખડો

બાઇજીને સાસરિયે ખનાવ દેવરજીને ખનાવ રાજજીશી ચાકરી

ઉબીછિ ધન આવરિયાકે બહાર કાગદ આયા હાડા રાવજીકા મારારાંજ

છોરી દાસી મેહેલાં દઃખ્સોત જોય કાગનજ઼ આંચા હાડા રાવજીકા મારારાજ

દઃખ્લો જોતાં લાગી બડ વાર ચાંદાકે ઉજ્વળે કાગળ બાંચલ્યો

એડે છેડે લખી છિ સલામ અદ બચ લખિયા મારૂણીકા આળંઆજી

મારારાજ

આળગડીઁ માકા સસરાજી ખનાય આપસી માણ઼ો ઉંચા ડાગલા

માકા રાજ

સસરાજીકા જોખા જોખા પૂત ઓકયું જવે સુંદર ચાકરી માકા રાજ

આળગડી માકા જોઠજી ખનાય થાં રત માણ઼ો ઉંચા ડાગળા

જોઠજીશી ધારાધૂરી નાર નત ઉડ માંડે સુંદર રસણ઼ોજી

આળગડી માકા દેવરિયા ખનાય થાં રત માણ઼ો ઉંચા ડગળા

દેવરિયાજ઼ી ગોણ઼ે આઇ નાર ॥ મેહેલાંમે ઝરપે સુંદર એક્લી

આળગડી થાંકાં ભાયલાં% ખનાય થાં રત માણ઼ો ડાગળા

ભાયલાંજ઼ી રૂપાં રૂડી નાર ઓંકયું જવે સુંદર ચાકરી.

આળગડી માંકાં નણુદોઇ બનાય

નણુદોઇ પરાયો પૂત ઓ કયું જવે સુંદર ચાકરી.

અતરામે ઇજીસકે પૂત મા કાંઇ રાજ ચાલ્યા ચાકરી

ચીતરામે થે ઇજીસપૂત થાંકાં ધિરાજ઼જ ઘોડલે ચડેજી માકા રાજ

ઉબી છિ+ ધન આવરિયાજ઼ી બ્હાર સરદ ગરમીકા ઓબોઇ એહે ગયો

લીનાં મારૂણી હીવડે લગામ આંસું પૂછ્યાં પીળી પામરી.

જતાં હસ્કર માંને શીખ જ્યું ચત લાગે થાંકા ચાકરી

જતાં ઇઁઆજ્યો થાંકે ગોય અશી ઘોડાકા આજ્યો પરગણ઼ો

---

*(અટક્ચાળા.) †a lamp. ‡wo men. ¶ (ચાકરી). ॥ (પેહેલ વેહેલી આવેલી) % friends. + was. §sorrow

જતાં ઈંથાન્યો થાંકો પૂત સાંરી છાગાંમે* જનન્ને પાલણ્ો
જતાં ઈંથાન્યો થાંકો ખ્યાહ્ો છોટીશી લાડી કટેલર ઘર આવન્જે

સાસ્ માંને સાંગરિયાશી+ હુંશ ડગભ્યાંx તોડણ્ સાસ્ ઉંચલી†
સાસ્ માંને ડગભ્યાં તોડયાં ચ્યાર ગોરા પૂંચામે કાંઢો બાગોયોજી
સરવર થારી ઉંચી નીચી સરવર પાળ પાંપ પતડાય‡ ઘોઅ્ા ઘોવતી
પાંડયા થારો પતડયો બાંચ સુણ્ાય કતરા દિનામે રાજન આવશે
ગોરી જતરા પીંપળ પાન અતરા દિનામે રાજન ઘર આવશે.

પાંડયા થારી કાઢું આાળુ જીભ આગ ઘતુરો થારે મુખ ભરૂ
ગોરી તૂ§ રૂપાં ધણી સરૂપ નેણ્ાંકે ભીતર તને લે ચલું
પાંડયા નેણ્ામે સુરમો સાર નાર પરાઈ થારી ન હોય માકા રાજ
ગોરી તું રૂપ ધણી સરૂપ ગાલ ચમટીમે લે ચલું
પાંડયા થારી ચમટીસે રૂપયા પરખરે નાર પરાઈ થારી ન હોય
ગોરી રૂપ ધણી સરૂપ ઢાલ પડઘટમે‖ લે ચલું
થારી પડઘટમે કેસરસુ પાર્યાં મેત નાર પરાઈ થારી ન હોય
ગોરી તું રૂપાં ધણી સરૂપ ઢાલ જગલમે સુંદર લે ચલું
થારી બગલમે દુપટા અંગુ ચાલે મેલ
પાંડયા થારા ઘરમે રાંડ કુરાંડ કોરા કળસ્યામે રાંધે ધુઘરી
આમ માર્જી માજમ રાત સુતી માર્ણી આણ જગાઈ
વાર બાઘજી થાંશી જીભ ખાંડ શેકાલી થાંકો મુખ ભરૂ

I.

From Durbar to શ્રીજીકા ભંડારકા ખીલાદર
ભટ લખમીનંદજી ગેરહાજર હુઆ. તાંકે બહુજહેં ખરચ સાર ઉધાર ખાતે દીનો રૂા. ૭૦૦૦ અંકે સાત હજાર એક હાલીકા. તીકો લિખ્યો મંડા લીનો. તિમ થાંકે સિરકારજી તરફ સો ગોવ ધરતી છ ને છ તનખવામેસું ને થાં કે પ્હોંચેગા થાંકા રૂપિયા બ્યાજ કસર સુ પ્હોંચાં નિકાલસ હોશિ. બીચ કોઈ ઉજર કરશી નહિ. પરવાનગી મુનશી રતનલાલ મિતિ J. S. 1 S. 1909. તાલીખ દફ્તર.

---

* સાળાં, પરસાળ. + સાગરિયો. x જુઘ. † નીકળી. ‡ આળ ટીપણું.
§ sing. ‖ ખોળ.

I. a.

શ્રી ભારફ્ત ભંઝરી જમનાદાસજી પાંડે ગોપાળજી કિસ્તુ શા. બ્યાજ
સુ ચુકયાં જમા હોયાં. આજીવિકા નિક્ષલસ હો જાશે મિતિ વૈશાષ
શુદ ૭ સં. ૧૯૦૯ દા. મેહેતા દ્વારકાલાક્ષ હાથકા. બહુજી માહારાજજી
હજૂર માંધ્યે ભારફ્ત પાસવાન ચમના એવીસ્સાઈ ્હાન્ન દેતુ ધની હજૂર
રાજ ખુસી સોને સહિ.

II. Receipt.

અસાડ બદિ ૧૦ રૂપિયા નગદી હજર દોય ઓર ચીઠી હજર દોય
ષી માસ બાસાખી લિકા અંકે રૂપિયા ચાર હજર હાક્ષીકા. માસ્ફૃત પાંડે
ગોપાળજી મુનીમ બલ્હૃદેવ્જી ફ્રેતદ્ધર નરસંગલાલ મેહેતા ગોપાળજી કિસ્તુ જ–
મા. હવેલીને બહુજી મહારાજજી પાસ્ફ હસ્તે મેહેતા દ્વારક્ષલાલ ફ્રાસવાન
ચમના ઓખે મંગલાકિસ્તું જમા ખર્ચં મિતિ સાવણ બદ૧ સં. ૧૫૬૦. ખત
પેટે આયા.

III. Gift.

અપરંચ કોટાદ્ધ રાજજી જાગિરી ગાંવ ડાહોવીજી. ધરતી નાગ જમીન.
દુકાના બાગ કુવો માફ્ષી પોતીકો નીમ સીમસે હવેલી બારે છે. શ્રી દરબાર–
ષી તરફ્થી પુન અર્થ તાંખા પતર પરવાના સોમાં ખાવાં પાવાં છાં જે
તાર તાર ભેટ છે પુજર્થ આગે સો એહ્નુખોટી મંદર ઉક્ષ છે જે. આખાં
પાયાં જાશેર્ઈ માફ્ક ભાર્ઘબંધ બગાબત લાગતી વળગતી કો દેવરજેઠ કોર્ઈ
આગે પાછે ઉરસો કરે નહિ કરે તો જૂઠો માલક હું ષું. સો મને ભેટ કરદીના
સો સદા સરવદા શ્રીજીજી સેવા અંગીકાર રહેશિ.

and concludes

મારાં સો વરસ પૂરાં હોયાં ચારો ઉત્તર કરમ ક્ષસ દીજે માખા ધરક્ષ
રીત માફ્ક. ફેર શ્રીજી માલક છે. ભારફ્ત પાંડે ગોપાળજીજીસું ધરમ કરમ
પતર શ્રી બહુજી મહારાજકા હુક્મસું માંધ્યો. શ્રીજીકા ચરણારવિંદામે
ચત મન સેવા ભેટ કરી મારા ચાકર ભેડકો રોજગાર પ્રતફ્પૂત ગૈલાયુગો
ખેડી દાહિતા કરી ખંદાડી કરે ને આગેશું ગુસાંઈજી મહારાજકા ધરમેં
રીત છે જીકો કરદીના જે ખાયાં પાયાં જાશે. ધને મેરે જે શ્રીજી થું એભુ–
ખ હોશિ. સભ તરહસે દુઃખ ધરમાં દેખશિ. શ્રીજી કા સરણો લીના છે
ફેર દગો ફોસીકો સગો છે નહિ ચો જવાબ રાજ ખુશીસું માંધ્યો છે. ભંડા–
રી જમનાદાસ મુનીમ બલદેવ ઈ ભંડારને ખેડંગો. જે ન સુણેગો જીકો અ–
પરાધ શ્રીજી આગે છે. મિતિ વૈ. શુ. ૧૦ સં. ૧૫૧૦

IV.

સાધેશ્રી ચિરંજીવ ગંબલા સોંબડડ બહુજી મહારાજક્ષી આસીસ
વંચને. અપરંચ બડા મહારાજકે ઓર છોટા મહારાજકે દોની ભાયાં કે
આપુસમે કબેજ છા તિ બાબત ગાંવજાગિરી અને દેખો ચુકાવા સાર શ્રીજી-
કા ભંડારને રૂપિયાં સાત હજાર અકે સાત રૂપિયા સાત હજાર લીના ઈ પેટે
તનખવા મેહેલ્યા અબ તુમને ગાંવજાગિરી અસઆખકો માલક તું છે મારે તે
સિવાય ઓર કુણ છે યાકા રૂપિયા ચુકયાં ગાંવજાગિરી યાંકાંથી સમાલલીને.
મિતિ જેઠ શુ. ૫ સં. ૧૯૧૧ ઘા. ગણુપતલાલક્ષ હાથથા. સાખ ત્રવાડી
આઉતરામની. સાખ ગોરાણી જમનાંબાઈક્ષ. સાખ મેહેતા જમેતરામક્ષી. બ-
જુ બાઈ રાધાક્ષી. ચિરંજીવ રામચંદરક્ષી. સાખ મેહેતા અરજનલાલક્ષી. સાખ
બાઈ ગંગાક્ષી. સાખ મેહેતા કૃતેહલાલ અમૃતલાલક્ષી. સાખ મેહેતા બલદેવક્ષી.

V.

Order addressed:—આને ગાંવોંકા બિલ્લાદાર પટેલ પટવારીદ-
સો યાંકા ગાવઅે ભટજી શ્રી મહારાજક્ષી ડોલ્યાંથી ધરતી વાહેદક્ષી ગાંવ શ્રી
જીકા ભંડારક્ષ બિલ્લાદારકા સુંપરત છે.

Partition made in 1908 and Fargati also given.

ભંડાર હાલાને માલુમ કરાધ સો આગે આજીવિકા સરકારને આધા
આદ બાંટ સં. ૧૭૭૮કા સાલમે દ્વારગ ત્યાં આપસમે મંડયા દીનિ છિ અર
અે દોને જુદા જુદા હો ગિયા વાંકા વાસ્તે માં સુરિયા નહિ યાંકા વાસ્તે
માંસુરિયા નહિ પાછે ભટજી શાંત હો ગિયે જબ સિરકારક્ષ હુકુમસુ ગાંવ
ડોલ્યાં વાંકા ઉત્તર કરમકા ખરચ પેટે ભંડારા બાંકા સુંપરત કરા દીના.

VI. VII.

મેને આકોધા નક્ષા બાંસથુનીકા ઉદકભટજી શ્રીજી મહારાજકે તિંક્ષ
પટેલ પટવારીદસે અપરંચ યેં ગાંવ શ્રી ગોરધનનાથજીકા બડા ભંડાર તાલકે
લેણામે તનખવાછો જે નિકીલેશકર ભટજીકર્ઈ પાછો બાલફર બક્ષો
છે સોધાંક બિલ્લાદારકે સવાધીન કર તહેશીલક્ષી કોડી આવે જે યાંહે
ભરજો ભંડારાલાઅે રૂપિયા અેકદીને મતો પરવાનગી શા ગણેશ રામ-
મુનીમ. મિતિ બાદરવા શુદ ૮ સં. ૧૯૨૪, માલીખ દઘતર.

VIII.

દરબારકો યો હુકુમ છે ઓર ગાંવડાંબ્યોક્ષી તેહેસીલ આપ કરાવો મતો
જમીદારા બેહિ જમા રાખો લેખોહોની પડખો સિરકારકા દઘતરમે મેલાઅો
ખેખારતે ખેણાહેણા કરેગા જે સરકાર કદાશિ હુકુમ પુગાદીનો છે. વા ક્રૈ-
જદારસે રૂખર કેહે દીની છિ. યાંકી તનખવાક્ષે યાંકા ગાંવઠા હોલ હોગા
જક્ષી તેહેશીલ ન કરાશિ. કાગદ બાંય હલકારોક્ષી લાર પાછે મોકલને
ઓર આધક્ષ બિલ્લાદારે બેજને. મિતિ ક્રા. ખુદ ૭ઠ સં. ૧૯૩૨.

GUJERATI ENTERPRISE IN THE 16TH CENTURY.

Here is a curious testimony to Gujerati enterprise in 1510 A. C. in commercial transactions between the Strait of Babel Mandeb and Malacca. The commentaries of Albuquerque make this important discovery :—

......" There is one fact brought into bold relief by the commentaries of Albuquerque, and it is this that the Guzeratees held naval supremacy from the Strait of Babel Mandeb and the mouth of the Persian Gulf to Malacca. They were the great carriers all over the Indian Ocean. The Hindoos are not generally credited with being a maritime people. But it is expressly said of those of Goa (1506) 'they were a maritime race, and more inured to the hardships of the sea than all other nations, built ships of great burden, and navigated the coasts.' And again, in respect to Ceylon and the Far East—' The Guzerattees understand the navigation of those parts much more thoroughly than any other nation on account of the great commerce they carry on in these places '.........
' This much is certain, that on the Asiatic Side, say from Malacca to Calicut, and from Calicut to Jeddah, the bulk of the overland traffic was carried on by the people of Gujerat all through the Middle Ages, whence their cargoes were trans-shipped on Arab buggalows to Cosseur, and thence by caraven to the Nile, which bore them on its flood to Rosetta."

Bombay Gazette, June 17th 1893 p. 4.

Specimens of Kachhi Songs.

(4.)

કચ્છી કાફીઓ.

૧.

કર કલમેજ઼ તવાર ગાફલ સાહેબ નામ સંભાર
મન મરીજ઼ વેને મૂરખ મનડા।૦ કર કલમેજ઼ તવાર૦ ૧.
જ્યાંનું આવ્યે તું હેઠ્લો સેં તુ ઓીઞા* સંભાર
જ઼મ અચીધો તોજે જીવ ગિનશુ તોકે મોકમાં ડીધો માર
મન મરીજ઼ વેને મૂરખ મનડા૦ ૨.
ખ્યો ને ખારાયો ઊયો નાં અલાજે હિકડો રંગ રખજ
બધી સમો તો ખંખજ એલી પાણુ માંધા પાર
મન મરીજ઼ વેને મૂરખ મનડા કર કલમેજ઼ તવાર૦ ૩.
ડુંગર સારો ડોયો જેકે ભિલ'સાં ચારો માર
ક઼ંધ અઆંગો પેઅનજે મથડે સંધડો ભાર
મન મરીજ઼ વેને મૂરખ મનડા કર કલમેજ઼ તવાર૦ ૪.
કલમું પડાં કુલધ઼ૃ‡ ભિજ઼ મુંજે તન મેં ઉન તવાર.
હિરો શા એ મુંરશીદ મુંજ ખુકે પલમેં લંગાએ એપાર.
મન મરીજ઼ વેને મૂરખ મનડા કર કલમેજ઼ તવાર૦ ૫.

૨.

ખુદા જે નાં ગિનાં થારો, રાયો રઙ§ મેં મું વિસાર્યો
ચિત ચાર્યો મું વિસાર્યો, વળી દિલડી દિલ વાર્યો
ભિંજ઼ રાયો ને'∥ નિભાર્યો છઉયો કુડખાંઢ સચ સાર્યો
ખુદા જે નાં ગિનો થારો રાયો ર મેં મું વિસાર્યો. ૧.
નિત નિમાજ઼ું જિકર પડો રખો રોજ઼ સાંઇ%‌ સંભાર્યો
ધણીજે ખ્રા ખ્રમ ધાર્યો મુછ઼રો સૈયદ સાર્યો
ધમ ગુજ઼ર્યો સજનુ સાર્યો ખુલી વાઢું ડી મ ગાર્યો

---

* દિવસ. † યમદ્ભૃત. ‡ સાચી યકિન. § જીવ. ∥ સ્નેહ. % ઈશ્વર.

પુણી પીર કે પાર પાર્યા ખણો નેજુન શાણુ* ન્યાર્યા
ખુદા જે નાં ગિના યારો રાખ્યો રૂ મેં મું વિસાર્યાં. ૨.
ઉમર ચે સુણો સખ યારો વસિલો પાક પીઆરો
લંગાંધ્ધે લખીઉ શિતારો પડો કલમો વાધેધ વાર્યો
ખુદા જે ના ગિના યારો રાખ્યો રૂ મેં મું વિસાર્યાં. ૩.

૩.

અલાજી નેસ અંધર ભિંજ યાર, ઉમર સાંગીડા વિડી સારીયાં
લિખાઈ અરજ મોક્ષી અષાણુન, અધા કાશિદ તો ન પુંજાઈ
અલા પાંજે માડુડન જ હાલ હવાલ, ઉમર સાંગીડા વિડી સારીયા
અલાજી નેસ અંધર ભિંજ યાર ૧.
ઉમર તુઇજા પટ ન પેરીંધીશ માગ માઠનજ ખીંણા જલોંધ
અલા પાંજ લોઈફ અબાણુજ લાલ ઉમર સાંઇગિડા વિડી સારીયાં
અલાજી નેસ અંધર ભિંજ યાર. ૨.
બિટન પાસે ચઢ્યા ચિંગારીન અલા તડતડ કન તવારૂ,
અલા પાંજ માડુડા ચારિયે ભિઢાં માલ ઉમર સાંગીડા વિડી સારીયાં
અલાજી નેસ અંધર ભિંજ યાર. ૩.
જીધ ચયે આઉઉનીને આઇઆં અલા શીનું કેંશાણુ સાઇઆં
અલા પાંજે માડુડનજ કોલકરાંર ઉમર સાંગીડા વિડી સારીયા
અલાજી નેસ અંધર ભિંજ યાર. ૪.

૪.

રખ શરમ તું કર ભંલાઈ અલા ડાઢી ધુનીયાં લોભ ઘણો
રખ શરમ તું.
સારી દુનીયા મતલબજ મતલબ સંગ સગાઈ
મતલબજ અધા માતપિતા અલા મતલબજ બેણ ભાઈ
અલા અલા ડાઢી ધુનીયાં લોભ ઘણો રખ શરમતું. ૧.
જે તું આવ્યે દેખશે બંધા સારી દુનીયા ભાઇ

---

*સામું. ઼તાર. ૌરેશમ. ડુખ્યો. ૨ દિલ કંને આપુ ?

જમ અચીંઘ્રિ ઓચ્યંઘો અલ્લા વેંઘો રામ રમાઇ
ડાઠી ઘુનીયા   ૨.
આડા પહેાર સંબાયો ક્યેા યાદ ઇલાઇ
સચ્ચેા નાલેા અલાને જિન ખલકત* દુલ બનાઇ
ડાઠી ઘુનીયા   ૩.
દુનીયાં મે જીયણ† થોડો એક દીન થાને રાઘ‡
હરદમ તાં મિશકીન ચવે મું ખેાની અલાસેં લાઇ
ડાઠી ઘુનીયાં   ૪.

૫.

અલ્લા મિલઘો મૂક કેડી ઘડી વાઠું તાં ન્યારીઆડું ખડી ખડી
ઉબીની વાઠું ન્યારીમાં શેણુનજી તાં ખડી ખડી. ૧.
હિનીની નેણે ન માણ્યો રેારેા લાઘ જડી
અલ્લા મિયાં વાઠું તાં ન્યારીયાં ખડી ખડી અલ્લા મિલઘો મુકે કેડી ઘડી ૨.
શેણુ અસાંજે હૈડે મેં વિસરેા તા ન ઘડી
અલ્લા મિયાં વાઠું ત્યાં ન્યારીયાં. ૩.
હરદમ તાં મિશકીન ચવે વેને મનડા મરી
અલ્લા મિયાં વાઠું ત્યાં ન્યારીયાં ૪.

૬.

અલ્લા મુંજે દિલ મેં શોખ ઇલ્લાઇ અલ્લા મુંજે મન મદિને મેં લગો
પાર ઉતારા તડેં થીંઘો જડેં માલક મેર કરીંઘો
વારસ શી હાણે વારસ થીંઘો મેર કરીંઘો. આપેં અલ્લા &c.
મુંજે મન મદિને મેં લગો મુંજે દિલ મેં શોખ ઇલ્લાઇ અલ્લા
હે હકીકત અલ્લા વાળી લાજ નખી ઐયો✠ કોષ ન વાળી
કુદરત કિનજી ન્યાર નિરાંની માલક અય મુખ્તારે અલ્લા
મુંજે મન મદિને મેં લગો   ૨.
હજ જકાત ફરજ હે કરના રોીશે રોજ નિમાજ પડના

----
* દુનીયા. † જીવવું. ‡ રાખ. § જેજ. ✠ ખીજો.

યાધ રખો આખર કે મરના ડાઢી* હૈ શિરકાર†
મુંજે મન મદીને મેં લગો ૩.
મિશકીન એ કર જિકર અલાઈ શ્રીં ક્યામત કામ જે આઈ
પાક નખી બરીંધા ગોવાધ,‡ કાજ થીંધા નિશ રોજ અલા
મુંજે મેંન મદીને ૪

———

૭.

માઐલે નરણે ન્યાર ભોરા મન માયલે નરણે ન્યાર૦
માંઐ છે નિરધસ નિરાત્કાર માઐલે નરણે ન્યાર
ચેત કરીને ચાલો પ્રાણી માયાજે મત લાભ. માયલે નરણે ન્યાર ૧.
કુડી કાયા કુડી માયા ખોટો અય સંસાર
ઝાંઝ પખાવાજ નોબત વાજે મુરલા કરે મલ્હાર
અમૃત જલ જિતે દ્વારા વરસે વરસે મેઘ મલ્હાર
માઐલે નયણે ન્યાર ભોરા મન માયલે નરણે ન્યાર ૨.
પેલા તો ગામના મિંદીર મોટા તેના છે બે પાર
એક શેરે શત્રુ છે ખીજ મિત્ર ભારી
માઐલે નરણે ન્યાર ૩.
ઉંચાતો દેવલ ધજ ફરકે મંજ જોગી જટાધાર
પીર ગોશમામદ દ્યાજ મંગે મંગે સમુદ્ર પાર
માઐલે નરણે ન્યાર. ૪.

———

૮.

ખ્યો ન કોય આરો જોગી સાહેબ ના' સંભારોરે૦
બિના મહમધ મિશકીન ચવે બિયો ન કોઇ આરારે
મોર નખુવત ડિયા નખીકું શાન કુરાન ઉતાર્યોરે
બિના મહમધ મિશકીન ચવે ૧.
હા દુનીયા દિન ચાર જિયારે,§ કુડો ફૂલ પસારોરે
બિના મહમદ મિશકીન ચવે ૨.

———

મોત ન માણ્યી લૂટે ગિરે દિન રાત વજાવે નગારાંરે
વિના મહમદ મિશકીન ચવે ૩.

૯.

મસ્ત પીઆઆલો પીતમડેંજે અલા જેંકે રંગ લગો રાજુલજે*
શુમળ મેડીજી મોલ અડાયો જેંકે રંગ લગો રાજુલજે
બેલા કારણ મજનું મસ્તાના દિલ લુટ લીયો લેલાજે
મસ્ત પીઆરસો પ્રીતમડેંજે ૯૦
હિનડે જાંધીકે† હુઃખડા પધડા અલા જેંકે પેચ પ્યો તે પુનલજે
મસ્ત પીઆલો ૯૦
આશક શાચે અઇઆં ઉનજે અશરફ શાચે ઐઆં ઉનજે
અલા જેંકે હાલ પ્યો હય હયજે
મસ્ત પીઆલો ૯૦

૧૦

મોલેતાં મિલાયો રબ વછોડે વિરાયો અધીજી પુનલજ મોલે મિલાયો
પાંઇજે પિરનજા ઉડતી સુંઝાણ્યા, ઉડતી સુંઝાણ્યા‡
આંઉ વાચા ન જાણ્યાં અધીઉ પુનલજય મોલે મિલાયો
મોલેતાં મિલાયો ૯૦
પાંઇજે પિર ચનલ્યા § આંઉ લંગલાં ભનાઇઆં
તેમેં જારીઉ છડાઇઆં, અધીજી પુનલજય મોલે મિલાયો
મોલેતાં મિલાયો ૯૦
પાંઇજે પીરનલા આંઉ કાગ ઉડાઇઆં
આંઉ△ ફાલ પુછાઇઆં અધીઉ પુનલજય મોલે મિલાયો
મોલેતા મિલાયો ૯૦
શા લતીફ ચવે કાશી હકાની કાશી એકાની÷ કલમે કુરાનીરે
અધીઉ પુનલજય ૯૦

---

* જીવ, આત્મા. † ખંદા feminine. ‡ ઓળખું. § આશક માશુક માટે.
△ ફાલ=ભવિષ્ય. ÷ હકાનીઃ સારી.

૧૧

સામીડા તુ નાં સંભાર કે દન અય તો જીવણુહાર૦
કોડી કોડી માયા જોડી જેતેં લાખો કરોં હજ્જર
વેધી વેરી જે અયા ખાલી વેરા હથ પસાર
કેદન અય તો જીવણુહાર સામીડા તું નાં સંભાર ૧.
પંચ વખત નિમાઝજ રોજ ત્રિ ગુજર યાર
કર સાહેબજી ખંદગી ઘડીએ પલક ક્રીમ વિસાર
કેદન અયતો જીવણુહાર ૬૦ ૨.
એક ઘમ ધારા દોસ્તન જો મું તાં વઘ વિઝાઘ અયજમાર
લેખો થીંઘા સાહેબસેં ઉતે આકઝખાર કોર્ન ન ક્રામ
કેદન અયતો જીવણુ હાર સામીડા ૬૦ ૩.
ડાઢા દીં અરઘ કિયામ તજ મિશકીન ચાવે તો પોકાર
કાજી થીંઘા કુલનજે રબ વાયઘ આપે આપ ક્હાર
કેદન અયતો જીવણુ હાર ૬૦ ૪.

૧૨

ખારોચી અય ઓલી શુણીયાંતાં માન શરઈ.: થીઆં
ઇઈ રંગીઈ ધીસ રતસે ચિતરાઘમ ચોલી
શુણીયાંતાં માન શરઘ થીઆં ૬૦
કોથે રંગાઈ મું કંજરી ચાઘર ને ચોલી
શુણીયાંતાં માન સરઘ થીઆં
દિઠી જામ પુનલજી લખ મથે (સીંઘી) ખોલી
શુણીયાંતાં માન શરઘથીઆં ૬૦
અધીરાં નું ઝાખ લનખી ચહે ડુંગર મથે ડોલી
શુણીયાંતાં માન શરઈ થીઆં ૬૦

૧૩

જિતે વેંઘો સારો જાય આંઈ પણુ વેંધીસ ઉન મકાન

.: ખુશી થાઈ. ૧રંગીશ-રંગ દઇશ.

ઉમર આયો ઓચંઘો ૫ખે મિંજ ૫ઙ
અરજુ* કરીયાંતિ બંધી આંઙ હલૈા જિત વેંઘૈ સારૌ જય
પેર ૫ટૌરા મારઘ ઉમરચે ડાલર લાય ઘણહાર
અરજું કરીયાંતિ બંધી આંઙ ૬૦
૫નનીા† સૌય ને ૫ટૌરૌ ઉમર મ્યાં, લખનજી અય મુંજ લૌઘ
અરજું કરીયાંતિ બંધી આંઙ ૬૦
અઘ‡ લાઇબિં તું કરીઐ ઉમરમીઆં વેને તું મનતાં મરી
અરજું કરીયાંતી બંધી આંઙ ૬૦
અઘીઙની શાખ્ય લતીબ્ચવે મીયાં ઘનેતાંન વરી
અરજું કરયાંની બંધી આંઙ ૬૦

૧૪

શાહેઅ નામ સંબારૌ વાલા, સાંઈ નામ સબ્સેં નિરાલા૦
તનજી તસખ્ખી કરલે હમેશાં, મનજી કરલે માલા
સાંઈ નામ સબ્સે નિરાલા શાહેઅ નામ સંબારૌ વાલા. ૧.
એક દિન નમડા જીવને જની કંઘૈા શેણુ ન વાલા
સાંઘ નામ સબ્સે નિરાલા ૬૦ ૨.
કર રૌશનાઘ મન મેં રજઞઇ હમેશાં અંઘર || મિંજ ઉજવાલા
ડીની અસર ને મિશકીન ઓલે પાક નખ્ખી કું હવાલા
સાંઈ નામ સબ્સેં નિરાલા ૬૦ ૩.

૧૫

ડે મૌકલ વેંઘી મરી મુંજ જાન જાનબ+ સેં જડી
જાન જાનબસેં જડી મુંજ જાન જાનબ સેં જડી. ડે મૌકલ ૬૦
ખડી હૌઇશ ખ્યૂવ△ ને આંજ% અચ્યુ લાય અંખ તે ફરઘ
લૌક ચૌંચા ૫ઘ ચરઘ મુંજ જાન જાનબ સેં જડી ડે મૌકલ ૬૦

---

*હાથ જોડી અરજ કરું છું. †તારા ૫ટવસ્ત્ર પાંચસૌના છે પણ
મારી ધાખળી લાખની છે. ‡જુલમ. §ઈશ્વર. || કૌડૌ (અંતઃકરણુમા.) +ઈશ્વર
△ કૂઆ. %તમારા આવવાને માટે મારી આંખ ફરકતી હતી.

ઉડામી વિજ તું ની કાગદ મુકે કે ખબર ખીં* જી ખરી
દોસ્ત ઘીધા દિલ ભરી મુંજ જાન જાનબસેં જડી કે મોકલ ૬૦
જમલ તોજે જોશ કાં દુઃખ સેં પવે નુંગર ફુરી
ફેર ડીધા/ દિલ ભરઈ મુંજ જાન જાનબસેં જડી કે મોકલ ૬૦
અધીકઈં શાખ લતીઅ ચવે મુકે મોખ† મિલંધા સો ભરી
આંઢ પણ વેંધીશ માગ ભરી મુંજ જાન જાનમસેં જડી. કે મોકલ ૬૦

૧૬

આયા જીખ જાન ઘર મેરે, મિલજીજ કયુંસ મેરબાની
મિલજીજ† કયુંસ મેરબાની અચજીજ કયુંસ મેરબાની
આયા જીખ જાન ઘરમેરે. ૬૦
બસેં આ/ખેં તું જી આવ્ખેં સજણ શિણુ શાણા સોફેરા
આંઢ આંખે ઘર કદમ તું ઘંખે, ફરીઆં જીખ જાન દુરબાની
આયા જીખ જાન ઘરમેરે. ૬૦
કુંજન કુણુકે અવાંજન શાણુ ખુદ તાં તેંનેં શરમાયા
મ ખુસી ચે મૂલ અય ખુલખુલ ગુલ સંઘા બા ગુલસ્તાની
આયા જીખ જાન ઘરમેરે. ૬૦
શિકાં સારીયાં જેંજી સોભત જેંજી ઉઝ્જ ઉઝ્આનાચો સિં
ભર્યા અંખ ભાગ બાદલજ વસાઇએ તું અંબર એશાની
આયા જીખ જાન ઘર મેરે. ૬૦
બચલા બાલ થી ઉનજો કે જેંજે જામ ક્રો અય સર
અસી અયઘર ઉઠી અતગર પીખારે જામ સો જાની
આયા જીખ જાન ઘર મેરે. ૬૦

૧૭

મિઠો અય નાસોઈ અલાજે સચો અય દીન નખીજે
શા કલંધર ધમ જુકે લાલ મિઠો અય નાખો અલાજે
દિલજા મિસળના હરગીસ જુલજ્ના, જુલજ્ના વાલા જુકેંતા
શા કલંધર ધમ જુકે લાલ મિઠો અય નાખો અલાજે.

અચ્ચૌ જિંયા રાંજ ચોસર ખેલેં
શવલા ઢારા મોંસે ઢાર્યો મસ્તક લંઘર ધમજુલે જલ
મિઠો નાલો અલાજે. ૭૦
પીરે મેં પીર સચ્ચા શિરાજશા જ્ાત્રુ અચ્ચેંતા હુમેશાં
શા કલંઘર ધમ જુલે લાલ મિઠો નાલો અલાજે. ૭૦
ખુમાર શિધી ચે આખર મરણું અલ્લા દુનીયા થીઘી સલ્ફ઼ાની
શા કલંઘર ધમ જુલે લાલ મિઠો નાલો અલાજે. ૭૦

<hr>

૧૮

દાતા તેરે ટેકરેમેં ખોલ્ઘાં ચંડૂલ
ઝારો ઝાર મેં તુંહિતું પાનો ઝાનમેં તુંહિ તું
તુંહિ તો ગુલાખીદા દ઼ૂલ દાતા તેરે ટેકરેમે ૭૦
રોધા જો રસૂલ ધાહિ અજબ બનાયા
બરસે જો સારા સારા નુર દાતા તેરે ટેકરેમે ૭૦
આંમે ફેરી ડાળ ઉપર પીંજરા ટંગાવારે
ખોલેરે નબીજી રસૂલ દાતા તેરે ટેકરેમે ૭૦
શા ફ઼ુશેના વલી ફ઼કીર ઓલાધા મેર્ * તાં કઘો મેહેબૂબ દાતા તેરે ટેકરેમે.

<hr>

૧૯

ઝલિયા મોતી સમાલો મોતીઝી ઓલડી
સેફ઼ી પરધર રેનરે† ભિયાં
ઝશ ખુંઘન મેં સો મોરે મનમેં
પીહી તું પિયાલડા મહોબત વાલુડા
શામ અચીંઘો શા મકાનજી ઓલા ઈશ ખુંઘનમે. ૭૦
ગ્યાન સેં હલણા ગ્યાન સેં ચલણા
શામ અચીંઘો શા મકાન જે મ્યા ઝશ ખુંઘનમે. ૭૦
મોતીઝી ઓલડી મોતીઝી ચોલડી શામ અચીંઘો ૭૦
શેર અલી શેર અલી મલંમ સમુઘે મ્યાં

---
* દયા. † રહેશે.

શૈયદ પાક રસૂલરે મિયાં. ૯ેશ ખુ ંધનમેં. ૬૦

૨૦

તોકે ધ્યાન લગો ધિલ ધિવાના ભાઇ સમજ સમજ મસ્તાના
જિતે અસાંજે સાહેબ્‍એ બિરાજે જિતે વેજંતા નોખત નિશાના
ભાંઇ સમજ સમજ મસ્તાના, તોકે ધ્યાન લગો ધિલ ધિવાના.
હિરારે માણુક કેરી ભરસે જેલી લાલ જવેરીધા પાના
ભાઇ સમજ સમજ મસ્તાના. ૬૦
ક્યિરે કિસીકે રંગમેં ને સંગમે દૂર દૂર કા જ્ઞાના
ભાઇ સમજ સમજ મસ્તાના ૬૦
ખોલ્યા **ભાકરશા** કિરપા કરીને રખલે અલક કેરા ધ્યાના
ભાઇ સમજ સમજ મસ્તાના ૬૦

૨૧

*અઇઆં શોબુ અસીલ, ઉમર મીઆં તુંની અંબઅે અમીર
ન્યૂલમ ન કર સૂમરા અઇઆં શોબુ અસીલ
†એડો જ્યૂલમ તું કરીએ ઉમરમીઆં બે ગુના તકશીર
ધણ્ણારનજ§ ગોલી ઉમર મીઆં નાં પેનુ‡ તેરા ચીર
ન્યૂલમ મ કર સૂમરા. ૬૦
મિશકીન ચવે ઉમર મીઆં સખરની નીંજે શીલ
ન્યૂલમ મ કર સૂમરા. ૬૦

૨૨

દિલ મેં રખો આંઇ નમીજે નાં સાર્યો સરતીઉ હરદમ અલા જેના
ભરી અય કલમા મહમદજ. હિંઆ કોન સંઘા અય કલામ
સાંઇ જે નાબે સાખત રોજ, ભેરીન બધંધા બધાય
સાર્યો સરતીઉ હરદમ નખી જેનાં દિલમે રખો આંઇ નખી જેનાં.
સચ્ચો નાબો અલાજે બ્ચ્યો સમો નખી જેનાં

અક્ષા ઇખી ખીખી ફ્રાતમા જે પુઆ છુંટ્યો સારો જમ*
સાર્યાં સરતીઉં હરદમ નખી જેનાં. ઇ૦
નીથ બધીને નિમાન પડજ ખોંધી ઉનીતા મલામ
ચારો યારો રસલજ હીજાં સચા પાયૈંને દીન સલામ
સાર્યાં સરતીઉં હરદમ નખી જેનાં. ઇ૦
ખાવંદ ખલકયો દોસ્ત ઇનીજ જિત કામલ પડે તાં કુરાન
સૈયદ હુશૈન શાચે સિક મુકૈ આંજ અર્ઈ મિલોતાં મજને જ જમ
સાર્યાં સરતીઉં હરદમ નખી જેનાં ઇ૦

૨૩

ખાક દના થી વેને મનડા નેઠ વેને ભરી મનડા
છો તું સજણ વિસારીએ જુઉઈ સાહેબી સૈયદ કે મીઆં અલા
ઉ ડીના દાતાર રે મનડા છોતું સજણ વિસારીએ
ખાધમ પીતમ જિનસે મીઆં અલા
જનમ ગુબરે વિઝી સેરે મનડા છોજું સજન વિસારીએ
સોડી સજે સુઝ મે ભિઆં અલા ક્ષિમ્ર કારૂ કંઘેરે મનડા
છોતું સજણ વિસારીએ.
હિંડો બીડૈ, બિટનને મિંઆ અલા
કડ કડ કંઘે તોજ હઙડૈ મનડા છોતું સજણ વિસારીએ.
ભચલ ચવે અધા ભાવરા મિઆં અલા
ગાબ ગાલાર્ઈ મે વિઝી ક્ષબ રે મનડા છોતું સજણ.

૨૪

છા મુંજે ખિલ જીતીઆ દીલઘર યાર કા જણાઇ કેર હુઆ.
ડાઢા ડુંગર નઝીઉં લડઈઉં હોથ પુનબ તો જીઉં અખીઉં અડઘઉં.
અરે સાંઈ મોબત જ મચ ખારે વે યાર. કા જણાઇ કેર હુઆ
ખાબ અથીનજો પલટયો ખાણુ
અરે સાંઇ તો લાખતી જેર હારે કા જણાઇ કેર હુઆ

---

* જમ-દુનીઆ. † તારા માટે તે રૂએ છે શોક કરે છે.

રા મુસાફર રાત દિઠાંસી
ષિલ દૈરાય અસી હાણુ વિઠાસીં
અવે સાંઈ કલમે શાણુ કાઢી ત્યા   કા જણાઘ કૈર હુઆ
અશરફ શા ચવે ઈશક લગોસીં
અરે સાંઘ ષિલમેં ખુંડા ઘુખાઈ વ્યા   કા જણાઈ કૈર હુઆ.

_____

૨૫

શા મુંજી ષિલ ધુતે તિન નેઠી આઉં, કીં કરીઆં
મુંજો વશન લગો શા મુંજી ષિલ ધુતે.
શાજન ભિલંધા શાંઘ શે ઈ જવ જડ્યો મુંજો જિનસાં રેઠી
પર મેં પમાર તિનખાં પઈ દૂર જિનીજે દેઠી   કિ કરીઆં.
માઠ સભર આઉં કિ કરીઆં ષિઆં જનમ ધારા આઉં ઝીદલજીઆં.
હાથૈા હંખૈા ખપખમ ષિલકે સાંઈ તાં મિલાંઘૈા શેષ.
કિ કરીઆં મુંજો વશન લગો.
નેણુ ખણ્યો આઉં ઉઠાઉ ત્યારીઆં
લઉં અખડીએં સે આઉં ખાગ ઉઠાઈઆં
હય હય કિમ કૈડા હંજુ તે હાર્ષે
જનખુજી પર થૈ રે અલા.   કિ કરીઆં.
મહુમદ ષૈાસ ચવે આલમ આંકે
ઈશ્ક અરંગ જી સુધ નાંઞે આંકે
વાર્ષૈા વારીઆં પલીઆં ષિલકે
તાન વ રેઠી વેઠી અલા. કિ કરીઆં

_____

૨૬

કૈર પંજે યાર જ વખાણુ, મુંઘંજે ઘસ્કરે ઠૈરાન ઝીયૈા
શચન ગાલ આય શાહેબમાંધા, નિઠ વડા નાધાન ઞિંઆં
હાજીએ રખઘે હાયડા ઞિઆં જિત થિઘે ત્રાણૈાત્રાણુ. મુંઘંજે.
શાહેબ ભિલઘે શચતે, જિતે લાવૈા દીન થ્યા લાલ ઞિઆં
અકલ હિઉ હથ હંઘ કર્ષૈા જિતે અગીઆને પરિયાણુ. મુંઘંજે.
જિન ભનાયા ભાગ જેસુ, જિમીનું અસમાન ખાં

તિન ખનાયા મોલ મેડીઉ મોતને મકાન ભિઆં.   મુંઈજો.
ખુરજ્ર શા ચવે જે દિલાસો તિખો અય તો ધાર ભિઆં
સભ ભંગાઇ'ધે લખીઉ જિતે કલમેજી તવાર ભિઆં. મુંઈજો. •

The Sindhi Kafis or the popular Sindhi sings.

૨૭

કુરજ્ર† અધો‡ કમનતસેં મોલાવું મેડીએ માઠેશાં
જડે વઐડા. કુરજ્ર ખધો કમનતસેં.
આઉ નમાણી આઇઆં નેઝુ નમાણા છાલ હોએ.   જડે વઐડા ૬૦
વિચાડી ને વિખરજી§ કલન પઇ કેંકે કા   જડે વઐડા.
વઝુન ને વિખરમેં લાંઉ જલ્યેતિ શાઇ.   જડે વઐડા.
અધીઉ ની શા અબ્હ લતીખ ચવે મન મેડાવો સદાઇ હોવે જડે વઐડા.

૨૮

મોલે તાં મિલાયો વિછોડે વરાએો, અધીઉ પુનલ જમ મોલે મિલાએો.
મુંઘજો પિરીયનલા આઉ ખંગલા ભનાઇઆં
ખંગલા ભનાઇઆં મેં જરીઉ છડાઇઆં.   અધીઉ પુનલજય.
મુંઘજો પિરીયનલ આઉ ઉઠની સુંઆણુ
ઉઠની સુંઆણુ આઉ વાચા ન જાણુ.   અધીઉ પુનલજય.
મુંઘજો પિરીયનલા ‖ આઉ કાગ ઉડાઇઆં
કાગ ઉડાઇઆં આઉ ફાલ પુછાઇઆં.   અધીઉ પુનલજય.
હુભદલ શાચે કાશી હકાની
કાશી હકાની યાર કલમે કુરાની.   અધીઉ પુનેલજય.

૨૯

જિનજ વયા દૂર તિનજો મારે શૂર
સે રભ આણીઘો જિનજ વયા દૂર.
કેથીઆની કરા તે કતાર્યા આઘેની વેલ અસૂર
વેઠી સારીઆં સે રભ આણીઘો. ૬૦

---

* સિંધી કાશી છે.   † દિલ.   ‡ બાંધ્યો.   § ઉધમ–કામ.   ‖ લા=માટે.

મારેની બ્યા માજુર કે કેચ કરી બ્યા ક્લુર વેઠી
ઊઠ કતારું હલઘઉ મઇઆ કરીઐતાં મજબુર વેઠી.
અધીઉં નીશા અબ્છ લતીબ્ય ચવે દશ પવે તો આંકે દુર.
સે રભ આણીઘા.

———

૩૦

ન માયા નીજે નાતે નાંય કો મરણુ મોરણુજે નમાયા
અચી પી જન તું જની, અય ધુનીયા ફનાફાની
અબ્બા ખાનન તોજી ખાની, લથા ફેરા ફેરણુજ્જ નમાયા.   ૧
અંગણુ આયા પરી સે હીં, ભગી ખિલડી જિનીરે હી
ભિહી મેરું થઘઉં પાંતે જેઅળા જુંજુર નેરણુલ નમાયા.   ૨
તોજી અખણીન લાઈ લાલી હળી થીઉં હોથ હ હાલી
ગુમનસેં ફી વચન ખાલી અથાંઉ ખમખાન ખોરણુજ્જ નમાયા.   ૩
મછણુ મન થીઐં માંઘા મુને મુરથીદ અલા આંઘા
લથો વઢ વેર બ્યા વાંધા નમાયા **ભિલ'ખ*** બંઉ તો કરે કઉં તો.

———

૩૧

સભે શીંગાર ક્યો સાજન ઘણુ મિંજ ગોર બાઘઘા
ખણુ ખંજર પિરી ખૂની આહે અન્જલત સંધી ઊની
પરાઊીઆં મોં મિંજ મુની બિલાશક બાલ બાઘઘા.   સભે શિંગાર.
જિક કે અકલન આડા તિને કે તુઠાઈન તાઢા†
ભસો બિશિયર બિરું બાલા નજર જે નાજ સેં નિઘા.   સભે શિંગાર.
કિતે જુસભ, કિતે શાની, કિતે ભધીયલ લય લાની
જઉં કે જહેર તેં જની. પશો અચી પેર પાંઘઘા   સભે શિંગાર.
ઇઘા કે રમન સેં રાજી, ભિલ'ધ ગવાર પિરી માજી
પિનજ પચ્ચેંનાર થી પાજી આખર અય સાનસેં ઇઘા. સભે શિંગાર.

———

૩૨

અછીઆં તોજે શાણુ નિત સારીયાં રોજ મેખાણુ

———

મિઠા મહમદ જમ શૈયદ આઈઆં તોને શાણુ
ઝધીનેં મહમદ આવ્યા તિંતે ફુફ્ર કયા કતલામ
ધિલ પર ધીન જગાઈ ગ્યો જિતે આશક કયો તે સલામ
મિઠા મહમદ ૬૦
ચારો યે યાર રસલજ અબા ભકર ઉમર ઓશમાણુ
પંજતન આંજીઓં પૂર્યાં કંધૈા ઙીડે સંધી હામ
મિઠા મહમદ ૬૦
હશણુ હુશૈન ઘૈા ચંદ અલીતેં અમર મઝાઉં એશાન
આલી શૈર* અલાને ઈ આપો આપ ઈમામ
મિઠા મહમદ.
અજજ ખાની આંઙી અવાંજ† ગોલી અઘઆ ગુલામ
ઙિરાની શાચે મુરશીદ મુંજ સૈયદ વઙ઼જ સલામ
મિઠા મહમદ.

૩૩

ધિલડી ઙૂરે તાં ગિડે પ્યારે નેઙુલે વારે
પ્રીતમ તો મુંસે પ્રીત ન પારઘ,
સુરી‡ ચાડે ને તો મુકે મારઘ.
ઙનિં ઉઙાણી ડુંગર તાં ઙડી પ્યારે નેઙુ લે વારે ૬૦
જતમ કરે મું ક્રિ઼ તો સેં થારી, ઙિન વિનોઙ ક્ષિઙતો વિજરી
જનભ દિને મુકે ઝેરજ જડી પ્યારે નેઙુલે વારે ૬૦
ઘાયલ થઈ આંઉ ગુંઘલ ગારીઆં થ્ર રેઙુનજ ઈ ઝિંજઙતી મારીઆં
વિસરો નતા મુકે ઙિકડી ઙડી પ્યારે નેઙુલે વારે ૬૦
નાનભાઈ ચઙ઼એ આંઉ કયાં શી ખજ઼ણી આંને ગુણુજી આંઉકેડી કરીઆં તારી‖
ગુંઘર ખડીઘે પીર ઘોસ કે મિઠા પ્યારે નેઙુલે વારે ૬૦

૩૪

ઙાઊઆ ઙોથ મોઈઆસ, ઘોસ્ત મોઈઆસ, લગી યાર લઙન તેં

---

* સિંઘ. † આંજી તમારી. ‡ ઝણા. ઙ જેની રીતે ડુંગર ઉપરથી
ઙડો ફેંક્યો હોય તેવી રીતે. ‖ કરું તારીફ.

થઇઅિશ ડાઈ દુંગરે ઘરઈ પાણુ† થઇઅશ, લગી યાર લકન તેં,
ઇસ્ક આઇાઇઅિશ જેડીઉ‡ હેઈા તાં ન હુઈશ, લગી યાર લકન તેં
ભતીઉં ઊધીસ લોક કે ચરઈ પાણુ થઇઅશ, લગી યાર લકનતેં.
અધીઉં શા અખ્ખ લતીબ થઅે કાઠેઆ કાઠઇઅશ§ લગી યાર લકનતેં

૩૫

△ કમીડી ને અલા કૈચ તેં શા પોંધી પચ્ચાર✛ શા પઇ પચ્ચાર
કમીડી ને અલા કૈચ તેં.
કમીડીજ કિત્રીઉં⚹ હાડ ભિંજ હજ્જર
શા પોંધી પચ્ચાર કમીડી ને અલા કૈચ તેં.
મું/ નમાણી% ને નજરે ભેરા ખણુજ ભતાર
શા પોંધી પચ્ચાર કમાણી ને અલા કૈચ તેં
વીંટજી બ્યા વણુન મેં વિઆડીની વાર,÷ શા પોંધી પચ્ચાર ઇ૦
અધીઉં શા અખ્ખ લતીબ ચઅે કિઢાં વઐઇ ક્તાર, શા પોંધી પચ્ચાર ઇ૦

૩૬

શા ડઈ બ્યા ડૈર ડઈ બ્યા ડૈર ઉજગા અખણ્ઝીન કેં =
હેડે શેર ભંબોર મેં જાત ન જાણ્ણા આંઉ કૈર, શા ડઇ બ્યા કૈર.✕ ૧
કંકુ વઐેણ્ણા* કપડા, મેંધી-રતડા પૈર,╱
શા ડઈ બ્યા ડૈર ઉજગા અખણ્ઝીન કે; ૨
હેડી વેર વણુનમેં આંઉ બાંઇઆરી કૈર
શા ડઇ બ્યા ડૈર ઉજગા અખણ્ઝીન કે. ૩
અધીઉં શા અખ્ખ લતીબ ચઅે અમર નજ્ઞાઉ તેહેર
શા ડઇ બ્યા ડૈર ઉજગા અખણ્ઝીન કે. ૪

---

† પોતે. ‡ જેવડી. § મને તેડાવી ત્યારે હું આવી. △ નવસીલી.
✛ ખબર. ⚹ કેટલી. ╱ હું. % રાંક. ÷ બિચારીના વાળ. = આં-
ખોને ઉજગા દઈ ગયા. ✕ કોણુ. * વર્ણુના-રંગના. ╱ મેંદી જેવા
રાતા પગ મેંદીથી રાતા-રંગેલા પગ.

૬૭

મોમે ભન ધારા ગાઅેયાં જીણુ મુંધજે¶
શિર દીંધીસ સંસારેકે ડોલ મથા તા ડોયોરે
ગાઅેયાં જીણુ મુંધજે મોઅે ભન ધારા૦
ઉડ મારીઁધીસ ઉનીજ, ટકર મથા વિઝી રાયોરે
ગાઅેયાં છીણ મુંધજે. ૧
પાડે ∴ માંધે પરીયનનૈ† ચડખો તાં મું વિઝી ચાયો
ગાઅેયાં જીણુ મુંધજે.
અધીઉ શા અબ્હ લતીઅ ચઅે ખેનર‡ તાં મુકે ભોયોરે
ગાઅેયાં જીણુ મુંધજે.

૩૮

લગો તિન શામીડૈઁજે ખાણુ, લગો તિન ભોગીડૈઁજે ખાણુ,
સામી સફર હલ્યા ડોય ન કયાંઉ પરીયાણુ,
લગો તિન સામીડૈ જે ખાણુ. ૧
ભોગી હુધા જુગ મેં જિતે રાતો ઝી અય રેયાણુ§
લગો તિન સામીડૈ જો ખાણુ. ૨
નાગા વઅેઓ / નિકરી આંઉ હયડા હણાતિ હાણુ
લગો•તિમ શામીડૈઁજો ખાણુ. ૩
મડીઉ ડિસ્સીન મીઝા મન ઠાર્ખ્બે‖ મુકે સુખ નતો અચે હાણુ
લગો તિન સામીડૈઁજો ખાણુ. ૪

૩૯

સમી થઈ વ્યાસીં અસીં તાં ભોગી થઈ વ્યાસીં
પુછી પંધ+ પુરભ* વેઁધાસી અસીંતાં ભોગી થીંધાસીં૦
 જત્રીઉ પાયો જનમેં અસીં ઘર ઘર ગુમ ધાસીં
પૂછીં પંધ પુરન વેઁધાસી ૧

¶ મુંજે–મારો.   ∴ શેરી.   † નખી.   ‡ ભેણુ–ભેન.   § ગમત.   / વ-
અેડા–વ્યા–ગયા.   ‖ ઘાસ મહમદનો ચેલો.   + પંથ.   * પૂર્વ.

E-42

આશણુ આધે શીનજ અસીં દુરે ડિસંધાસી
પુછી પંધ પુરવ વેંધાસી—૨.
ગિલાંઉ ગીબતું ગામજડું અસીં શિર તે સોંધાસીં
પુછી પંધ પુરવ વેંધાસી—૩.
ઝડીઉ ડીસી મીઉ મન્ઠાર ચઝ઼ે અસી ખગલે પોંધાસી
પુછી પંધ પુરવ વેંધારી—૪.

૪૦

કડે થીંધા નેઠ અલા અસાંજો કડે થીંધા નેઠ
આંઉતાં મારઈ ઉનીજે મેઠ અલા અસાંજો.
રિક્યારઇ ડિસાં ત આંઉ કિન છડીઆં
આંઉ બીડે જલીઆં બેઠ અલા અસાંજો—૧.
ચઢ વઢી મોયા પટૈ ન આયો છે અલા અસાંજો.
રાતું ગણીઆં,† ક઼ીણ્ણા ગુઝર્યા, મહિનો આયો નેઠ અલા અસાંજો—૨.
પીર ધ઼ાસ ઓઝે આંઉ શિક મૈં તિ સારીઆ
ઝનડા મરી વેને નેક અલા અસાંજો કડે થીંધા નેઠ.—૩.

૪૧

× અંગણુ આયોશી વલા માડુ અંગણુ આયોશી૦
નિઝો આંકે સારે જીવડો હિ, વલા માડુ અંગણુ આયોશી૦
નેણુલા વિછાઇઆં, વારલાં વિછાઇઆં, પ્રીતમ પેરે દહિ =
દુખીયન ને ડીલજી ખ ત્રે ગાલીણિ શુણ્ણા આંધ વઘ
વલા માડુ અંગણુ આયોશી—૧.
પ્રેમ રસીલા પાસે મ થીઝ મુકે હેડી હીઆરીજ઼ુ દઘ
શીઠ ચઇને ને આંઇ ખોલાયો ત લખનેરામાં આંકે જી
વલા માડુ અંગણુ આયોશી—૨.
ધિલની ધુતે તો ગિડેની ધુનારા તો ખુંસે કેડી ક઼િર્

---

‡ ભેંસ. § અક્ષ્વાર. † રાત-ગણ્. × વહાલા માણુસ–આંગણે આ-
વવાનું કારણ. = દેહ–શરીર. ✿ હૈયાધાણુ.

ધિલકે વારીઆં કૉન વરે નેણુલે અવાજે મુઈ
વલા માઢું અંગણુ આયોશી—૩.
જલ વિના જ઼ મછલી તલખે તીં તલખે અસાંજો જીવ
પીર ધોરા ઓલે પ્રીતમ પ્યારા પ્રીતડી જઘવજી
વલા માઢુ અંગણુ આયોશી—૪.

૪૨

%કિરાં તોજે ઘર ઉમર આંઉ કિરાં તોજે ઘર△
મુંજ માઢુઙા થ્યા વિઝી ઘર ઉમર આંઉ, કિંરાં તોજે ઘર૦
જિનજી આંઉ નઘ તિનજી આંઉ લાઈ
હિઙો મુંજો કેડો ક્દર ઉમર આંઉ કિરાં તોજે ઘર—૧.
પોતીની ક઼ળ અંઘ શીખવતી સુમરા
જેડી અવાજ઼.: પર, ઊમર આંઉ કિરાં તોજે ઘર—૨.
માઢુની ભિઙા મુંઘ કે લગે આંઉ ઉકંઙ઼ ઉનીકે અપર
ઉમર આંઉ કિરાં, તોજે ઘર—૩.
ઉની ડાઙણેજો= ધોરા એ મિલંધા અધીર્ત઼ન
લઘ તાં વેંધા ગ઼ધર ઊમર આંઉ કિરાં તોજે ઘર—૪.

૪૩

અચ તું ઓરૈ રે જની આંઉ તોજી નિત વાઢું ન્યારીઆં
પાંઈ જે પાણુ તું છાનું ઉખાડીંએ સુતડા સૂર વ્યા ચોરે ચોરે
આંઉ તોજી નિત વાઢું ન્યારીઆં૦
કાયા માયા ભલો કરીઆં આંતા કુલભાની ॥
×ડીંધીસ કાગન કે આંજી કોરેકોરે આંઉ તોજી નિત વાઢું ન્યારીઆં—૧
અનડ઼ા ન ભાને અલા નિંદ્ર ને આને
મારૂંઈશ આંજે આંઉ હોરે હોરે, આંઉ તોજી—૨.

% તારે ઘરે હું કેમ રહી શકું મારા માણસો થળપારકર ગયા છે.
△ ઘર ઘર. ∴ અવાજ-આંજી-તમારી. = શરીર માવિત્રાનો. ૈ ન-
જીક-પાસે. ॥ આંતા=તમારા ઉપર કુલભાની=કુરબાન. × તમારા માટે
હું મારૂં શરીર જો તમે કહો તો કાગડાને કોરી કોરીને આપું.

પીર વ્હાસ ઓલે પગલે મથા આંહ તાં વેંધીસ ઘોરે ઘોરે
આંહ તોજી નિત વાઢું ન્યારીઆં—૩.

———

૪૪

વખત હલણુજ કેડા ટાણા, આંઠિ ફી ન જાણા;
વખત હલણુજ કેડા ટાણા૦
ઍડોની અય કોય ખરધ મટાવે, ઍડો અય કોય ખેરી શેણા,
આંહ ફ઼ીંન જાણા વખત હલણુજ કેડા ટાણા—૧.
મટી મેં મિલ મિટી વેંધી ગહઆં ચર શણુગાર,
વખત હલણુજ કેટા ટાણા—૨.
જીવ ગીની ને વેંધા જાયે જંગલ મેં થીંધા થાણા
વખત હલણુજા કેડા ટાણા—૩.
મિશકીન ચવે મુરશીદ મુંજા તો વિન બ્યો કોઈ નાંઆે ઠેકાણા.
વખત હલણુજા કેડા ટાણા—૪.

———

૪૫

હરદમ ધિલમેં તોજો ના સરવર જામ
હરદમ ધિલમેં તોજો નાં૦
પાક મહમધ મુસ્તફા મીઠ મધીને જો સરવર જામ
હરદમ ધિલમેં તોજો નાં—૧
કલમાં ની પડીયો પાક નખીજ
સાંભત રખજા સિધકોઅ* ઈનાન
હરદમ ધિલમેં તોજો નાં—૨.
આખીૈ ને વેળા દીંની હશરજી
તાં પણુ પોંધો તોસે કમ હરદમ દિલમેં તોજો નાં—૩
મિશકીન ચવે તુંઇજી મિલણ જી
હિઠડેમ|| તલપ તમામ, હરદમ ધિલમેં તોજો નાં—૪.

———

* Day of Judgment-ક્યામતનો રોજ (?) ¶ આખીૈ=મુશ્કેલ. ||હેઠામાં.

૪૬

હાજી મંગા પીર અસાંકે અલા માંડુ મેડીએ ✱

કરામતું† કામિલ પીર જયું જ્યાન મેં નિજીંગો જર

અસાંકે અલા માડુ મેડી એ૦

ખોરીએ લેખો નાંહે કાર્ધકા સાબત લંગાધએ મુંજા પીર

અસાંકે અલા માડુ મેડીએ ૧

✗જેંની મમધ મન્યો મેંકે ખારાધએ ખનું ખીર

અસાંકે અલા માડી એ ૨

શિધી મુબારક આંજો સવાલી પૂરીજ પુજાધએ મુંજા પીર

અસાંકે અલા માડુ મેડીએ ૩

૪૭

હજરત મીરાં પીર અસાંજી અલા આશ પુજાધએ§

પરચેની મીરાં પીરજે જગ મેં અચ મશહુર

અસાંજી અલા આશ પુજાધએ૦

ચોડાં તજાકું∴ મેં નોબત જેંજી કુલ પીરેંજો પીર

અસાજી અલા આસ પુજાધએ ૧

પુરીજી થીધીઉ મનજીજી અલા પુતર દીધો પીર

અસાંજી અલા આસ પુજાધએ ૨

મિશકીન મદદ તોજે કામલ ધુધો+ પીર

અસાંજી અલા આશ પુજાધએ ૩

૪૮

અધીજાં તાં કુલ ભલાય ટલી,÷ ખાવધ કધા ખેર ભરી

પીરાણુ પીરજી ખાવન લગી, અધીજાં કુલભલાટલી૦

✱ મેળવી દે. † કરામતા. ✗ જેણે મહમદને માન્યો તેને તું દુધ-ખાંડ ખવરાવે છે=આપે છે. § પહોચાડી દે. ∴ ચૌદ લોકમાં—જગ્યામાં. + દ-લ્હો=દુલ્હો-ઉદ્ધાર. ÷ તારી કુલ બલા ટલી.

સત જમીન અસમાન મેં ચોદાં તબક મેં શેશન△ પડી
અધીજાં કુલ ભલા ટલી. ૧
અયની મોથાજ હમેશ મીરાંજ પીર ફકીર અમીર વલી
અધીજાં કુલ ભલા ટલી. ૨
નાતાની પાક રસૂલ શૈયદ જ ડાડા હજરત શા અલી
અધીજાં કુલ ભલા ટલી ૩
મુરીધ તાં મિશકીન ચચ્ચે પીર ઓલી મેં થીજ ધણી
અધીજાં કુલ ભલા ટલી ૪

૪૯

†વલો ધોસલ પીર ભેની મુકે વલો ધોસલ પીર૦
ઉને જરેમેં અસીં ન નાછજાં નાછિ નિર્મળ નીર
અચોરે વલા આંકે ખારાછઆં, સક૨+ ને વરી ખીર+
જાંચી અગાસી ન્યારે વર્ચો એડો ન દિઠો અમીર.
×નિજરે સિક મેં નાનઆઇ કે ભિઝયા હૈઉ મેં રખો ધીર.

૫૦

શેણુ ઝુસજોડીં સંભરધાં રાણુ ધારા ડીં કીં ગુજરધાં
નેઝા બધી જો નીઆં ઉને થીધિ
જિતે સરા જે તોલે તુરંધા. શેણુ સજોડીં૦
સાજન વરંધા પાને વતન તેં વાર્યા કેં જ ન વરંધા
શેણુ સજોડીં સંભરધા ૧
મલક ઇંધે મોત સંધા કોા જાણુા કેડી પર કંધા
શેણુ સજોડીં સંભરધા ૨
શૈંન્ર હુશેન શાચે મોત ભિણીને ક્ષિલર ધાખલ વિઝી કરીંધા =
શેણુ સજોડીં સંભરધા ૩

△અજવાળુ. †વલો=વ્હાલો. +સાકર ને વળી દૂધ=ખીર. × જ૭=
ગાઝી=ઝિક=છતેજરી. ‡ સજો=આખો. = જઇને ક્લમમાં દાખલ કરશે.

૫૧

માંધિ અછઆં રે મેઆર, મુંદે પોચાઇઆં પુંઆર.
સન ખુણથો વિહી આંઉ સારીઆં, માંધી અઇઆં રે મેયાર.
આયેની મુછજેઈ કરમગ્ના કેડા ડોગ ડીઆં કુંભાર,
માંધી અઇઆં રે મે યાર ૧
લોરીઅેની લેખા નથીઅે અચી શણુક્ષો સંભાર
માંધી અઇઆં રે મે યાર ૨
ધડોની ખણુ ઘેઉમેં અંચીંની થીજ આધાર
માંધી અઇઆં રે મે યાર ૩
ભલાની છાલ ભિલંધ ચે ઘણુ થીજ ઘણાર
માંધી અઇઆંની મે યાર ૪

___

§ મુંજે=મારા. ¶ દોપ.

ERRATA·

Page.	Line.	Incorrect.	Correct.

(PREFACE.)

I.	5	1887.	1886.
I.	7	centributed	contributed.
III.	27	(insert after "Congress") with us.	

(INTRODUCTION.)

VI.	17	Cardlides	Carolides.
VII.	11	Campain	Campani.
VIII.	2	ह	द
IX.	footnote line 2.	1650	1050
IX.	Ibid line 8.	mentions	makes
X.	2	(omit)	"to it"
X.	8	Hârânti	Hârâ–u–ti
XI.	17.	(insert after "Vans'âvali")	the Dwârka S'ankarâchârya Pattâvali.
4.	26.	(insert after "first")	"paper".
5.	24.	Univerite'	Universite'.
6.	20.	Koninkligh	Konniklich.
9.	24.	vertually	virtually.
14.	25.	Count Angelo Gabernatis	Count Angelo Gubernatis.
14.	30.	D∴	Dr.
15.	8.	(insert between "with" and "third")	"the"
15.	17.	was	were.
25.	21.	*Sama-diu-bahuka*	*Sama–dvi–bâhuka.*

Page.	Line.	Incorrect.	Correct.
26.	9.	Bridhanka	Brihadanka.
27·	9.	(insert between "each" and "them")	"of"
29.	1.	(insert before "Jaina")	"a"
30.	2.	Zeli	Zeij.
31.	7.	(insert after " of ")	"the"
31.	10.	Kiug	King
31.	13.	समाभिद्याराुहितेन प्रणिते.	समभिधाराूहितेन प्रणिते.
31.	15.	बभुव	बभूव
32.	·9.	समाद्ययांदि.	समाह्वयादि.
32.	13.	प्मो	०
82.	15.	घै	द्यै.
33.	19.	(insert after "worthily")	styled.
37.	15.	(insert after "has")	not
38.	15.	Silpa Sutras	Sûlva Sûtras.
38.	18.	debries	debre's
41.	4.	Griceson	Grierson.
42.	6.	Elttarah	Uttarâh
42.	29.	(Omit) âvartta,	
43.	12.	(Omit) also.	
47.	24.	Haranti	Hârâ–u–ti.
51. foot note. line 8.		13, 204, 968.	13, 214, 968.
51. Ibid line 12.		044	0. 44.

Page.	Line.	Incorrect.	Correct.
53.	foot note line		
	3.	(insert after "and")	"it."
54.	19 & 20.	Barrus	Burras.
57.	8.	century	centuries.
59.	13.	which	whom.
61.	15.	Chalukyas	Chalukya Rajputs,
61.	16.	(insert before " off ")	"and"
63.	17.	सूदि	शुदि.
63.	18	अणहिलवाड ३	अणहिलवाडइ.
63.	19.	राउानि.... ....छरू	राउनी.... .... छइ.
65.	3.	*thai*	*hoi*
67.	17.	(omit *Soma Parvan*	of
68.	14.	worth	work
73.	7.	(insert after " editions")	"of two poems"
73.	19.	which	whom
73. 27 also 75. 23.		Godhra	Gothda
89.	8.	Vallabhi	Valabhi
89.	9.	कर	पुर
90.	3.	Saidhar	Sardhar
92.	14.	green	grey
93.	25.	Mityaropadarsaka	Satyabhâmâ-rosha-dar-s'ikâkhyâna
104.	20.	(insert before "Buddhist")	" the "

Page.	Line.	Incorrect.	Correct.
109.	17.	Indical	Indica
109.	18.	Pronodosa	Frondosa
118.	9.	Prasamapura	Prasannapura
120.	5.	Chabhua	Chhâbuâ
122.	12.	Saura–	Sarva–
132.	1.	S′. S′.	K. S.
134.	13.	Sun or	Son of
149.	29.	Yarundi	Varudi–
153.	8.	on	of
161.	19.	के	कै
162.	12.	bannerests	bannerets

APPENDICES.

Page.	Line	Incorrect.	Correct.
A. 6.	21	Diliman	Dillman
A. 6.	25	De.	Dr.
A. 13.	25	Konimgen	Koningen.
A. 15.	3	Kashmirian	Kashmirian.
C. 1.	26	by.	by."
D. 1.	14	Hand-	Hend-
D. 1.	27	my	his
E. 1.	15	લીદી	લીંદી
E. 2.	6	ધડાવે	ધડાવે
E. 5	19	દળીઆત	રળીઆત.
E. 7	16	સાઢે	સાંઢે
E. 13	29	ચંદલો	ચાંદસો
E. 20	7	મારારાંજ	મારારાજ
E. 21	6	પાંપ પતડાય‡	પાંડયો પતડાય‡
E. 21	footnote	‡ ખ્રાળ	‡ ખ્રાહ્મણ